D1590599

Sexual Deviations in the Criminal Law

CLARKE INSTITUTE OF PSYCHIATRY Monograph Series

1. *Psychiatry in Transition, 1966–1967*, edited by Aldwyn B. Stokes. Papers delivered at the formal opening of the Department of Psychiatry in the Clarke Institute of Psychiatry.

2. *Sexual Deviations in the Criminal Law: Homosexual, Exhibitionistic, and Pedophilic Offences in Canada*, by Alex. K. Gigeroff.

Sexual Deviations in the Criminal Law

HOMOSEXUAL, EXHIBITIONISTIC, AND
PEDOPHILIC OFFENCES IN CANADA

ALEX. K. GIGEROFF

Published for the CLARKE INSTITUTE OF PSYCHIATRY *by*
UNIVERSITY OF TORONTO PRESS

KE
G53x

Foreword

Criminal offences are invariably defined in terms of personal, social, and legal factors. Although it is easily recognized that these factors are inter-related, the separation of professions and academic disciplines leads to disjunction and insulation, in practice as well as in study. The clinical professions such as psychiatry, psychology, and social work will tend to concentrate on the personal characteristics of the offender; the social scientist will tend to look for community factors, and the lawyer, whether he is prosecuting, defending, or adjudicating, will tend to see an offence in terms of what the law prescribes. Increasingly, however, the various disciplines are calling on each other for assistance in solving problems. To be mutually helpful they have to be able to communicate in a way which is understandable to all concerned. Communication and the sharing of information on complex matters depend, as we know, on how well the various frames of reference are mutually understood, how well the various terminologies relate to each other, and how much of a common basis can be identified. This may be seen as the primary concern of this study.

When in 1956 the Government of Ontario established a Forensic Clinic in conjunction with the University of Toronto as part of the Toronto Psychiatric Hospital, research into the nature of sexual offences became one of its major objectives. In the research programme that was developed, attention was first given to the clinical and social dimensions of sexual deviation. It was soon found that although a good deal of attention had been given to problems arising out of maladaptations of the sexual drive, very little was in fact known about the nature of sexual deviations and their social significance. Since pedophilia, exhibitionism, and homosexuality emerged as the most commonly identified forms of problem behaviour, the studies concentrated on these deviations, and *Pedophilia and Exhibitionism* was published as a handbook by Mohr, Turner, and Jerry. In these studies, it became quite clear that further understanding would be limited if the criminal law relating to these forms of behaviour was not carefully examined. This recognition led to the present volume by Mr. Gigeroff who, with the benefit of a great deal of empirical data at his disposal, inquires into the development, logic, and operation of the law, and thus builds a bridge between psychiatry, the social sciences, and the law. Although this study looks at problematic sexual behaviour with a focus on legal aspects, it does this with the purpose of clearing the ground, as it were, so that the normative judgments which the law represents can be seen in terms of actualities of human behaviour. Further studies which are coming to fruition from this on-going research programme will deal more specifically with the patterns of sexual offences, their nature, and their consequences, and eventually we should be in a position to re-define human and social problems in a consistent way, so that clinicians and social scientists as well as the makers and the guardians of law can bring their concerted efforts to bear on the increasingly complex human situation.

Kenneth G. Gray, M.A., Q.C.
Professor of Forensic Psychiatry
University of Toronto

Preface

Historically the social control of sexual behaviour in England was largely exercised by the Church through its system of ecclesiastical courts. It was not until the latter part of the fifteenth century that the secular arm of the law began to intrude into this area. A brief historical account of the development of the specific sexual offences is given in this study against a general backdrop of the burgeonings and contractions of the criminal law as a whole. This is important partly because it confronts us with a dynamic view of the development of the law which so often appears in its present manifestation as a static state. There is recurring need to re-examine and re-evaluate the views and ideas expressed in the past in order that man's intellectual investment, which is small enough in this area, should not be lost, but consolidated for our present and future use.

With Confederation in 1867 came an urgent need for a nationwide criminal law which Canada met principally through the wholesale borrowing, with minor adaptations, of English statutes. The focus thus moves at that point to a consideration of the evolution of Canadian legislation from its earliest beginning to the present. All of the legislative changes have been explored in detail, and the paths which have been taken are clearly plotted. Concurrently, there is a report on the parliamentary debates in every instance where discussion occurred in order to glean as much of the expressed intentions of the legislators as are publicly available. There has been one extensive revision of the Criminal Code since it was borrowed from the English Draft Code of 1892, and that was made between 1949 and 1954. The process which was followed during this period, from the appointment of the first commission through to the fourth and final draft bill adopted by parliament, is critically examined with a view to understanding the mechanism, resources, and methods used in criminal law reform at the peak of its expression in this country. This procedure is contrasted with the process of law reform in relation to homosexual offences in England during the period 1954 to 1966. The object behind the discussion of this dimension of the legal process is first of all to gain a realistic appreciation of the manner, kind, and degree of legal "reform" experienced a scant dozen years ago, but

more importantly, to consider how to improve on this procedure in the
period of change that is surely to come.

The third part of this book is devoted to a critical look at the only
readily available permanent record which the legal system keeps of its
decisions: the case law. The cases which appear in the law reports are
the basic source materials which are resorted to by all who have been
trained in the law, whether they are legislators themselves or staff legal
departments of government, whether they sit on the bench or form part
of the bar as crown attorneys or defence counsel. Virtually all of the
cases reported in criminal law are appellate court decisions which reveal
the interpretation placed on the statutes by the judiciary. More promi-
nently, these cases represent a continuing discussion of the evidentiary
and procedural problems which arise in the administration of criminal
justice. The emphasis has been placed on Canadian decisions, not from
a parochial attitude, but out of a conviction that so little has been
gathered here that this must be done by someone at some point. The
case law has severe limitations in terms of its usefulness in criminal law
reform, partly because it serves to clarify the existing law and does not
concern itself with changes to that law and partly because there is no
systematic reporting of facts. Perhaps this latter limitation is especially
apparent in the area of sex offences, the subject matter of which the
courts on occasion find "disagreeable to discuss." But the most serious
limitation is seen in the fact that only a minute fraction of all cases ever
get reported, and there is no way of determining whether what is
reported is typical or not; the case law does not admit of any quantitative
breakdown. Law reform is a problem which requires much more cogent
information and evidence than can be provided by a series of isolated
and unrelated decisions of particular problems.

To prepare information for the use of law reformers it is necessary
to look beyond the case law into the everyday decisions of the courts.
For example, an analysis is presented based on every case of gross
indecency occurring in a one-year period in Metropolitan Toronto and
resulting in a conviction. The empirical data show that this one offence
is used to cover many different kinds of behaviour; two-thirds of the
cases involved homosexual acts between consenting adult males in public
places, and the remaining one-third involved smaller groupings of homosexual acts between adult males and adolescent boys between the ages
of 14 and 18, heterosexual and homosexual pedophilic acts, heterosexual
acts between adults, and an assortment of other cases. The study of what
kind of actual behaviour constitutes an offence is particularly important
because it brings us closer to the reality of the events which are falling

under a particular law and enables us to assess how well or poorly the legal formulations we have made in the past are working. This kind of analysis could provide a criminological balance sheet for the legislative directors who set social policy.

A sound social policy not only must be based on understanding but must also be understandable by all those who participate in the process of criminal law. Without being exhaustive, the list must include the police, judges and magistrates, crown attorneys and defence counsel, probation officers, staffs of the mental health services including psychiatrists, psychologists, and social workers, personnel in the penal institutions or within the parole structure, as well as the social agencies and volunteer after-care workers. Beyond this group who are directly involved, the social policy must make sense to the informed and intelligent layman. When some laws are out of tune with the times, either because they are unenforced or because no one regards them with the same concern as they were seen with many years previously, the law as an expression of social policy is confused and contains a scrambled message. The absence of a clearly enunciated and understandable social policy reduces the work of those who deal daily with these problems to a specious and arbitrary activity.

The offences discussed herein represent the majority of sexual offences committed in the community and as such are of special concern. Other offences of less frequent occurrence, for example rape and sexual intercourse with female persons in prohibited age groups, are also being studied.

This volume on the Criminal Code offences in relation to homosexual, exhibitionistic, and pedophilic acts emerges from a comprehensive research programme on sexual behaviour, society, and the criminal law, aided by financial assistance from the Ontario Mental Health Foundation under Grants no. 22 and no. 46.

Dr. K. G. Gray, Professor of Forensic Psychiatry, University of Toronto, has been the principal investigator of the project on sexual behaviour and the law. His background in both law and psychiatry has given him a unique perspective on the problems in this area, and his guidance and encouragement have been invaluable. Dr. R. E. Turner, Assistant Professor of Psychiatry, formerly Director of the Forensic Clinic of the Toronto Psychiatric Hospital, and now Chief of Forensic Services at the Clarke Institute of Psychiatry, has supported my endeavours and actively involved me as a full participant in the teaching and study programmes within the Forensic Services. He also very kindly tolerated my "roaming at large," as it were, within the clinic which was so helpful in enabling me to orient myself to a psychiatric setting.

Dr. J. W. Mohr, Assistant Professor in the Department of Psychiatry and Head of the Social Pathology Research Section of the Clarke Institute of Psychiatry, has spent a great deal of time with me over the past four years discussing not only the immediate problems associated with this project but also the wider implications, aims, and responsibility of scientific research in this area. It is a great pleasure to thank publicly such a humanist, scholar, and friend.

This work in its original form was prepared as a master's thesis in law, and Professor J. Ll. J. Edwards of the Faculty of Law, University of Toronto, and Director of the Centre of Criminology at the same institution, stimulated me to dig deeply into original sources, provoked me into a clearer statement of the fundamental issues, and made me aware of the problems involved and the dimensions and difficulty of legal reform. The process was not an easy one for me, perhaps even less so for him, but in retrospect my gratitude grows.

To my clinical friends and colleagues who were part of the team at the Forensic Clinic I owe a debt of gratitude for their friendly and ready acceptance of a "lawyer" in their midst and for generously providing me with an understanding which I could never have otherwise obtained of the clinical aspects of these problems. I would particularly thank Dr. A. Zajac, now Director of Out-Patient Forensic Services at the Clarke Institute, and Dr. S. Jedwab, Consultant to the Forensic Services, not only for their "free tuition" in psychiatry but in appreciation of their stimulating and inquiring minds and warm friendship. Miss Mary Wildridge, a colleague in the Social Pathology Research Section, offered assistance far beyond duty in collecting material and typing and editing innumerable drafts, and May Jones typed the final manuscript.

My thanks go also to Mr. Owen Shime, barrister-at-law, for the use of materials, and to Mr. Joseph Pomerant, also a barrister, who has worked exclusively at the criminal bar, for reading the manuscript and generously sharing his practical experience and his insightful comments on the operation of our laws. The Metropolitan Toronto Police Department and the Ontario Provincial Probation Service have generously co-operated in the research programme.

This work would not have been possible without the support of the Government of Ontario, Department of Health, and more recently the Clarke Institute of Psychiatry under the directorship of Dr. C. A. Roberts and the Board of Trustees.

A.G.

Contents

Contents

1

The Formulation of the Criminal Law:
An Historical View

Leslie Stephen in his *Life of Sir James Fitzjames Stephen* says, "At every point the system is determined by the circumstances of its growth; and you can no more account for its oddities or its merits without considering its history than you can explain the structure of a bat or seal without going back to previous forms of life."[1] Stephen himself concludes that the criminal law as a whole can scarcely be said to have a history. "The law as to perjury and the definition of the crime of murder have each a history of their own, but the criminal law regarded as a whole is like a building, the parts of which have been erected at different times, in different styles and for different purposes."[2] One can trace back the sex offences in the present Criminal Code of Canada to our earliest criminal legislation in 1869, only to find that most sections had been borrowed almost word for word from earlier English statutes.[3]

In order to gain an understanding of the heritage of our legislation, it is important to consider some of the leading writers on English criminal law, whose lives taken together span almost 350 years, from the middle of the sixteenth century to the end of the nineteenth. The work of four of them – Sir Edward Coke (1552–1634), Sir William Blackstone (1723–1780), Jeremy Bentham (1748–1832), and Sir James Fitzjames Stephen (1829–1894) – deserves particular attention, but reference must also be made to various texts on the pleas of the crown written by Sir Matthew Hale (1609–1676), William Hawkins (1673–1746), and Edward Hyde East (1764–1847), and to a *Treatise on Crime and Indictable Offences*, by William Russell (1785–1833). These last four authors introduced very little new material and to a large extent reiterated in a more perfunctory way what had already been set out in statute and by Sir Edward Coke in the third part of the *Institutes of the Laws of England*.

Sir Edward Coke had been Speaker and later Attorney General in the

1 Leslie Stephen, *The Life of Sir James Fitzjames Stephen* (2nd ed., London, 1895), p. 414.
2 Sir James Fitzjames Stephen, *A History of the Criminal Law of England* (London, 1883), I, 6.
3 *Infra*, part 2, Legislative Genealogy.

House of Commons before becoming Chief Justice of the Common Pleas in 1606, and in 1613 Chief Justice of the King's Bench. It was at this time that he wrote the *Third Institute*, one of the first detailed and systematic accounts of the criminal law since Bracton's treatise, *De Corona*, written in the thirteenth century.[4] Coke had a great influence for some two hundred years on the law of England, and some would say far in excess of what his work merited. What he was able to do was to bring together all of English penal law and give an account of it as a whole. It was a work of consolidation, not innovation; but in restating and clarifying the then primitive state of the law, he accomplished the necessary preparatory work for later development. Some idea of the dimensions of the work may be gained from Stephen's estimate that if the penal law as it stood in Bracton's time had been codified it could have been put into an act of perhaps twenty sections, while in Coke's time the same subject might perhaps fill eighty sections.[5]

Shortly after Coke's death, and during the period of the Commonwealth (1649–1660), the urge for change became more apparent, and much attention was paid to law reform, culminating in a far-reaching proposal presented to the "Barebones Parliament" in 1653 but not adopted. The measures were prepared by two committees, one composed of members of parliament and headed by Oliver Cromwell, the other of persons not in parliament, the first named of whom was Matthew Hale. Hale, who was made Lord Chief Justice in 1671, died in 1676 leaving one of his major works, *The History of the Pleas of the Crown*, to be published posthumously. The seventeenth century was a period not of great development, but of ripening.

The eighteenth century was to see a new era of criminal legislation. The state of the law was excessively crude, and this became more and more apparent as it was found that numerous types of acts of violence, fraud, and mischief were not adequately covered or punished by the existing provisions. A common result was that for any novel situation which arose, a new statutory felony or misdemeanour was created. The result of this process during the eighteenth and early nineteenth centuries was an immense accumulation of new enactments which did not grow out of any design but were in a sense bracketed onto the existing structure. The process was additive.

4 Staundford's *Plees del Corone* and Lombard's *Eirenarchia* were published about the same time. Both these works are regarded by Sir James Fitzjames Stephen in some particulars as better than that of Coke, but Coke's great reputation has overshadowed them. See Sir James Fitzjames Stephen, *A General View of the Criminal Law of England* (2nd ed., London, 1890), pp. 36–37.
5 Stephen, *History*, II, 206.

This extensive development is illustrated by the work of two writers, Sir Michael Foster, whose *Report of Criminal Cases* appeared in 1762, and Sir William Blackstone, who published the first volume of a four-volume work, *Commentaries on the Laws of England*, in 1765. Stephen who regarded Blackstone as "neither a profound nor an accurate thinker" gives him a prominent position as being the one who "first rescued the law of England from chaos."[6] One gains the impression that there was a reaction against the pell-mell additive process and a need, once again, to consolidate, to clarify, and to structure what had been developed.

Blackstone's great achievement lies in his "reducing to lucid and systematic statement the disordered bulk of laws accumulated over the centuries."[7] The *Commentaries on the Laws of England* resulted from a series of law lectures which were given by Blackstone at Oxford between 1755 and 1765.[8] He went to great pains to provide reasons for the law in history and logic, and at times in "natural law." Blackstone could observe that "the criminal law is in every country of Europe more rude and imperfect than the civil," and yet the overall tenor of his writing tended towards a defence of the existing order.

But even with us in England, where our Crown law is with justice supposed to be more nearly advanced to perfection; where crimes are more accurately defined, and penalties less uncertain and arbitrary; where all our accusations are public, and our trials in the face of the world; where torture is unknown, and every delinquent is judged by such of his equals, against whom he can form no exception nor even a personal dislike; —even here we shall occasionally find room to remark some particulars that seem to want revision and amendment.[9]

Having gathered and organized into an interrelated whole the criminal law which had until then been scattered in reports, statutes, abridgements, and commentaries, Blackstone provided the intellectual framework against which reformers could thrust. Jeremy Bentham, while still a young man of 16, attended Blackstone's lectures in 1763, but "he heard them, for the most part, 'with rebel ears,' detecting, as he thought, several fallacies in Blackstone's reasoning."[10] It was eleven years later,

6 *Ibid.*, II, 214.
7 William Blackstone, *Commentaries on the Laws of England*, vol. IV, *Of Public Wrongs* (Oxford, 1769), ed. Charles M. Haar (Boston, 1962), p. xxvii.
8 Blackstone was the first person to give readings in English law at an English university. In 1758 he was elected first professor of the newly established Vinerian Foundation at Oxford.
9 Blackstone, *Commentaries*, IV, 3.
10 Jeremy Bentham, *A Comment on the Commentaries*, ed. Charles Warren Everett (Oxford, 1928), pp. 10–11. After working on this book for a year and a half, Bentham laid it aside and never prepared it for publication.

in 1774, that Bentham began his *Comment on the Commentaries*, a critical attack on Blackstone's Commentaries. Bentham was impatient with what seemed to him to be the anomalies and the absurdities of law as it was, and the *Commentaries* were "chiefly objectionable because, on account of their tremendous popularity, they bade fair to fix the law in its then state." Bentham was concerned with "law as it ought to be" and devoted most of his life to law reform. His "Offences against Taste"[11] wherein he discusses sex offences, is considered herein, not because Bentham's work has been effective in the evolution of the law in this area, but because his approach provides such a strong contrast to the work of Blackstone.

"Codification (to use the word he himself invented) was the passion of Bentham's life," and although he had several versions of the principles upon which he intended to draft a penal code, Bentham "never completed the penal code which was the first of his great projects, and which in fact led on to all his other efforts at codification."[12]

Although efforts were made at reform of the criminal law by the appointment of royal commissions, notably in 1833, 1837, 1845, and codifying measures were prepared in 1852, this enormous effort produced only the Criminal Consolidation Acts of 1861[13] relating to offences against person and offences against property. In 1863 the idea of codification was revived, and a commission was appointed in 1866 which approved the project, but by 1871 the thrust for reform had again spent itself.

It was against this background and with the advantage of it that Sir James Fitzjames Stephen, whose *General View of the Criminal Law of England* published in 1863 had already won for him the reputation as a scholar of criminal law, began to use the weight of his influence in support of reformation, which made codification once again a principal issue.[14] In 1874 Stephen was asked to prepare a second edition of his *General View* but, as he says, "I found myself met at every step by the difficulty that I was unable to refer to any work in which the contents

11 Jeremy Bentham, *The Theory of Legislation*, ed. C. K. Ogden (London, 1931), p. 476. The title "Offences against Taste" is given by Ogden to his edited version of two unpublished works by Bentham which is included as an appendix to the above edition.
12 Margery Fry, "Bentham and English Penal Reform," in George W. Keeton and George Schwarzenberger, eds., *Jeremy Bentham and the Law* (London, 1948), pp. 38–41.
13 It was essentially from these acts that the Canadian legislation in 1869 was copied.
14 L. Radzinowicz, *Sir James Fitzjames Stephen*, Selden Society Lecture delivered in the Senate House of the University of London, July 30, 1957 (London, 1957), pp. 17–21.

of the criminal law as it is were shortly stated."[15] In 1877 he published his *Digest of the Criminal Law, Crime and Punishments*.[16]

In August of that year, he was appointed as an independent drafts-man, and after the introduction into parliament of his draft bill in June of 1878, he was appointed a member of the royal commission. The com-mission reported in June of 1879, and the appendix thereto, containing a "Draft Code embodying the Suggestions of the Commissioners," has come to be known as the English Draft Code (EDC). Although never adopted in England, the Code was carried to New Zealand, Queensland, Western Australia, and Tasmania, as well as several of the colonies, and is "the specific basis of the Canadian Code"[17] of 1892.

In 1883 Stephen published a *History of the Criminal Law* and, with the help of his eldest son, a *Digest of the Law of Criminal Procedure*. In 1890, in his preface to the second edition of his *General View of the Criminal Law of England*, Stephen writes, "Of these works, I think I may fairly say that collectively they constitute a pretty complete account both of the actual contents of the Criminal Law of England, and of the various circumstances which led to its assumption of its present form."

The following sections will examine the treatment four writers afforded some of the sex offences: Coke, because he described the early founda-tion; Blackstone, because he tried to give some order to what had been erected; Bentham, because he argued for a new design; and Stephen, because he made the structure livable.

15 Stephen, *A General View*, p. v.
16 "When the *Digest of the Criminal Law* was written it occurred to me that with a little alteration it would make a Draft Penal Code." Stephen, *History*, I, vi. See Radzinowicz, *Stephen*, p. 19 and p. 46, n. 35, re "improvement of the law by private enterprise."
17 J. C. Martin, *Martin's Criminal Code* (Toronto, 1955), p. 2. Martin notes that much of the substance of both the English Draft Code and the Canadian Code had its basis in Peel's Acts of 1826–28 and the Acts of 1861.

Sir Edward Coke

Many of our present-day offences did not exist in the early seventeenth century when Coke wrote the third part of the *Institutes of the Laws of England*. What is included in that work which directly concerns the topic at hand is chapter 10, entitled, "Of Buggery, or Sodomy."[1]

1 Eduardo Coke, *Institutes of the Laws of England* (London, 1817), third part, pp. 58–59.

Coke gives no explanation as to why it was necessary to use both terms in the title.[2] With one exception, he uses the term *buggery* throughout, and we can only presume that for Coke the two terms were synonymous. One can pass over this question of terminology with the easy buoyancy of Coke himself but it does represent a hidden hazard. The underlying problems of basic categories, terminology, and nosology will be more fully discussed later. Suffice it to remember that Coke unwittingly introduces us to this problem with his first four words.

Curiously, Coke devotes almost twice the amount of attention to this offence as he does to that of rape. His review of the legislative history in his opening paragraph gives an indication of his arrogance and inaccuracy: "But it is to be known, (that I may observe it once for all) that the statute of 25H.8. was repealed by the statute of 1 Mar. whereby all offences made felony or premunire by any act of parliament made since 1H.8. were generally repealed, but 25H.8. is revived by 5 Eliz." What he did not say was that the original statute of 1533 (25 Henry VIII, c. 6) was to endure only until the last day of the next parliament, that it was made perpetual in 1540 (32 Henry VIII, c. 3), that the penalty was altered in 1548 (2–3 Edward VI, c. 29) before being repealed in 1553 (1 Mary, c. 1) and revived in 1562 (5 Eliz., c. 17).[3]

The statute makes "the detestable and abominable vice of buggery committed with mankind or beast" a felony, and goes on to provide that "no person offending in such manner in any such offence, shall be admitted to his clergy."[4] In his opening sentence, Coke refers to the offence as follows: "*If any person* shall commit buggery with mankind or beast; . . . this offence is adjudged felony. . . ." (Italics are mine.) It appears from this statement and from the face of the statute that the offence applied to males and females alike. But Coke goes on to give a fuller description of the offence, and in doing so also shifts his position to give a more limited application to the statute. "Buggery is a detestable, and abominable sin, amongst christians not to be named, committed by carnall knowledge against the ordinance of the Creator, and order of nature, by *mankind with mankind,* or with brute beast, or by *womankind with brute beast.*" (Italics are mine.) He does not make it at all clear at this point whether he is using the term "mankind" in its larger sense to mean "human beings" or in its narrow sense to mean

2 "A more disorderly mind than Coke's and one less gifted with the power of analysing common words it would be impossible to find." An opinion expressed by Sir James Fitzjames Stephen, *A History of the Criminal Law of England* (London, 1883), II, 206. See also footnote 1.
3 See *infra,* Blackstone, p. 15, n. 4.
4 25 Henry VIII, c. 8.

"male persons." A reading of the whole chapter, however, shows that Coke was using the term "mankind" in its narrow sense, thus limiting the offence to "male persons with male persons, or beasts," and "female persons with beasts." Coke supports this interpretation by citing in full Leviticus xviii, 22–23.[5] It is quite clear from a reading of the biblical text that the term "mankind" refers to "male persons."

Coke later affirms this position in discussing the application of this offence to women. "For the words be, if any person, &c., which extend as well to woman, as to a man, and therefore if she commit buggery with a beast, she is a *person* that commits buggery with a beast, *to which end this word* (person) *was used.*" (Italics are mine.) It is essential to notice that Coke here is referring to *his own interpretation* when he says the words are "if any person," and he is in fact misquoting the statute which refers to "the . . . vice of buggery." Whether Coke deliberately misquoted the statute or not, what he emphatically states is that female persons are only liable under this statute in cases of bestiality. His explanation for this kind of act being included as an offence is surprisingly not the biblical text, but rather that "somewhat before the making of this act a great lady committed buggery with a baboon, and conceived by it, &c."[6]

What is of paramount importance is that Coke takes the position that acts of anal intercourse between a male and a female person are not within the purview of this act. He does so even though he was aware that ancient punishments applied to both parties involved in heterosexual acts of anal intercourse. "But in ancient times, in that case, the man was hanged, and the woman was drowned, whereof we have seen examples in the reign of R. 1. And this is the meaning of ancient franchises granted *de furca, et fossa,* of the gallows, and the pit, for the hanging upon the one, and drowning in the other, but *fossa* was taken away, and *furca* remains." He does not, however, relate this discussion to his other conclusions. Can it be that Coke reasoned that, because the punishment of drowning was meted out to females and subsequently taken away, therefore females were no longer punishable for acts of anal intercourse? Or did he deliberately limit the offence to male homosexual acts of anal intercourse because of the biblical texts on which he relied? What lends great weight to Coke's interpretation is that he was

5 "22. Thou shalt not lie with mankind as with womankind: it is abomination: 23. Neither shalt thou lie with any beast to defile thyself therewith: neither shall any woman stand before a beast to lie down thereto: it is confusion." (Authorized King James Version.)
6 This is a biological impossibility. I leave it to the reader to conjecture whether Coke was passing on a folk myth, or gossip involving a case of mistaken identity or paternity.

closer in time to that particular piece of legislation than any subsequent writer, that he was attorney-general 32 years after its passage, and chief justice of the King's Bench at about the time the *Institutes* were written.

Before proceeding with the rest of Coke's discussion, it is of interest to pause here to consider how later writers dealt with this point. Sir Matthew Hale, writing some fifty years after Coke, undoubtedly was familiar with the *Institutes*, although he made no reference to them. He follows the position taken by Coke that "a woman may be guilty of buggery with a beast within this statute."[7] Hawkins, who wrote in the early 1700s, reduced his whole discussion of the subject to some twelve lines, including modes of ancient punishment, legislative origin, and key words in the indictment. In this highly condensed version, what emerged is: "All unnatural carnal copulations, whether with man or beast, seem to come under the notion of Sodomy."[8] Blackstone swathed himself in a cloak of propriety and avoided the issue, as will be seen later. East, who cited all of the authors referred to above, states, "This offence (Sodomy) consists in a carnal knowledge committed against the order of nature, by man with man, or in the same unnatural manner with woman, or by a man or woman in any manner with beast."[9] Russell, in 1819, repeats East word for word.[10] It can be seen that it was after Hawkins' terse speculation that subsequent writers broadened the interpretation placed on this offence by Coke and Hale.

Coke identifies the word "bugeria" as an Italian word, which he says has the same meaning as he gave the term, and says that "pederastes" or "pederestes" is the Greek word signifying "lover of little boys," which he regarded as a species of buggery. He reports that it was complained in parliament that the Lombards had introduced the shameful sin into the realm.[11]

With respect to punishment, he notes that the ancient authors all say that the offence deserves death, but vary in the means to be employed; Britton gives the penalty as burning, while Fleta and the Mirror held

---

7 Sir Mathew Hale, *The History of the Pleas of the Crown* (London, 1800), I, 669–70.

8 William Hawkins, *A Treatise of the Pleas of the Crown* (8th ed., London, 1824), I, 357. Hawkins gives no explanation as to why he drops the term buggery in favour of sodomy. Is nothing more involved than linguistic custom or style?

9 Edward Hyde East, *A Treatise of the Pleas of the Crown* (London, 1803), I, 480.

10 William Oldnall Russell, *A Treatise on Crimes and Indictable Offences* (London, 1819), I, 815.

11 Coke cites Rot. Parl. 50 Eliz. This attribution to aliens should be considered along with the fact that the Lombards were a wealthy class of Italian merchants, brokers, and bankers, formally banished during Elizabeth's reign.

that "Those who commit unchaste acts with animals and sodomites are to be buried alive."

From these passages, one is left with the impression that Coke was reporting by rote. There is a generous sprinkling of Latin phrases but there is a distinct lack of any critical or analytic discussion in depth on any issue. For example, he writes of "lovers of little boys" as "a species" of buggery, but he does not elaborate. What factors make up this species? What other "species" exist? What are their elements? What are the differences which might be important for the law? Again, characteristically, Coke passes over these problems.

Coke enters into a phrase-by-phrase discussion of his definition:[12]

(i) *Detestable and abominable.*] Those just attributes are found in the act of 25 H. 8.

(ii) *Amongst Christians not to be named.*] These words are in the usual indictment of this offence. . . .

(iii) *By carnall knowledge, &c.*] The words of the indictment be, *contrary to the ordinance of the creator, and the order of nature, he had sexual relations and carnall knowledge of the said boy, &c.** So as there must be *penetration,** that is, *the thing in the thing,** either with mankind, or with beast, but the least penetration maketh it carnall knowledge.

(iv) Both the agent and consentient are felons: and this is consonant to the law of God. *If any one lie with a man as with a woman, both have committed an abomination, let them die the death.**[13] And this accordeth with the ancient rule of law, *those who do it and those who consent to it are to be punished with like penalty.**

(v) *Ejaculation of seed** maketh it not buggery, but is an evidence in case of buggery of penetration: and so in rape the words be also, *had carnall knowledge of,** and therefore must be penetration; and *ejaculation of seed** without penetration maketh no rape.

Coke's treatment of this part of the chapter is a rambling admixture of words taken from the statute, indictments, the Bible, and common law principles. There is a strong reliance on scripture although many of his references point to little more than the story of Sodom being destroyed by fire. The impression remains that he uncritically copied a biblical concordance. There is a lack of arrangement; for example, following his discussion of the term "carnal knowledge," he includes, without comment, the biblical explanation of how the Sodomites came

12 The single square brackets and the italics in the following passages are those found in the original text. The asterisk signifies that the preceding quotation or phrase has been translated from Latin.
13 Coke cites Leviticus, xx, 13. The Authorized King James Version reads: "If a man also lie with mankind, as he lieth with a woman, both of them have committed an abomination; they shall surely be put to death; their blood shall be upon them."

to this practice through pride, excess of diet, idleness, and contempt of the poor. ("The idle man thinks of nothing except his belly and Venus.") Seemingly to round off the chapter, but unrelated to the preceding discussion, he gives an unidentified Latin quotation on the four "crying sins" (*clamantia peccata*), known as such because in the Bible these were the sins which cried out to God for punishment. "The voice of shouts, the voice of blood [Cain and Abel], of Sodomites, the voice of the oppressed and the unpaid wages of labour."

In fairness to Sir Edward Coke, although his approach is a desultory and uncritical one, it must be said that his treatment of the subject is more forthright and complete than that afforded the topic by his successors, including Hale, Hawkins, Blackstone, East, or Russell. He gives a narrow interpretation to the statute, as has been shown, but utterly fails to give any explanation as to the inconsistency between his views and those of the ancient authors. Coke was a strong and persuasive figure in his time, and it may be that he was aware of the inconsistency and chose to ignore it to give greater authority to his own position, supported as it was by scripture. But there is the lurking suspicion that he was so certain of his own view that he was blind to the inconsistency which faced him.

One might be critical of his use of words, his inaccuracy with respect to the legislative history, and his failure to attempt any classification; one might be disappointed at not finding a more closely reasoned work. Coke is open to such criticism, but he also provided an open, informed discussion of the topic and gave at least a firm biblical position for his views. Over the intervening three and a half centuries our legal position with respect to this offence has not altered appreciably, nor have our jurisdictions coped consistently with the terminology of buggery and sodomy, and who can lay claim to having identified the "species"?

Sir William Blackstone

About 150 years after Coke's *Institutes*, Blackstone published his *Commentaries on the Laws of England*, and it is volume IV, *Of Public Wrongs*, dealing with crimes and misdemeanours, which contains sections relevant to this study.

Coke made no attempt at classification, but Blackstone, faced with a far greater number of offences, was obliged to do so. He was not equal to the mammoth task. His classification gives the immediate impression of creating order out of what must have been chaos, but his decisions with respect to the few offences which concern us here do not make sense.

Blackstone classified what he termed the "crime against nature" with "such other crime and misdemeanors, as more particularly affect the *security of his person,* while living."[1] In this category he also included mayhem, forcible abduction, and rape. But the one element present in each of the other offences, which is not necessarily present in the offence of buggery, is that of force. It would be entirely understandable if Blackstone had in mind cases of non-consenting, forcible acts of anal intercourse, but he makes it clear that consenting parties to the act, that is, both agent and patient, if both are of age, are liable under the statute.

What "security of person" is protected in the punishment of acts between consenting parties? Is the "security" with respect to the agent who does the penetrating different from that of the patient who is penetrated? Is there a physical danger to both parties, even though they are consenting? If the answer is yes in the case of the patient, is it the same for the agent? None of these questions is answered by Blackstone, and the impression remains that participation in the act alone constitutes the danger. But danger to what? What may be operating here is the whole conception of what the human body is. If it is conceived as a holy vessel, into which the Holy Spirit has been poured, or a house of God, then an entry of the kind in question can be regarded as a defilement of the body seen in that light. If this is the basis for his classification, then Blackstone must have had in mind the spiritual aspect, the spiritual concept of a person, when he classified this offence as one against "security of person." In this sense, participation in this kind of act is an offence or an affront to the spiritual aspect of man. Seen in this way the consenting parties are not victims of each other in any physical sense, but both can be considered as hurt, or victims, because of the spiritual implications of the act. As they share the responsibility for the occurrence of the act, they are also the offenders.

How different this is from the other kinds of cases Blackstone places in the same category – mayhem, forcible abduction, and rape. In those cases, first and foremost, the physical security of one person is protected from injury by the forceful acts of others, and one can designate, on the surface at least, one party as the offender and the other as the victim.

In cases of buggery with an animal, or bestiality as we now term it,

1 William Blackstone, *Commentaries on the Laws of England,* vol. IV, *Of Public Wrongs* (Oxford, 1769), p. 205. Italics are mine.

the only "person" involved is the offender himself. If Blackstone gave any thought to this offence at all, which is doubtful, he must have had in mind some self-inflicted harm, which once again is different from the other offences in the section. It is nothing but confusion to classify "open and notorious lewdness" under the "Offences against God and Religion," and to classify this offence, which he justifies by reference to scripture and "the express law of God," as an "Offence against the Person of Individuals." One might well ask what sense there is anyway in classifying under one heading acts of physical aggression aimed at killing or disfiguring another, acts prompted by economic motives ("stealing an heiress," as forcible abduction was vulgarly known), sexually aggressive though not necessarily "perverted" acts, and sexually deviant acts? What would we think of medicine as a discipline if it considered sunburn, measles, bruises, and skin cancer under one category because they all manifested themselves on the body surface?

The closest Blackstone comes to a definition or a description of the offence is "the infamous *crime against nature,* committed either with man or beast."[2] He makes no mention of the interpretation given to the statute by Coke, whereby females are liable under the offence only in cases of bestial acts. What is more objectionable is that he totally abandons the terms "buggery" and "sodomy" in favour of the phrase "crime against nature." One can assign any term an exact meaning, but Blackstone does not do so here. Taking the phrase alone, and without prior knowledge of the meaning he chooses to give it, one is free to conjure up such diverse ideas as the artificial fluoridation of water or the incautious use of insecticides. Blackstone was in fact reaching for another level of abstraction from his subject matter.

The subject was obviously repugnant to Blackstone, as can be seen from the trail of adjectives and epithets he leaves in his wake: "a deeper malignity," "an offence of so dark a nature," "the very mention of which is a disgrace to human nature," and "miscreants." In not discussing the subject, he claims to imitate "the delicacy of English law, which treats it, in its very indictments, as a crime not fit to be named." He must have been aware that the statute itself names the crime.

Blackstone's adoption of the more abstract expression, his epithetical treatment of the subject matter, and his defence behind a porous veil of custom all suggest that he was in fact displaying a very typical human reaction in shying away from an unpleasant topic. But though normal, this reaction may be all the more reason why we require a more exact terminology, as technical as medical or scientific language, to enable us

2 *Ibid.,* IV, 215–16.

to discuss such things with precision, as unhampered by general emotional reactions as possible.

Having avoided any adequate discussion of the offence out of a sense of propriety, Blackstone is not so constrained on the topic of punishment. "This the voice of nature and of reason and the express law of God, determine to be capital. Of which we have a signal instance, long before the Jewish dispensation, by the destruction of two cities by fire from heaven: so that this is an universal, not merely a provincial, precept." There is not a scintilla of doubt in Blackstone's account that the punishment provided for this offence is the only right one. He speaks of it as "A crime, which ought to be strictly and impartially proved, and then as strictly and impartially punished." In his earlier discussion of capital punishment, he was of the opinion that it was inflicted in these cases "after the *example* of the creator, in his positive code of laws for the regulation of the Jewish republic; as in the case of the crime against nature,"[3] whereas in cases of murder the punishment was a direct command of God himself to all mankind.

Only by glossing over the legislative history of this offence is he able to give it the appearance of universality. Enacted for a temporary period in 1533, it was made perpetual in 1540. In 1548 the penalties were reduced, and although still capital, could no longer affect the property of the offender. In 1553 the offence was totally repealed; it was re-invoked nine years later in 1562. Blackstone's account rather tends to underplay the temporal character of the offence.[4]

3 *Ibid.*, IV, 9.
4 A more detailed account of the legislative history is as follows: In 1533 a statute (25 Henry VIII, c. 6) was passed, in part as follows: "Forasmuch as there is not yet sufficient and condign punishment appointed and limited by the due course of laws of this realm, for the detestable and abominable vice of buggery committed with mankind or beast: (2) it may therefore please the King . . . that the same offence be from henceforth adjuged felony. . . ." The statute provided penalties, "such pains of death, and losses and penalties of their goods, chattels, debts, lands, tenements and hereditaments," and was to be without benefit of clergy. The statute was enacted to be in force until the "last day of the next parliament." In 1540 the statute was made perpetual (32 Henry VIII, c. 3) in these terms: ". . . shall continue and endure in their full force and strength, and be observed and kept forever." Eight years later, in 1548, the statute was repealed in part by 2-3 Edward VI, c. 29, a statute remarkable in its brevity: "An offender in buggery being attained by confession, verdict or outlawry, shall suffer death as a felon, without loss of lands, goods or corruption of blood."
The resoluteness of 1540 vanished in 1553 when the first statute was repealed by 1 Mary, c. 1, which also abolished all offences made felony since the first day of the reign of Henry VIII. Her purpose in doing so is admirably set out in section II: "The Queen's most excellent Majesty, calling to remembrance that many, as well as honourable and noble persons, as others of good reputation within this her Grace's realm of England, have of late (for words only, without

It was easier for Blackstone to criticize capital punishment when discussing the subject generally, removed from specific offences.

A multitude of sanguinary laws (besides the doubt that may be entertained concerning the right of making them) do likewise prove a manifest defect either in the wisdom of the legislative, or the strength of the executive power. It is a kind of quackery in government, and argues a want of solid skill, to apply the same universal remedy, the *ultimum supplicum*, to every case of difficulty. It is, it must be owned, much *easier* to extirpate than amend mankind: yet that magistrate must be esteemed both a weak and cruel surgeon, who cuts off every limb, which through ignorance or indolence he will not attempt to cure.[5]

Blackstone was not able to carry over these observations to his consideration of the punishment for buggery. He was not one to argue strongly for changes of the established order, and he saw his duty as permitting him only to "hint them with decency to those, whose abilities and stations enable them to apply the remedy."[6] In this instance, Blackstone did not even hint at a change in surgical procedure; he was no reformer.

Assault with Intent to Commit Unnatural Crimes

Blackstone does not group this offence with those "more immediately against the personal security of the subject," but terms it an "inferior offence," as "a breach of the king's peace, an affront to his government, and a damage done to his subjects. . . ."[7]

As in case of an assault with intent to murder, or with intent to commit either of the crimes last spoken of [Rape and Unnatural Crimes]; for which intentional assaults, in the last two cases, indictments are much more usual,

---

other opinion, fact or deed) suffered shameful death not accustomed to nobles; her Highness therefore of her accustomed clemency and mercy, minding to avoid and put away occasion and cause of like chances hereafter to ensure, trusting her loving subjects will, for her clemency to them shewed, love, serve and obey her Grace the more heartily and faithfully, than for dread or fear of pains of body, is contented and pleased that the severity of such like extreme, dangerous and painful laws, shall be abolished, annulled and frustrate and void." In 1562 a statute, 5 Eliz., c. 17, revived in full force the original statute of Henry VIII, for the following reason, "since which repeal [that of Queen Mary] so had and made, divers evil disposed persons have been the more bold to commit the said most horrible and detestable vice of buggery, aforesaid, to the high displeasure of Almighty God."
5 Blackstone, *Commentaries*, IV, 17.
6 *Ibid.*, IV, 4–5.
7 *Ibid.*, IV, 217.

than for the absolute perpetration of the facts themselves, on account of the difficulty of proof: And herein, besides heavy fine and imprisonment, it is usual to award judgment of the pillory.

In Blackstone's description of the common law practice of his day can be seen the early rudimentary forms which were only later to emerge as statutory offences. What is of interest to us here is that the offence which we now refer to as "assault with intent to commit buggery" was not originally seen as a concrete entity, a separate offence from the complete act of buggery, but was deliberately developed to meet a practical difficulty, that is, to provide a sanction where proof of the full act was difficult to obtain. Robert Malcolm Kerr, one of the early adapters of Blackstone's *Commentaries*, added the following passage: "When both parties are consenting to an unnatural attempt, it is usual not to charge any *assault*; but that one of them laid hands on the other with intent to commit, and that the other permitted the same with intent to suffer, the commission of the abominable crime before mentioned."[8] It can be seen that in cases of consenting parties, where the existence of the consent was a good defence to the concept of assault, the early innovators of the day were able to circumvent the difficulty by resorting to a very direct description of the behaviour, "one of them laid hands on the other" and "the other permitted the same." As will be seen later, when consideration is given to the legislative development of this offence, subsequent classifiers were to group this offence under "Assaults," thus misconstruing the character and intention of the early indictments.

Open and Notorious Lewdness

Blackstone includes under the heading of "Offences against God and Religion," "such crimes and misdemeanors, as more immediately offend Almighty God, by openly transgressing the precepts of religion either natural or revealed; and mediately, by their bad example and consequence, the law of society also; which constitutes that guilt in the action, which human tribunals are to censure."[9]

8 William Blackstone, *Commentaries* (1769), adapted by Robert Malcolm Kerr, ed. Charles M. Haar (Boston, for Beacon Series in Classics of the Law, 1962), p. 217. The *Commentaries* received instant and immense success and were imported in great numbers by the American Colonies. The first American editions were printed in 1771–72. The exact date of the Kerr adaptation is not given in this edition.
9 Blackstone, *Commentaries*, IV, 43.

Although it may now appear difficult to find a relationship "more immediate" than "immediate," Blackstone's circular reasoning enabled him to enclose a rich diversity of offences, including apostasy, heresy, witchcraft, drunkenness, and open and notorious lewdness. "The last offence which I shall mention, more immediately against religion and morality, and cognizable by the temporal courts, is that of open and notorious *lewdness*: either by frequenting houses of ill fame, which is an indictable offence; or by some grossly scandalous and public indecency, for which the punishment is by fine and imprisonment. [Citing] 1 Siderf. 168."[10] Blackstone does not go so far as to tell us how this offence is "more immediately against religion," and he may have been copying Hawkins before him, who classified this and certain other common law offences as "more immediately against God not capital." Hawkins had been rather more forthright with his description of the offence: "Fourthly, All open lewdness grossly scandalous; such as was that of those persons who exposed themselves naked to the people in a balcony in Covent Garden with most abominable circumstances."[11] The reference in both Hawkins and Blackstone is to the case of Sir Charles Sidley, which was decided in 1663. Part of the original case report (translated from the Norman French used in reporting the cases in those days) is as follows:

Sr. Charles Sidley was indicted at common law for several misdemeanors against the peace of the King and which were to the great scandal of Christianity, in that he showed his nude body in a balcony in Covent Garden to a large multitude of people and there did such things and spoke such words etc. (giving then particulars of his behaviour) . . . [the court] wished him to know that this Court is "custos morum" of all the King's subjects, and it is high time to punish such profane actions which were against all modesty . . . Christianity and also morality. . . . The Court considered which judgment to give him, and because he was a gentleman of a large family (living in Kent) and his estate was encumbered (not intending his ruin but to reform him) they fined him 2000 marks and he would be imprisoned for 1 week without bail and be of good behaviour for 3 years.[12]

It is important to note that, having taken place before a "large multitude of people" in Covent Garden, the offence was "to the great

10 *Ibid.*, IV, 64.
11 William Hawkins, *A Treatise of the Pleas of the Crown* (8th ed., London, 1824), I, 358.
12 1 Sid. 168; 82 E.R. 1036. The case is also reported in 1 Keb. 620; 83 E.R. 1146, where the accused's name is spelled "Sydlyes" and the place where the offence occurred is given as "Convent Garden." From other information available it is almost certain that the place was not then a convent although it might very well have been the site of such an institution in earlier days.

scandal of Christianity," and that it was against, not specific persons, but "all modesty . . . Christianity and also morality." It is the public character of the act which provoked censure, the public sense of decency, the general modesty, morality, and Christianity which was offended against. This is again made clear by the court's reference to itself as "custos morum" of *all* the King's subjects. The court referred to these acts as "profane" not in the sense of "secular" but in the sense of being irreligious or irreverent. Blackstone's reference to this offence as "notorious" lewdness also suggests that the act or acts were well known, widely but unfavourably talked about.

When Blackstone abstracts this offence to "grossly scandalous and public indecency" and then neglects to deal further with it, he contributes towards its eventual confusion with "indecent exposure of the person." He also lays the foundation for another offence, that of "gross indecency" which was later to take on a character quite different from the kind of act aimed at in the original indictments. Once again it must be pointed out that the absorbing power of abstracted phraseology which lacks a clear definition contains hidden dangers for subsequent misunderstanding.

One must acknowledge with some gratitude Blackstone's work in raking together the leaves of an abundant century. Though he added no precision to his definitions, yet his work, like Coke's before him, established another plateau in English law. Perhaps it does not fall to those who consolidate to be also critical and analytical. Certainly Blackstone was neither of these.

Although he undertook to classify the offences, it cannot be said of him that he advanced the nosology of crimes. His categories were too contrived, his processing of the offences too perfunctory. His sense of propriety gave him a predilection for the abstract phrase, decorous but inappropriate for a work of this kind. For those who must know the function of bones and muscle, it is pointless to deliver a panegyric on the soul. It may be said of Blackstone, as Stephen observed, that he rescued the laws of England from chaos, if this is taken broadly to mean that he gave them some sort of organization. But where the subject matter was distasteful to him he obscured and confused what existed, thus adding another kind of chaos and in a way which has been perhaps more insidious, for the laws in those instances have not yet been rescued from his influence.

Jeremy Bentham

Bentham heard Blackstone's lectures in 1763, but it was not until 51 years later in 1814, at the age of 67, that he turned to his own systematic analysis of sex offences. His first attempt was in connection with part of his penal code, and two years later he returned to the subject again with the intention of preparing a separate treatise. Neither was completed and only a much condensed version, a welding of the two works, has been published.[1] The fragment available is too highly edited to provide a fully satisfying exposition of Bentham's treatment of the subject, but notwithstanding this limitation, his division of the subject matter and particularly his analysis of proscriptions merit consideration.

Bentham referred to the sex offences as "offences against taste," attempting by the use of neuter terms to avoid as much controversy as possible which turns on a projection of feelings.[2] It is significant that Bentham took "sex offences" together as a group for purposes of his examination and in this respect anticipated the Canadian Code by about 150 years.

To delineate the scope of his subject, Bentham begins with the following definition: "Any act having for its object the immediate gratification of the sexual appetite may be termed *an act of sexuality.*" Bentham proceeds to classification, using the "dichotomic" or "exhaustive" method.[3] He divides sexual acts into two classes, those regularly exercised, "i.e. in a manner conformable to rule, viz. the rule prescribed by public opinion," and those irregularly exercised, "i.e. in a manner unconformable to that same rule." The first class he divides into those potentially prolific and those not potentially prolific. The

1 Jeremy Bentham, *The Theory of Legislation*, ed. C. K. Ogden (London, 1931), pp. 473–97. The original manuscripts run to some two hundred closely written pages of foolscap which have been reduced by Ogden to some twenty pages. Consequently it is difficult to determine to which specific offences the arguments raised by Bentham relate. Whether this shortcoming should be attributed to Bentham or his editor cannot be decided without reference to the original manuscripts.

2 *Ibid.*, p. 515, a note to page 78 regarding "neuter terms." See also p. xii, Ogden's opinion that "Orthology, the science of correct symbolism . . . was the corner-stone of Bentham's system."

3 Elie Halévy, *The Growth of Philosophical Radicalsm* (London, 1928), p. 60. For Bentham's description of the method see *The Works of Jeremy Bentham*, ed. John Bowering (New York, 1962), I, 493.

second class he analyses at length, prefacing his remarks with the words, "Now comes the task of moral anatomy: now comes the case in which disgust awaits the reader, and, through that disgust, reproach the author." His divisions are made according to whether the operation takes place between persons of the same sex, persons of different sexes but under age, unmarried, and married but outside legal bond. Ogden has abridged these classifications, so that for a full account of them resort must be had to the manuscripts contained in Portfolio 74b, University College, London, England.

Bentham completely ignores the existing sexual offences and begins by delineating what he regards as sexual acts, including those of which society approves as well as those of which it does not. From the meagre account available, it can be seen that he begins, not with *specific acts* such as buggery, but with a system of broad categories established by using primary parameters, to distinguish different kinds of *relationships*. To spell it out further, using the parameters of "male" and "female," he distinguished homosexual relationships from heterosexual relationships. He went on to use the simple parameters of age and marital status, but how precisely he used these is still unforgivably locked in his unpublished works. It is not yet known whether he went on to relate specific acts within the various relationships to form even more precise categories. Bentham's great insight was that the kind of system of classification which was needed must take into account the relationship between the parties involved and not rest solely on an unrelated act. What is of major importance is that here for the first time is a deliberate attempt, however crude, to proceed systematically in identifying the "species" which Coke, two hundred years earlier, had intuitively glimpsed.

Using the principle of utility, Bentham goes on to argue that there can be only one source of reference, that is, the effect of an act on the sum of happiness. An act is noxious (hurtful, harmful, injurious in a moral sense) or it is not. Until it can be proven to be noxious, it must be acknowledged as beneficial (for unless attended with pleasure it is never performed) and not simply as innoxious. He then sets out five classifications:

1. Noxiousness to the operator himself and him alone on the score of health.

2. Noxiousness to the operator himself and him alone on the score of reputation.

3. Noxiousness to one of two or more parties, the party or parties being actually repugnant or at least not consenting.

4. Noxiousness with reference to a third person or determinate individual.

5. Noxiousness with reference to third persons at large, i.e., to individuals indeterminate in respect of identity or number.

Bentham deals only with the first two categories, and holds that they demand prudential care on the part of the individual or his guardian but no interference on the part of the legislator. He does not elaborate on the last three divisions.

One need not agree with Bentham's principle of utility, the basic philosophic position which gave him a consistent perspective, but it was at least an enunciated one. He recognized, though he did not complete the task himself, that one must spell out the attending evils before a sanction was imposed. It was important to know not only who was injured, but in what way they were injured. This close examination of consequences, the quest for specific, was Bentham's reaction against the abstractive tendency of Blackstone before him, and a call for detailed discussion to replace rhetoric.

In examining the "State of the Public Mind in England in Relation to the Irregularities of the Sexual Appetite," Bentham acknowledges that "it will not be possible to compress any such representation as shall approximate in any degree to the truth." The cause of so vast a difference of opinion, he concludes, "will probably be found in a great measure in the state of the law." "Whatsoever may have place in practice, decency, according to the notions generally attached to the word, will in general keep it excluded from the field of conversation: the cases in which it makes its appearance in that field are those in which it is dragged into it by the hand of the law." He describes the prevailing English attitude as one which is indulgent to the "noxious" class of case (e.g., adultery) but reserves its fury for the "innoxious"; but even in this it is not consistent, for while it pays little regard to intercourse between two females, it makes up this deficiency when it is between two males.

Bentham deals briefly with the terms "unnatural," "odiousness," and "abomination." His comments on the first two terms are quoted here in full, because resort to them and their like still occurs.

1. *Unnatural* – The imputation senseless. Considered as indication of any quality as having place in the practice itself, it is difficult to find for it any detrimental import.

The truth is that by the epithet *unnatural*, when applied to any human act or thought, the only matter of which it affords any indication that can be depended upon is the existence of a sentiment of disapprobation, accompanied with passion in the breast of the person by whom it is employed: a degree of passion by which without staying to inquire whether the practice be or be not noxious to society, he endeavours by the use thus made of this inflammatory word to kindle and point towards the object of this ill-will the same passion in other breasts for the purpose of inducing them to join with him in producing pain in the breast of him by whom the passion has been excited.[4]

2. *Odiousness* – The man who, on the ground of the odiousness of the practice – i.e. the disgust excited in his mind and that of others by the idea of it – calls for punishment to be inflicted on those by whom the unpleasant emotion is produced, sets up a principle of which, if adopted, nothing less than the extirpation of the human race would be the result. That without any other ground the bare existence of the affection of hatred should afford a sufficient justification for the gratification of it – did any notion more atrocious than this, or more universally destructive, ever gain entrance into the human breast?[5]

One can see here the ferocity of Bentham's attack against the kind of treatment which Blackstone, for example, with his abundant use of adjectives and epithets noted earlier, afforded the same topic.

Bentham proceeds to expound his views on the underlying "ill-principled" causes of proscription: *asceticism* which springs either from a "love of reputation," i.e. the desire to become an object of admiration by maintaining a line of conduct which others do not, or "love of amity," i.e. the desire to ingratiate oneself to an almighty being; *that antipathy of which every diversity of opinion may be subject*, which is only mischievous when transferred from the act itself to the agent; *notions attached to the words "purity" and "impurity"*; *envy*, apt to be excited in the breast of every man through contemplation of an enjoyment which is out of his power; *desire of praise on the score of virtue*; *opportunity to gratify the passion of antipathy* without incurring the slightest disrepute; and, a precautionary *defence* against the imputation of the same propensity when well grounded or an apprehension that it may be made. Bentham concludes that these principal causes have given

4 The term "Unnatural Offences" was a general heading under An Act Respecting Offences against the Person, and covered the offences of buggery, bestiality, assault with intent to commit buggery, and indecent assault on a male (S.C. 1869, 32–33 Vict., c. 20). The term has made a more recent appearance. A banking and commerce subcommittee substituted "unnatural sexual act" for the term "gross indecency" when the Criminal Code was in a draft stage as Bill H-8 before the senate in the Spring of 1952. The change was adopted by the full committee but not incorporated in subsequent drafts (Senate, Canada, Standing Committee on Banking and Commerce, 1952, p. 18). The term "abominable" was also used in relation to the offences mentioned above in 1869, but dropped in 1886.
5 Lord Patrick Devlin (*The Enforcement of Morals* (London, 1965), p. 17) employs the word "disgust." For his defence against his many critics on this point, see the preface, p. viii.

rise to a violence of antipathy which in the British Isles, more than in all other countries, "nothing less than the heart's blood of the victims marked out for slaughter . . . has hitherto been unable to satisfy." In his view, "whatever fault there is has for its seat the breasts, not of those who are the objects of the antipathy, but those who harbour it."

He then sets out to meet the reasons given for legal punishment, reasons which he classifies as "alleged mischiefs." The first argument dealt with, and the most plausible, is that there may be *injury to population*. Bentham's rebuttal is based on three grounds: these laws are incapable of having any effect on population; that, if there were any effect, and that effect was in depletion of the population, this is beneficial because much of the misery which affects the civilized part of the globe flows from an excess of population; and lastly, if the behaviour in question had any unfavourable effect on population, punishment applied to such practices would not be a proper course for filling the supposed deficiency. The second argument is based on *enervation*, i.e. detriment to health and strength. Bentham agrees that it cannot be reasonably doubted that there may be detriment and probably has been but in reply he raises three questions: Suppose there was evil resulting, is it of such quantity and value as to be preponderant over the good which results? If yes, does it merit the use of such rigorous legal sanction as the English laws require? And lastly, is it more enervating than "other irregularities," such as "the solitary mode" (presumably masturbation), which are not punishable? The third alleged mischief is that the behaviour leads to *indifference towards the opposite sex*. Bentham dismisses this argument on the following basis: To human beings of either sex there is no danger in seeing "a rival in any degree formidable in an animal of a different species"; there is little likelihood that women will become indifferent to men to any mischievous extent because (presumably) of lesbian activity; and lastly, as for men growing indifferent to females, there is evidence in abundance to show the strength of the influence females have over males for good or evil. He argues that such indifferences are conceivable, but it is unreasonable to hold that because they are conceivable they are probable. Nothing in support of the probability of this result has ever been deduced either from the general principles of human behaviour or from anything found in history.

Bentham then turns from the above "imaginary evils" to what he regards as the "real ones." He unequivocally states his position in the following passage: "Irregular – unnatural – call them by what names of reproach you will, of these gratifications nothing but good, pure good, if pleasure without pain be a pure good (mischief from excess being implied out of the case), will be found. But when the act be pure good, punishment, for whatsoever *purpose*, from whatsoever *source*, in whatsoever *name* and in whatsoever *degree* applied in consideration of it, will be not only evil, but so much pure evil."

Bentham then enumerates the "Real Mischief from the Punishment and Restraint applied in these same cases." He first notes the punishments meted out by the legal and political sanctions, the popular (presumably social) sanction of infamy, and the religious sanction through the fear of hell torment. He lists the punishment inflicted on the innocent in consequence of false evidence. He includes the fear of punishment in delinquents, resulting in self-banishment, as well as that fear experienced by non-delinquents. There is also the loss of enjoyment through the fear of punishment and the pain resulting when such fear causes a violent restraint on behaviour. In conclusion, Bentham points to the most serious kind of evil, blackmail: "How easy it is to fabricate out of the dread of an accusation of this nature an instrument of extortion is but too obvious."

Drawing an analogy between intolerance to these acts and religious intolerance, Bentham asserts that the Englishman regards with abhorrence men being burnt alive by the Spanish *auto da fe*, "Yet in a subject of infinitely less importance, for a divergence not in opinion, but merely in taste, with no other difference than that between hanging and burning, will the same man with indefensible satisfaction behold the same punishment inflicted on a fellow-countryman in every other respect void of offence. For heresy in religion, no; but for heresy in taste, what can be more reasonable?"

Bentham's "analysis of the existing proscription" is by far the largest part and perhaps the most satisfactory part of the work. Acknowledging the attitude of the society around him, he launches a violent criticism against it on many levels: its verbal expressions, its hidden psychological motivations and philosophical premises, its rational arguments, as well as the harmfulness, as he sees it, of the external and internal pressures resulting from the laws. This is not a section-by-section analysis of the existing law, but mounted on a much higher sociological, psychological, and philosophical plane. One is hampered by not knowing precisely which offences Bentham is discussing, nor can one come to any decision as to how much of the fault lies with Bentham and how much lies with Ogden, his editor.

Bentham then presents his case of "all comprehensive liberty" under the heading of "Beneficial Tendencies of Certain of These Modes." (He was aware that such a title would provoke extreme impatience in some readers and in others a far angrier and defensive response, but unless such an investigation was made, he concluded, the interests of truth, public utility, and justice would be sacrificed.) In the first place, he writes, there would be an addition to the mass of pleasure, for although the source of such pleasure might disgust and horrify some, we cannot in logic deny using the word pleasure "to an appetite the gratification of which has been sought by such multitudes at the risk and frequently to the sacrifice of life. Whether or not a man is the *proper* judge, every man is, in fact, the judge and the sole judge to the purpose of his conduct, of what is agreeable or disagreeable to himself." Secondly, without elaboration, he lists "Prevention of the injury liable to be done to health by solitary gratification." Thirdly, he views pederasty as free from the "dangers which accompany fornication," such as conception out of wedlock, the loss of reputation, and, to prevent that, the hazard of procuring abortion and infanticide, as well as the inevitable consequence of prostitution in many cases. Fourthly, he includes the "diminution of the amount of female prostitution" regarded by him as a greater net balance of "evil" from which pederasty is free. He cites in particular the despondency of prostitutes, the contempt in which they are held, the disease resulting from excess and contagion, and the alcoholism resorted to as a palliative. Lastly, he considered one of the benefits to be that if the destiny of a wife was to have a rival, her mortification would be less and there would be less to fear if the rival were one of her husband's sex rather than her own.

Bentham's conclusion: "All comprehensive liberty proposed. Punishment in no case justifiable without proof of the demand for punishment; the proof lies with him by whom punishment is proposed or advocated." Only on the last point does he elaborate, "It is by this means alone that the powers thus exercised can be distinguished from *tyranny*, the offspring of *caprice*."

He argues that benefits to genuine morality in general (excluding false and spurious morality) would result, and sets this out as one of the "Advantages from Proposed Liberty." Bentham holds that man's character is chequered, and as he cannot achieve perfect conformity to the rule of right, some deviations are not incompatible with whatever degree of excellence he can attain, therefore he might better yield to transgressions[6] which are innoxious, rather than those which are noxious.

6 Bentham nowhere seems to define this term, but he believed there were in law a number of offences which were really *against oneself* – what he at other times called "vices and imprudences" – from which no injury to another person results, or if it does it is but the consequence of injury done to oneself. It is likely that "transgressions" would fall into that class.

Bentham's approach is almost the antithesis of that taken by Blackstone: where the latter set out to gather the law as it existed, Bentham set out to make his own analysis; where Blackstone defended and reflected the attitudes in the existing state of the law, Bentham attacked those attitudes and was aware that he was leaving himself open to the criticism of public opinion.

Bentham's wisdom cannot be reached by comparing him with Blackstone. He saw the relatedness of sex offences as a whole, and he recognized the need for classification which he then set out rationally and intellectually to construct. In seeking the principle of natural classification, Bentham tried to adapt the methodology of botany and chemistry, to create a workable scientific nomenclature.[7] The classifiers in those sciences had been able to define significant differences quite precisely between species and between elements, based on empirical data, but Bentham did not have such data before him. He lacked – and perhaps it was his only lack – the scientific tools to match his own insights. His powers of observation were phenomenal and carried him a long way towards a new science, but never to a consummation. The morality of his system was rooted in a controversial philosophical principle, and as utilitarianism waned, so did the influence of Bentham's ideas for constructing a criminal code. But medicine and mathematics,[8] the two sciences from which he drew his inspiration, may yet prove to be the correct models for the science he struggled so hard to establish.

The approach taken by Bentham has not been followed in the development of the law in relation to sex offences. He never so much as added a brick to the standing pile, but his criticism of what existed then and to a large measure still exists, and the solution toward which he pointed, represent an important part of the historical picture. Bentham stands as the critic and would-be reformer of Blackstone's orthodoxy.

7 Halévy, *Philosophical Radicalism*, pp. 29, 30.
8 Bentham, *Works*, III, 224.

Sir James Fitzjames Stephen

No single person has had such a direct and powerful impact on the criminal law as we know it in Canada today as that nineteenth-century barrister, codifier, essayist, and judge, Sir James Fitzjames Stephen. From 1855 until his death some forty years later he was a prolific writer, whose range of subject matter and depth of learning are not even hinted at by his reputation as the father of the English Draft Code. He was well prepared for his eventual role as "the greatest draftsman and codifier of criminal law which Great Britain ever produced."[1] For fifteen years he led a double life as a barrister and journalist whose taste for writing essays developed into a passion which threatened for a time to absorb his energy and impair his health. In 1863 he published his *General View of the Criminal Law of England*, regarded as the first scholarly and literary introduction to the study of the history of English criminal law. He exhibited a veritable thirst for legislation during two and a half years of prodigious activity (1869–1872) as legal member of the Governor-General's Council in India, where a criminal code was already a *fait accompli*. Within two years (1875–1876), he published his *Digest of the Laws of Evidence* and *Digest of the Criminal Law*, both enthusiastically received. When he was first asked to prepare a draft bill for a criminal code and a code of criminal procedure in August 1877, at the age of 48, he had already completed much of the preparatory work on his own.[2]

In June of 1878 his draft was submitted to parliament and in December it was referred to a royal commission. Their report, drawn up by Stephen, was ready by June 1879, and all seemed ripe for the adoption of a criminal code in England. It was never passed by parliament. Stephen's supreme effort had come to nothing.

Unexpectedly, in that same year, he was appointed a judge of the Queen's Bench Division. Within four years, in spite of his arduous duties on the bench, he had produced his *magnum opus*, the *History of the Criminal Law of England*, in three volumes, published in 1883.

Stephen held the view that the only great improvement at once desirable and practicable was the codification of the law, which he explained meant only its reduction to an explicit systematic shape, and the removal of technicalities and other defects that disfigured it.[3] It would, he argued, give unity and a literary form to the existing system, and would be a great convenience to the administration of justice. "The matter is one which does not press," he wrote, since ". . . the existing law is perfectly well understood and is administered without the smallest difficulty or confusion."

Perhaps Stephen's recent experience on the bench had radically

1 L. Radzinowicz, *Sir James Fitzjames Stephen*, Selden Society Lecture (London, 1957), p. 22. A mere list of Stephen's published life's work occupies over thirteen closely filled pages. See pp. 49–62.
2 Stephen, "Improvement of the Law by Private Enterprise," *The Nineteenth Century* (August–December 1877), II, 198.
3 Stephen, *A History of the Criminal Law of England* (London, 1883), III, 347, 366.

changed his views compared with those he expressed in his *Digest*, written six years earlier. Discussing the Consolidation Acts of 1861, he wrote, "The Act also is so long that it is hardly possible for any memory to retain its different provisions," and also, ". . . Sections of an Act of Parliament . . . consist of single sentences of enormous length, drawn up, not with a view to communicate information easily to the reader, but to preventing a person bent upon doing so from wilfully misunderstanding them. The consequence is that sections of Acts of Parliament form sentences, thirty, forty, or fifty lines in length."[4] The Second Schedule to the EDC lists sixty-seven separate acts of parliament, beginning with an act from the thirteenth century under the reign of Edward I and ending with an act passed in 1874–75 under the reign of Victoria, which were to be repealed in whole or in part and superseded by the Code.[5] The Schedule, prepared no doubt under Stephen's guidance, if not directly by him, stands in mute opposition to his later opinion.

The impression remains that Stephen as critic and codifier could condemn the confusing forms and expressions of the law, but that after four years on the bench, Stephen the judge, mindful lest he give offence to his brothers, had lost some of his candour when he described the law as "perfectly well understood and administered without the smallest difficulty or confusion." What had changed was neither the complexity of the law nor anyone's comprehension of it, but the viewpoint of Stephen himself.

Stephen was a writer, a literary man of vast talents, and it should come as no surprise to anyone that he conceived of a code as a "literary work," as a contribution to his country's "serious literature." He was a stern, disciplined man with a deep sense of respect for history, for whom a code would represent "nothing less than the deliberate measured judgment of the English nation on the definition of crimes and on the punishments to be awarded in respect of them, that judgment representing the accumulated experience of between six and seven centuries at least."[6]

His father was an earnest evangelical who took part in a movement for moral reform of the nation based on religious revival; his mother could trace her family back through a long line of clerical ancestors to Elizabeth I. Stephen himself, at the age of 22, seriously considered whether he should enter the church, the bar, or medicine. It is consistent with that background that Stephen saw the criminal law as an expansion

4 Stephen, *A Digest of the Criminal Law* (St. Louis, 1878), p. xiv.
5 *Report of the Royal Commission Appointed to Consider the Law Relating to Indictable Offences*, Appendix, Second Schedule, p. 205.
6 Stephen, *History*, III, 366–67.

of the second table of the ten commandments, and believed that "The statement in the Catechism of the positive duties of man to man corresponds step by step with the prohibitions of a Criminal Code." Religion and Law were for Stephen the two pillars on which morality rested, and he was deeply concerned that the religious sanction had been immensely weakened by liberal thought on religious and moral subjects. Stephen viewed his age as in dire need of a "sermon in the most emphatic tones": "A man may disbelieve in God, heaven, and hell, he may care little for mankind, or society, or for the nation to which he belongs – let him at least be plainly told what are the acts which will stamp him with infamy, hold him up to public execration, and bring him to the gallows, the gaol, or the lash." (p. 367)

This moral rectitude, based on religious principles (seen earlier in a less highly pitched form in Blackstone and Coke), was coupled in Stephen with a highly detailed historical grasp of the development of the criminal law. It is understandable that when Stephen turned his well-worn pen to write that "emphatic sermon," he would think of it as serious literature, and strive to give it the clarity, succinctness, and strength to match his purpose. He gave the criminal law a livable form and a new starting point.

Some of the sex offences already formed part of statute law. In order to note the kind of changes which Stephen proposed, and also to set out as complete a record as possible, it is helpful to consider together the existing legislation (and the gaps therein), the relevant sections from the *Digest*, and the EDC.[7] Any specific discussion which Stephen gives to any of these offences in either the *General View* or the *History* is also included.

Unnatural Offences

Existing Legislation

The Offences Against the Person Act.
Unnatural Offences

Section 61. Whosoever shall be convicted of the abominable crime of buggery, committed either with mankind, or with any animal, shall

---

7 To avoid needless repetition, Stephen's Draft Criminal Code (1878) is not included, inasmuch as it differs only slightly from the EDC. Any differences were set out in the *Report of the Royal Commission* and have been noted where necessary. An examination of the changes which occurred in the Canadian legislation following the EDC is made in the following chapter.

be liable, at the discretion of the Court, to be kept in penal
servitude for life or for any term not less than 10 years. (24
Vict., c. 100, s. 61 (1861))

Digest

Chapter XVIII – Offences against Morality
Article 168 – Sodomy – p. 115
Every one commits the felony called sodomy, and is liable upon conviction thereof, to penal servitude for life as a maximum, and to penal servitude
for ten years as a minimum, punishment, who
(a.) Carnally knows any animal; or
(b.) Being a male, carnally knows any man or any woman (per anum).
Any person above the age of fourteen years who permits himself or herself to be so carnally known as aforesaid is a principal in the first degree in
the said felony.
          Article 254 – p. 191
(3.) Carnal knowledge means the penetration to any slightest degree of
the organ known by the male organ of generation. [ref. to 24 and 25 Vict.,
c. 100, s. 63]
Note X (To Article 168) – p. 377
This crime was anciently punished by death, if we are to believe Britton
and Fleta (Cit. Br. c. 9; F. 1, 37.); but the silence of Bracton on the subject,
the contradiction between Britton, who speaks of burning, and Fleta, who
mentions burying alive (Cit. cf. Tacitus, Germany, ch. xii.) as the punishment, and the fact that the offence was made felony by 25 Hen. 8, c. 6, lead
me to believe that till Henry VIII's reign it was treated as an ecclesiastical
offence only.
It was punishable by death from 1534 till 1861 (though of late years the
sentence was seldom executed), when the present punishment was provided
by the Offences Against the Person Act. It is almost the only case in which
recent legislation has affixed a minimum punishment to any offence whatever.
I think the proper place for the crime in a Code is that in which I have
placed it. Where there is no violence, it hardly seems appropriate to describe
it as an offence against the person, and where the crime (as is almost always
the case) is committed with an animal, the impropriety of such a classification is more distinctly marked.

EDC

Part XIII – Offences against Morality
Section 144 – Unnatural Offence – p. 95
Every one shall be guilty of an indictable offence, and shall be liable upon
conviction thereof to penal servitude for life, who commits buggery either
with a human being or with any other living creature.
This offence is complete upon penetration.
Every one charged with any offence under this section may be arrested
without warrant, and shall be bailable at discretion.
[Ref. is made to:] By 24 & 25 Vict., c. 100, s. 61, ten years' penal servi-
tude is the minimum punishment for this offence.
Report of the Royal Commission – p. 22

With regard to offences against morality, we think it expedient to do away with the minimum punishment of ten years' penal servitude, at present inflicted in certain cases. It is the only, or almost the only, minimum punishment still retained, and experience shows that in this, as in other cases, circumstances greatly affect the nature of the offence.

In his *General View of the Criminal Law*, Stephen makes but scant reference to the offences against morality. He acknowledges that in the great majority of cases an immoral act is punished as a crime only when it involves an outrage on some particular person. Like Blackstone before him, Stephen found the subject "not a pleasant one, and it involves little curiosity or interest." He refers to the offence again briefly in the *History of the Criminal Law*, with reference to the withdrawal of certain offences from the Ecclesiastical Courts.[8] "The statute of Henry VIII is wholly inconsistent with the opinion that the authors cited (Fleta, Britton, Mirror) stated the law correctly, whereas it is not only consistent with but suggests the notion that the offence was till then merely ecclesiastical."

Stephen attempted in his *Digest* to replace the ancient "abominable crime of buggery" with a much more specifically defined offence of "sodomy,"[9] to bring into the wording of the offence the interpretations and decisions which had been previously established in case law. The EDC did not go as far as the *Digest* in this direction. With respect to punishment, the removal of the ten-year minimum, as recommended in the EDC, indicates that although the principal aim was to clarify the expression of the law, thought was at the same time given to changes which experience with it suggested. The offence was also reclassified from "Offences against the Person," where it had been placed by Blackstone and kept by the existing legislation, to "Offences against Morality."

Attempts to Commit Unnatural Offence

Existing Legislation

The Offences against the Person Act
Unnatural Offences
   Section 62. Whosoever shall attempt to commit the said abominable crime,

---

8 Stephen, *History*, II, 429. For an account of the ecclesiastical jurisdiction and sanctions against "immorality" without specific reference to this offence, see pp. 411–12.
9 The issue raised by Coke's use of the two terms "buggery" and "sodomy" was still not resolved 250 years later.

or shall be guilty of any Assault with intent to commit the same, or of any Indecent Assault upon any Male Person, shall be guilty of a Misdemeanour, and being convicted thereof shall be liable, at the discretion of the court, to be kept in Penal servitude for any Term not exceeding 10 years and not less than 3 years, or to be imprisoned for any term not exceeding two years, with or without Hard Labour. (24–25 Vict., c. 100, s. 62)

Digest

Chapter XVIII – Offences against Morality
Article 169 – Attempt to Commit Sodomy – p. 115
Every one who attempts to commit sodomy is guilty of a misdemeanor, and is liable, upon conviction thereof, to ten years' penal servitude as a maximum punishment. [Cites:] 24 & 25 Vict., c. 100, s. 62.
Assaults, Aggravated and Common, Punishable on Indictment
Article 242 – Punishment of Assaults with intent to commit Sodomy – p. 182
Every one is guilty of a misdemeanor, and is liable, upon conviction thereof, to ten years' penal servitude as a maximum punishment, who is guilty of any assault with intent to commit sodomy, or of any indecent assault, upon any male person.
[Stephen adds this footnote: "The last words of this enactment would cover the case of an indecent assault by a woman on a man; but this can hardly have been intended."]

EDC

Part XIII – Offences against Morality
Section 145 – Attempt to commit unnatural offence – p. 95
Every one shall be guilty of an indictable offence, and shall be liable upon conviction thereof to ten years' penal servitude, who attempts to commit buggery, or assaults any person with intent to commit buggery, or who being a male indecently assaults any other male.
Every one charged with any offence under this section shall be bailable at discretion.

Here again the problem of classification can be seen. Should the three offences contained in the section continue under the classification of "Offences against Morality" or should the latter two be classified as "assaults"? Stephen follows the second procedure, but does not tell us why. How helpful it might have been if there had been available to him information which could show whether the cases which arose in this area were ones involving, say, bodily injury due to aggression, or were more usually in the nature of "technical assaults." It was pointed out in the discussion of Blackstone that subsequent classifiers were to misconstrue the development and purpose of these offences; Stephen does so here without explanation.

Public Indecency, Indecent Exposure, or Indecent Act

Chapter XVIII – Offences against Morality
Article 171 – Public Indecencies – p. 116

Every one commits a misdemeanor who does any grossly indecent act in any open and public place in the presence of more persons than one; but it is uncertain whether such conduct in a public place amounts to a misdemeanor if it is done when no one is present, or in the presence of one person only.

A place is public within the meaning of this article if it is so situated that what passes there can be seen by any considerable number of persons if they happen to look.

Chapter XX – Vagrancy
Article 193 – Rogues and Vagabonds – p. 132
A rogue and vagabond is a person who (inter alia)
(e.) Wilfully, openly, lewdly and obscenely exposes his person in any street, road, or public highway, or in the view thereof, or in any place of public resort, with intent to insult any female.

[The punishment upon conviction is set out in Article 195 as "imprisonment with hard labour for any term not exceeding three months."]

[Cites:] 5 Geo. 4, c. 83, s. 4 [the same, in both wording and punishment, as the provisions in the Digest].

EDC

Part XIII – Offences against Morality
Sec. 146 – Indecent Act – p. 95.
Every one shall be guilty of an indictable offence, and shall be liable upon conviction thereof to two years' imprisonment with hard labour, who wilfully
(a) Does any indecent act in any place to which the public have or are permitted to have access; or
(b) Does any indecent act in any place, intending thereby to insult or offend any person.

There was an attempt made to establish the common law misdemeanour of public indecency as a statutory offence. The offence of wilful, open, lewd and obscene exposure of the person had long since had a statutory existence, under the Vagrancy Act. The proposal made in the EDC was that these two offences should be fused under the common notion of "indecent act." Subsection (a) is directed towards behaviour in the nature of public nuisance and the essential element of publicity which may or may not involve a sexual motive. Subsection (b) is directed towards an act which essentially involves the exposure of the person (genitals) with the intention of insulting a person (usually a female) in public or private; this is, unlike the previous act described, essentially sexual.[10] The clarity so eagerly sought by Stephen eludes him in this instance. In forging these two offences together under a common terminology, he may have succeeded in giving a formal structure to the common law offence of public indecency, but at the cost of blurring the historic outline and the risk of losing the original intention of both offences. Once again can be noted the tendency towards and the danger of the more abstracted terminology which one meets in Stephen's case far less frequently than in Blackstone's.

Indecent Assault Female

Digest

Chapter XXVII – Assaults, Aggravated and Common, Punishable on
               Indictment
Article 245 – Assaults punishable with two years' imprisonment – p. 183
    Every person commits a misdemeanor, and is liable, upon conviction, to a maximum punishment of two years' imprisonment and hard labour, . . .
(d.) or who indecently assaults any female, or attempts to have carnal knowledge of any girl under twelve years of age; [Cites:] 24 & 25 Vict., c. 100, s. 52

EDC

Part XIX – Assaults
Section 204 – Indecent assaults – p. 106
    Every one shall be guilty of an indictable offence, and shall be liable upon conviction thereof to two years' imprisonment with hard labour, who
(a)   *Indecently assaults any female; or
(b)   Does anything to any female by her consent which but for such consent would be an indecent assault, such consent being obtained by false and fraudulent representations as to the nature and quality of the act; or
(c) **Attempts carnally to know any girl under the age of twelve years whether he believes her to be of or above that age or not.
    [Cites:]   *24 & 25 Vict., c. 100, s. 52
              **24 & 25 Vict., c. 100, s. 52

Stephen's grouping in the *Digest* of various kinds of assaults in terms of the maximum two years' imprisonment, thus laying a special emphasis on the punishment they hold in common, is a most unsatisfactory way of categorizing offences. Once again, the recurring problem of classification arises. Both the EDC and the *Digest* contained chapters on "Rape,

10 L. Radzinowicz, ed., *English Studies in Criminal Science*, vol. IX, *Sexual Offences* (London, 1957), pp. 357, 427.

Knowing Children and Procuring Abortion," and yet the offence of *attempt carnal knowledge of a girl under 12* is found under "Assaults," with no explanation produced.

With respect to the sex offences considered here, Stephen's rearrangements of the traditional classifications are clearly less than successful. Although he modifies the offences a little, he does not recast them in any fundamental way; indeed, in some instances his modifications serve to obfuscate rather than clarify. There is a curious contradiction in all of this. Taking a broad view, we must credit Stephen with considerable accomplishments across the whole field of criminal law, but on closer inspection in this particular area his accomplishments seem of slighter value. He appears like a skilled but undiscriminating lapidary, who polishes every stone he finds but can appraise the value of none of them.

Perhaps with a wisdom all her own, Britain did not accept Stephen's Draft Code, but made it available for export to the colonies which were in those days without the resources or the manpower to develop to any great extent their own criminal law. A compact, easily available digest of English law in the form of a code had many advantages when the machinery for administering the law was in its infancy. It was a good code, and the best that any one person or any one commission had ever produced. It was the legacy that Canada inherited.

In retrospect we see two poles in the approach to law, represented by Stephen, who distilled, consolidated, sharpened what had gone before, and Bentham, who set out to design an entirely new code, unfettered by historical precedent and based on a clearly defined philosophical principle. There must be a middle ground between these positions. We need not uncritically preserve the laws as they have been handed down from the past, but no more have we licence to abandon what is valuable along with what is not. The problem, of course, is to decide what is valuable. Implicit in the problem is a basic question of research: What information do we need in order to make our evaluation?

2

Legislative Genealogy (1869-1954) and the
Process of Criminal Law Revision

Homosexual Offences

Buggery and Bestiality

Neither buggery nor bestiality has been defined by statute at any time. The meaning ascribed to the terms by the courts will be discussed in the following chapter, but for clarification at this point the first term applies to "carnal knowledge, or sexual intercourse, by man with man per anum, man with woman per anum," and the second term to "man or woman with beast in any manner."[1]

Enacted in 1869,[2] the relevant Canadian statute followed the identical wording (but not the penalty) as an act passed in England in 1861.[3] Minor word changes by way of clarification were made in a revision of 1886,[4] and no substantive change appears in the Criminal Code of 1892.[5] No changes were made in the general revisions of 1906[6] or 1927.[7] A change of terminology was made in 1953–54 and the penalty was reduced.[8]

The offence was originally contained in an Act Respecting Offences against the Person under the general heading of "Unnatural Offences," following the confused classification of Blackstone discussed in part one. In 1886 the offence was included under An Act Respecting Offences against Public Morals and Public Convenience, and in 1892 under the "Offences against Morals" which followed Stephen's classification in the Digest and the EDC.[9] Sexual offences were classified as such for the first time in 1953–54, and these offences were of course included with them. It will be recalled that this classification was suggested by Bentham in 1814.

1 L. Radzinowicz, ed., English Studies in Criminal Science, vol. IX, Sexual Offences (London, 1957), p. 345.
2 S.C. 1869, c. 20, s. 63.
3 Offences against the Person Act, 1861, 24–25 Vict., c. 100, s. 61.
4 R.S.C. 1886, c. 157, s. 1.   5 S.C. 1892, c. 29, s. 174.
6 R.S.C. 1906, c. 146, s. 202.   7 R.S.C. 1927, c. 36, s. 202.
8 S.C. 1954, c. 51, s. 147.
9 Sir James Fitzjames Stephen, A Digest of the Criminal Law (St. Louis, 1878), Article 168, p. 115; Report of the Royal Commission to Consider the Law Relating to Indictable Offences, Appendix, s. 144, p. 95. Stephen actually used the term "morality" rather than "morals."

It is at the level of classification that the most significant change with respect to these offences has occurred. The shifts in classification aptly illustrate the underlying problem surrounding the questions of personal harm and morality. The present classification, "Sexual Offences," avoids that controversy, but without solving it. By classifying these and other acts by a descriptive term which identifies the subject matter, the elements of personal harm and morality may be more easily identified and distinguished. Before that is possible, however, it will be necessary to be much more specific about other elements than the deceptively simple, all-inclusive term "buggery" at present allows.

"The abominable crime of buggery committed either with mankind or with any animal," as the offence was set out in 1869,[10] is not much changed from "the detestable and abominable vice of buggery committed with mankind or beast," as one finds it in the original statute of 1533, passed during the reign of Henry VIII.[11] The inclusion of the terms "Sodomy and Bestiality" as a marginal note in the statute of 1869 was no doubt intended as a clarification, identifying "sodomy" with "buggery with mankind" and "bestiality" with "buggery with any animal." On the basis of this alone, one would conclude that "buggery" was the more inclusive term, encompassing what was conceived as two kinds of acts. However, many of the learned authors, including Hawkins, East, Russell, and Stephen in his *Digest*, used "sodomy" as the inclusive term. Where the legislators were using one term, the writers were using the other, and the seeds of confusion planted by Coke, who used the terms interchangeably, were successfully perpetuating themselves in both fields.

In 1886, the offence was somewhat clarified and broadened; "abominable" was dropped as a descriptive adjective, "mankind" was clarified to "human being,"[12] and the term "animal" was changed to "any other living creature."[13] No other changes of this kind were made until the Criminal Code revision of 1953–54. The offence was then simply set out as "buggery or bestiality"; the two terms stand alone, with nothing more. Thus, "buggery" has been given a restricted meaning and now presumably applies only to acts involving humans, and "bestiality" is introduced into the substantive legislation for the first time, and presumably applies to acts involving persons and other living creatures. No one has suggested that the two terms standing as they do in the alternative are interchangeable.

The punishment provided in 1869 was a maximum of life and a minimum of two years.[14] The English statute from which the section

10 S.C. 1869, c. 20, s. 63.   11 25 Hen. VIII, c. 6.
12 Thus laying to rest Coke's narrow interpretation once and for all.
13 R.S.C. 1886, c. 157, s. 1.   14 S.C. 1869, c. 20, s. 63.

was copied provided for a minimum imprisonment of ten years.[15] In 1886 the two-year minimum was dropped but the maximum of life imprisonment was retained. No change was made in the Code of 1892. In our most recent Code of 1953–54, the maximum term was lowered to 14 years.[16]

But what does all of this measure up to? The changes which have occurred have made no essential difference to these offences, for they have been of a nominal kind and the content remains virtually the same.[17] "Bestiality," the new term introduced, is nowhere defined, and one still must make recourse to the earlier legislation and case law to find an historical meaning for it. Neither Hansard nor any legislative committee has recorded any discussion of these offences. The terminology in current use is still crude and primitive, and it obscures important distinctions which can be made on the basis of differences of sex, relationship, marriage, age, force, duress, consent, and public or private place.[18] It is impossible to cover with any clarity the wide range and variety of human sexual behaviour involved by using only two words. The basic error is that the descriptive terms are based solely on the acts involved and do not allow consideration of the circumstances or the "events" in which the act occurs. Although there was a conceptual consistency in including both the offence of buggery and that of bestiality in one section when they shared the common terminology of "buggery," there is no longer any valid reason to do so. To continue carrying them in one section, as though they somehow dealt with the same or similar behaviour, reveals an unthinking fidelity to the past in relation to these offences. In my opinion, it is idle to comment on the punishment set out in the Code before we have undertaken the task of identifying the "species" of buggery that Coke hinted at so long ago. The punishment provided may well have merit for some kinds of cases, but before we can decide this, before we can begin to discuss "cures," we must first learn what different kinds of "diseases" exist.

It is thus difficult to see what difference there is between our present offence and what existed four hundred years ago. The difference, if there be any, does not represent the four centuries of experience we have had with this offence, nor does it reflect any analysis. It strongly savours of neglect.

15 Offences against the Person Act, 1861, 24–25 Vict., c. 100, s. 61.
16 S.C. 1954, c. 51, s. 147.
17 A Senate subcommittee, considering the most recent change, referred to it in its report as "a change in form only." Senate, Canada, Standing Committee on Banking and Commerce, 1952, p. 34.
18 See Appendix II for a discussion of the amendments proposed on December 21, 1967, by the then Minister of Justice, the Hon. Pierre Elliott Trudeau.

Attempt Buggery and Bestiality

In 1869 the offence of attempt buggery and bestiality was included in a section which also contained the offences of assault with intent to commit buggery and indecent assault on a male.[19] Minor word changes were made in 1886,[20] but the offence continued to be included in the same section with the other two offences until 1892, when it was given a separate section.[21] No changes were made during the general revisions of 1906[22] and 1927.[23] In the amendments to the Code in 1953–54, "Attempt Buggery" was eliminated as a separate section, but the offence is still punishable under a general attempt section which covers all offences for which no express provision is made.[24]

Originally, the offence was set out as "Whosoever attempts to commit the said abominable crime," following the wording of the English section passed in 1861. This obtuse adjectival description of the offence was remedied in 1886 to read, "Everyone who attempts to commit buggery." The classifications for this offence have been the same as that of the full offence of buggery and what was said earlier applies equally here.

The ten-year maximum term of imprisonment set down in 1869 remained unchanged until 1953–54. Now, a person convicted under the general attempt section is liable to imprisonment for a term that is one half of the longest term to which a person who is guilty of the offence is liable. The effect is to reduce the maximum term for attempt buggery or bestiality by three years, from ten to seven.

Assault with Intent to Commit Buggery and Indecent Assault on a Male

These two offences, together with attempt buggery, formed part of one section in 1869[25] and had been adopted from an earlier English statute.[26] In 1886 indecent assault male was restricted to male persons who might commit the offence, thus creating the first distinct male homosexual offence.[27] In 1892, under the first Code, there was a change in classifi-

19 S.C. 1869, c. 20, s. 64.
20 R.S.C. 1886, c. 157, s. 2.
21 S.C. 1892, c. 29, s. 175.
22 R.S.C. 1906, c. 146, s. 203.
23 R.S.C. 1927, c. 36, s. 203.
24 S.C. 1954, c. 51, s. 406.
25 S.C. 1869, c. 20, s. 64.
26 Offences against the Person Act, 1861, 24–25 Vict., c. 100, s. 62.
27 R.S.C. 1886, c. 157, s. 2.

cation, terminology, and punishment,[28] and corrective alterations were made in the same year by a subsequent session of parliament.[29] No changes were made in the general revisions of 1906 and 1927.[30] In 1953–54 these offences were reclassified, and minor word changes were also made.[31]

Like the offence of buggery, these offences were contained in the Offences against the Person Act, under the subheading "Unnatural Offences," in 1869, and in 1886 they were reclassified under "Offences against Public Morals." Under the Code of 1892 they were once again placed under "Offences against the Person and Reputation," but this time under the subheading "Assaults," where they remained until 1953–54.[32] At present they are included in the chapter "Sexual Offences, Public Morals and Disorderly Conduct," under the subheading "Sexual Offences."

Their present classification is certainly the one to be preferred and no alteration of it seems necessary or desirable. The confusion which has surrounded these offences is worthy of comment. It must be remembered that it was the difficulty of proving the full offence of buggery which gave rise to the indictments for "assault with intent to commit." These were much more usual, Blackstone says, than indictments for the full offence. Also, where the parties were consenting, it was "usual" not to charge any assault but to charge that "one laid hands on the other with intent to commit."[33] The first of these forms was directed towards forceful acts of buggery and the latter towards consenting acts of buggery. But both were developed to provide a sanction against persons involved in an act of buggery. With the development of the law with respect to attempts, however, persons charged with the actual commission of the offence might be convicted of the attempt, which encompassed not only forceful acts of buggery but consenting ones as well, and thus the distinction was obliterated.

It is understandable why the section which included both the offence of attempt buggery and the offence of assault with intent would follow the classification given the full offence of buggery itself, first as offences

28 S.C. 1892, c. 29, s. 260.   29 S.C. 1892, c. 32, s. 1.
30 R.S.C. 1906, c. 146, s. 293; R.S.C. 1927, c. 36, s. 293.
31 S.C. 1954, c. 51, s. 148.
32 The classification made in 1869 follows that of the English statute of 1861, while in 1886 the classification follows the recommendation of the EDC. The Code of 1892, on the other hand, follows the classification Stephen made of these offences in his *Digest*.
33 William Blackstone, *Commentaries on the Laws of England*, vol. IV, *Of Public Wrongs* (Oxford, 1769), ed. Charles M. Haar (Boston, 1962), pp. 217, 243.

against the person, and later as offences against morals. Stephen in his *Digest*, however, cast the offence of attempt as an "Offence against Morality," and the offence of assault with intent under "Offences against the Person," under "Assaults." In this he was not followed by the EDC, but was followed in the Canadian Code of 1892. Stephen apparently came to his conclusion by analysing the problem in this way: "Every crime against a person must of necessity involve an assault. An assault is not less an assault because it is intended to be the first step towards murder, or rape, or robbery."[34] What made this kind of characterization more logical was that "indecent assault on a male" also formed part of the section. He failed to give adequate attention to the fact that the original intention of this form of charge was to impose sanctions for completed acts of buggery which could not be proven as such. Seen in this light, the offence is as much an offence against morality as the offence of buggery was itself. To classify it as Stephen did was to over-emphasize the element of assault, the general principle underlying all offences against the person, rather than the specific content, the sexual nature of the act.

Changing Statutory Provisions

Assault with Intent

Originally set out as "Whosoever . . . is guilty of any assault with intent to commit the same [buggery],"[35] the offence was reworded as "Everyone who . . . assaults *any person* with intent to commit buggery" in 1886,[36] thus making it clear that the offence might be committed against either male or female. In 1892 the offence was erroneously amended to read "assault . . . with *attempt* to commit *sodomy*,"[37] then later corrected to "*intent* to commit sodomy."[38] The term "sodomy" was thus introduced, following Stephen's *Digest* (but not the EDC),[39] although the wider legislative term "buggery" was still reserved for the full offence. No discussion of the change is reported in the bill's passage in either the House of Commons or the Senate. No changes were made in the general revisions of 1906 and 1927.[40]

In 1953–54 the offence was limited for the first time to male persons

34 Stephen, *A History of the Criminal Law of England*, II, 221.
35 S.C. 1869, c. 20, s. 64.   36 R.S.C. 1886, c. 157, s. 2.
37 S.C. 1892, c. 29, s. 260.   38 S.C. 1892, c. 32, s. 1.
39 Stephen, *Digest*, Article 242, p. 182; EDC, s. 145.
40 R.S.C. 1906, c. 146, s. 293; R.S.C. 1927, c. 36, s. 293.

as agents, but it could still be committed against any person regardless of sex. However, the change is not as significant as it first appears. The offence refers to an assault intending anal intercourse, and it is difficult to imagine a case in which a female person would assault another person with the intention of having anal intercourse. The change is virtually meaningless. The term used to describe the intended act reverted back from "sodomy" to the earlier "buggery." This change is in keeping with the present restricted meaning given to buggery under Section 147, discussed previously, but it signifies no actual change. Indeed the changes in the description of this offence over the last seventy-five years represent nothing more than a mere surface manipulation of words.

Indecent Assault on a Male

In 1869 this offence was set out as "Whosoever . . . is guilty of . . . any indecent assault on a male person," and in 1886 it was restricted to "male persons" who might commit the act.[41] This offence was not changed in either 1892, 1906, 1927, or the most recent code of 1953–54.

The maximum penalty was set out in 1869 as ten years. In the code of 1892, the period was reduced to seven years but a provision for whipping was added. When errors in the Code were corrected by the subsequent session of parliament, the term was increased back to ten years and the whipping provision retained. No discussion of these changes is reported by Hansard. The present provision retains both the maximum term of ten years set out in 1869 and the provision for whipping added in 1892. It is remarkable that whipping at no time formed part of the punishment for the full offence of buggery.

It is difficult to understand why these two offences continue to be included together under one section. The one prescribes certain acts having as their ultimate aim anal intercourse, either homosexual or heterosexual. The other prescribes male homosexual acts which may have quite other aims than anal intercourse. (Contrary to some popular beliefs, not all homosexual activity is directed towards anal intercourse, and it may well be that that activity forms but a small minority of homosexual acts.) Can their joint historic evolution have such a powerful and paralysing influence on us that we maintain these offences together for that reason alone?

41 The citations set out for the offence of assault with intent are equally applicable here, as both offences form part of the same section.

Gross Indecency

Gross indecency has never been defined in statute. In a later chapter I will demonstrate a method for uncovering the various ways this offence has been used, illustrating in the process the confusion which directly results from the failure on the part of legislators to define or express with any precision what they were intending to proscribe. In order to discover their intent, attention will be given at this point to the legislative discussions which have preceded the formulation of this offence.

The offence was introduced into statute law in 1890 and covered "any act of gross indecency" committed in public or private between male persons, together with anyone who was a party to the commission of the offence, or who procured or attempted to procure its commission.[42] The punishment was set out as a maximum of five years with a proviso for whipping. No changes were made to the offence either in the Code of 1892 or in the general revisions of 1906 and 1927.[43] In 1953–54 the offence was simplified and expanded to, "Every one who commits an act of gross indecency with another person," thus leaving the section open to cover male and female acts of homosexuality as well as heterosexual acts.[44] The provision for whipping was dropped.[45]

In 1890 Sir John Thompson, in moving second reading of Bill 65 in the House of Commons, justified the introduction of this offence into the criminal law on the basis that there was very little law on the subject, and that certain offences which were notorious in another country were beginning to make their appearance here.[46] When the section was considered by the House of Commons sitting as a Committee of the Whole, Sir Richard Cartwright raised the following objection:

I entirely approve of the purport of this Act as regards the offence which, I presume, the Minister has in view, but is it not possible that the words he has used, "gross indecency" are not sufficiently precise, and might lead to consequences that he does not intend? Of course, I am quite aware that the

---

42 S.C. 1890, c. 37, s. 5. The section follows the identical description set out in the English statute (Criminal Law Amendment Act, 1885, 48–49 Vict., c. 69, s. 11) except for the punishment which was "imprisonment for any term not exceeding two years."
43 R.S.C. 1906, c. 146, s. 206; R.S.C. 1927, c. 36, s. 206.
44 S.C. 1954, c. 51, s. 149.
45 Under the provisions of s. 641(1) of the Code, no female person can be whipped in any event.
46 Debates, H.C., Canada, 1890, II, 3161.

particular crime which he has in mind is one which, I very much fear, has been on the increase in certain sections of society, and can hardly be punished too severely. In my opinion the words are not legal words, and it strikes me that consequences might flow from this phraseology which the honourable gentleman does not contemplate.[47]

Sir John Thompson gave the following reply:

I think it is impossible to define the offence any better. The provision is the same as the English provision of Chapter 69, 48–49 Vict. It is impossible to define them any better, for the reasons that the offences which are aimed at are so various. The notorious cases I mentioned a few moments ago[48] are not the same in their characteristics, and the description which would cover them would not apply to these cases which have been brought to my attention, as occurring in Canada within the last few months. I think it is better to leave it in this form. It is not more vague than the English Act.

Sir John shifted his ground in these remarks. In his opening statement he justified introducing this section on the basis that certain notorious cases in another country were beginning to make their appearance here, i.e. implying a similarity between the two. In the passage quoted he appears to say that the notorious cases are not homogeneous, and even if one could describe them, that description would still not apply to what was occurring in Canada. In the face of this it is difficult to understand how he could urge the adoption of the section, which used exactly the same terminology as was used in another country (England) and defend his motion on the grounds that it was not "more vague." The discussion on this section up to this point had been entirely unsatisfactory, for members of the House had been given no clear idea of what was involved in the notorious cases, or the cases in Canada, or what the differences were. In short, they did not know exactly what behaviour they were being asked to make criminal.

Mr. Mitchell objected that the term "gross indecency" was also used in the following section, but the Minister pointed out that in that section the words referred to "indecent exposure," while in this section they referred to "improprieties between two males." Mr. Blake then expressed his doubt that there was "any other class of cases in which there is more danger of brutalizing people than in the class of cases dealt with in this Clause 3," and suggested that the penalty of whipping be added. The

47 *Ibid.*, II, 3170.
48 A reading of the full debate shows that Sir John Thompson did not actually give an account of any cases and the reference is merely to the fact that he had previously mentioned certain offences which were "notorious in another country."

Minister promptly proposed that the words "to be whipped" be added, but no discussion of the change followed.[49]

Mr. Mitchell made another plea that the offence be made specific:

I still think that in so serious a matter as one involving an imprisonment for five years, the specific act characterized as "gross indecency" should be put in the statute. I do not think there ought to be any uncertainty about it. If there is a term to apply to it, the Minister ought to put that term in the Act. Suppose a person is charged with an offence of this kind in one of the county districts before a Justice of the Peace. There are 50 kinds of gross indecency. The term may mean one thing in one case and a much more serious thing in another. I hold the Minister ought to put the exact name of the crime in the statute, so that there may be no mistake about it. No false modesty should restrain us from protecting the liberty of the subject in a case like this.

The section was carried in the House and there was no discussion on it in the Senate debates. From all of this, one can get no clear idea of what the intention of parliament was.

In 1892 the same objection to the vague terminology was raised, and the same defence, "it is impossible to define these cases by any form of words," was given. Mr. Mills, however, pointed out that these offences (against morality) had crept into the law from earlier ecclesiastical courts, and that they were sins rather than crimes, not being attacks upon property or life or upon any other members of the community. He then questioned whether crimes of this sort should be punished by long terms of imprisonment and suggested rather that "flogging, or something of that sort" and discharge of the prisoner was preferable and a far better deterrent than anything else. Sir John Thompson, in reply, drew a distinction and said, ". . . we only punish them as crimes where they are offensive to the people or set a bad example." He indicated that he would have no objection to reducing the term of imprisonment considering that whipping accompanied the offence, but no amendment of the kind was put forward.

The Senate's Standing Committee on Banking and Commerce con-

49 There was another exchange in the debates which is mystifying. Mr. James asked to what extent the Minister applied the words "or is a party thereto." Sir John Thompson replied, "Any person who is an accessory before the fact, I should say, would come under these terms." He then added, "As to the *compulsion to whip* that is left in the discretion of the courts." (Italics are mine.) The phrase "compulsion to whip" may simply be a ministerial slip of the tongue or the reporter's error; it may refer to nothing more than the provision for whipping which had just been added as an amendment. Or does it refer to acts of sadism which might have been the subject matter of those cases which had been brought to Sir John Thompson's attention? Was it with reference to sadistic acts that Mr. Blake spoke of the "danger of brutalizing people?"

sidered a report of its own subcommittee on June 11, 1952, when the present Code was in the form of Bill H-8 before the Senate.[50] The amendment to the previous section 206, which was limited to male persons, proposed that the offence be widened to "Every one who commits an act of gross indecency with another person," as we have it today. Objection was taken to the amendment on the ground that, "This has been carried into the bill omitting any reference to sex, and so may cover anything which the Court may in its opinion deem indecent, which is much too unguarded. Evidently it is sexual indecency that is in mind and the subcommittee is of opinion that the clause should be amended [to substitute 'unnatural sexual act' for 'gross indecency'], as set out above." The following discussion then took place:

HON. MR. DAVIES: What is the difference between "gross indecency" and "indecent assault"?

HON. MR. ROEBUCK: Well, you get the definition of "assault" to begin with. It is the application of force or the threat of force on the person of somebody else when the person threatening is in the position to carry it out. That is in substance the definition of "assault."

THE CHAIRMAN: "Indecent assault" might proceed quite involuntarily as far as one of the parties is concerned.

HON. MR. ROEBUCK: Yes. There are two parties to an indecent assault, the person assaulting and the person assaulted. But an act of gross indecency may be perhaps by only one party.

HON. MR. DAVIES: Something like indecent exposure.

HON. MR. ROEBUCK: But what is "gross indecency"? I don't know, because it has never been defined. It was not defined in the old code, because the term was always used in connection with the act of a male person which imported the sexual idea. They dropped that out, but left "gross indecency" in the open, so anything which you or I might think indecent is covered by this clause as we now find it in the Bill.

HON. MR. DAVIES: But to constitute indecent assault there must be some assault on a person.

HON. MR. ROEBUCK: Yes, there must have been some person assaulted.[51]

This must represent the low water mark of discussion with respect to this offence. The confusion and uncertainty about the distinction between this offence, indecent assault, and exposure of the person cannot be laid solely at the feet of the members of the committee. The members of the subcommittee complained that there had been a lack of satisfactory explanatory notes appended to the bill received from the royal commission, which made their work tedious and difficult.[52]

The amendment which was proposed was accepted by the Standing

50 Senate, Canada, Standing Committee on Banking and Commerce, 1952, p. 18.
51 *Ibid.*, p. 39. 52 *Ibid.*, p. 6.

Committee, but Bill H-8 was not proceeded with. Five months later, in November, the bill was re-introduced in the Senate as Bill "0," and the original wording of "gross indecency" was restored, replacing the term "unnatural sexual act." No subsequent discussion is reported at any of the stages of the bill's passage.

After looking at these debates, it should come as no surprise that the term "gross indecency" has never been defined in statute. No definition of it has ever been given to the legislators. It is not clear what the term "gross indecency" means, and objections have been raised in 1890, 1892, and 1952 without avail.[53] The danger of leaving the offence in these open terms for the courts to interpret has been repeatedly emphasized.

But the clue to the problem can be seen in the frustration contained in the remark that offences aimed at are so various that it is impossible to define them by any form of words. The dilemma was created by attempting to use too few words to cover too many different acts. The objection that the words selected to be used are too subjective misses the other crucial problem that they are in fact too abstract. With the abstraction comes the danger of including more than one intended, which is illustrated so clearly by the example of the legislators' bringing into the discussion the offence of indecent exposure. If the danger was apparent when the offence was restricted to males, it was compounded by extending the offence to persons of either sex.

It is understandable why the legislators have difficulty discussing "gross indecency": it is not *an* act but a term representing many kinds of different acts. But are there really *many* kinds? Are the *kinds*, the classes, as "various" as Sir John Thompson thought they were? Are there fifty as Mr. Mitchell suggested? Are we not up against the problem of identifying "species" of gross indecency, and is this not the same kind of problem which revealed itself in Coke's intuitive recognition of "pederastes" as a "species" of "buggery"?

53 Proposals have been put forward recently to amend this section. This development is discussed in Appendix II.

Exhibitionistic Offences

The clinical term exhibitionism is defined as "the expressed impulse to expose the male organ to an unsuspecting female as a final sexual gratification."¹ One does not, of course, find the same term used in the criminal law. Offenders are usually charged under section 158 of the Criminal Code, which covers indecent acts in a public place in the presence of one or more persons, or in fact in any place where the intention of the act is to insult or offend any person. Although not generally regarded as a serious offence, it is one of the most common offences, and consequently one with which female members of the community are more likely to be confronted.²

The provisions of the Vagrancy Act of 1869 which applied to this offence were copied from the similar statute enacted in England in 1822.³ Although the English act had been amended in 1824,⁴ the earlier version was the one adopted here. There was a change in penalty in 1874,⁵ and a further clarification in 1881.⁶ In 1886 the Vagrancy Act was made part of a larger statute, An Act Respecting Public Morals and Convenience, but essentially the provisions did not change.⁷ In 1890 the offence was reformulated along new lines,⁸ and in 1892 it was changed once again to follow the EDC.⁹ No changes were made in either 1906 or 1927.¹⁰ In 1953–54, while changes were made in the punishment and characterization, and a broader definition was given to "public place," the substantive offence remained essentially unchanged.¹¹

The Vagrancy Act of 1869 provided that certain persons were to be deemed vagrant, loose, idle, or disorderly if they committed one of a wide variety of acts, or lived a particular kind of life. Under this act were included the unproductive and irresponsible, such as beggars and those who refused to support their families, as well as those who interfered with or inconvenienced peaceable passengers by loitering on the streets or obstructing footpaths, or caused a disturbance by singing, screaming, or swearing, or by being drunk. It also included the prankster who broke windows or defaced signs, and the immoral members of

1 J. W. Mohr, R. E. Turner, and M. B. Jerry, *Pedophilia and Exhibitionism* (Toronto, 1964), p. 116.
2 J. W. Mohr and A. K. Gigeroff, "A Study of Male Sexual Offenders Charged in Court Over a Twelve Month Period: Report on the Development of the Study with an Inventory of the Data Collected and a Basic Analysis" (Forensic Clinic, Toronto Psychiatric Hospital, May 1964, mimeographed). This study shows that the offence of indecent act accounts for about one out of every five sex offence cases in Metropolitan Toronto.
3 S.C. 1869, c. 28; Vagracy Act, 1822, 3 Geo. 4, c. 40, s. 3.
4 Vagrancy Act, 1824, 5 Geo. 4, c. 83, s. 4.
5 S.C. 1874, c. 43.   6 S.C. 1881, c. 31.
7 R.S.C. 1886, c. 157, s. 8.   8 S.C. 1890, c. 37, s. 6.
9 S.C. 1892, c. 29, s. 177; EDC, s. 146.
10 R.S.C. 1906, c. 146, s. 205; R.S.C. 1927, c. 36, s. 205.
11 S.C. 1954, c. 51, s. 158.

society, the prostitute, the nightwalker wandering in the fields, and those who lived on avails or gambling or crime. It covered persons who were in the habit of frequenting bawdy houses who could not give a satisfactory account of themselves. Many others were swept into this group, among whom can be found those who "openly or indecently expose their persons." Taken as a whole, the statute was aimed not so much at individual acts as such, but at certain types of undesirable persons in the community. The particular act served to identify the individual as belonging to a certain class of persons. The reasons underlying the creation of this class were partly economic, partly an attempt to establish social order, and partly to provide a sanction against immoral behaviour. Vagrancy was a variegated social crime.

In 1886 the act was reformulated along the lines suggested in Stephen's *Digest* of 1877.[12] Various offences were each given a separate subsection, and the act was entitled An Act Respecting Public Morals and Public Convenience, but the classification of vagrancy, covering "loose, idle and disorderly" persons, did not disappear. One can see that this was a most interesting transitory stage. At one level, the character of the harm was more clearly emphasized, and at the same time the individual actions and modes of behaviour were being distinguished one from the other, while the earlier general classification of "vagrant persons" was not yet abandoned.

In 1890 the characterization of Public Morals and Convenience was maintained, but the classification of vagrant persons was dropped, and "indecent exposure of the person" became the offence. Now the action as such, not the person, was the subject matter for purposes of classification.

In 1892 the description of the offence was made more abstract (it was changed from "exposes the person" to "does an indecent act"), and the offence was classified as one of the "Offences against Morals." It remained this way until 1953–54, when the categories "Offences against Religion, Morals and Public Convenience" were changed to "Sexual Offences, Public Morals and Disorderly Conduct." Three choices presented themselves to the commissioners who framed the 1953–54 offence. Why it was decided to classify this offence as "Disorderly Conduct" and not in either of the other two categories is not known, for no reasons are given in their report. It is the only major sexual deviation not identified in law as a "Sexual Offence." It will be noted that part of the earlier terminology ("loose, idle, *disorderly*, or vagrant persons")

---

12 Sir James Fitzjames Stephen, *A Digest of the Criminal Law* (St. Louis, 1878), Article 193, p. 132.

was re-introduced, this time in relation to the conduct and not the person.

The classification may not be inappropriate. Most cases which fall under this category involve a deliberate exposure of the genitals to an unsuspecting female person with or without a conscious experience of sexual gratification. In most cases of clinical exhibitionism, not only is the victim a stranger but the offender does not seek any further relationship and is in fact afraid of it.[13] There is a sexual component, but whether or not this is predominant or central to the phenomenon is still in doubt. What is clearer is that the act almost always occurs in public places and it is the very inappropriateness of the act which is so disturbing to unsuspecting females. There is in many cases an aggressive-defiant element in the act which seems intended to evoke fear and shock rather than pleasure from the victim. At this time, there appears to be more certainty about the disruptive intention and effect of this behaviour than there is about the sexual content. On these grounds, the classification of "disorderly conduct" seems at present to be more justified than either of the other two categories.

The original phrase used to cover this offence was a direct description of the act, expressed simply as "indecently exposing their persons." In 1890, the offence was reworded, intending thereby "to remove doubts as to whether there is an offence when only one person is present where there is improper exposure."[14] But instead of simply adding the words "in the presence of one or more persons," the amendment went farther than this, to read "any act of gross indecency in any public place in the presence of one or more persons." In debate during committee, Mr. Mitchell pointed out that the term "gross indecency" was also used with respect to another offence.[15] The then Minister of Justice, Sir John Thompson, made the following proposal: "I will amend the section by inserting the words, 'everyone who commits an indecent exposure of the person in any public place.' " What was undoubtedly intended as a clarification resulted in a greater confusion, for the offence as amended read, "Everyone who commits any indecent exposure or act of gross indecency in any public place . . ." The words "of the person" were somehow lost in the amendment.

It was objected in the Senate that the phrase "indecent exposure" was not defined and that innocent persons or children might be subject to the penalty provided.[16] To meet this objection, the word "wilfully"

13 Mohr *et al.*, *Pedophilia*, pp. 118, 115.
14 Sir John Thompson, Debates, H.C., Canada, 1890–91, II, 1403.
15 *Ibid.*, pp. 3170–71.   16 Debates, Sen., Canada, 1890, p. 650.

was inserted before the word "commits,"[17] and the wording thus revised was accepted by both the Commons and the Senate without further discussion. No one discussed what "gross indecency" in this context meant. Was it merely an alternative expression for "indecent exposure," or did it refer to other unspecified acts? What resulted, in an almost accidental way, was an amalgam of two notions, one dealing with the specific act of "indecent exposure" in a public place, and the other reaching towards the common law offence of public indecency. But it failed in this respect, for the term "gross indecency" had already been applied to impropriety between two males; moreover, the hybrid expression laid stress on a *type* of indecent act rather than on the element of publicity.

Two years later, in 1892, the offence was once again restated, this time following closely the EDC.[18] The offence was divided into two sections which read:

[Every one . . . who wilfully]
(a) in the presence of one or more persons[19] does any indecent act in any place to which the public have or are permitted to have access; or
(b) does any indecent act in any place intending to insult or offend any person.[20]

Subsection (a) represents the acceptance into statutory law of the common law offence of public indecency and is an improvement on the phrase "act of gross indecency" introduced in 1890.

Subsection (b) contains exactly the same wording as that used in the corresponding subsection in the EDC. Owing to the fact that the earlier Canadian enactments had followed the English Vagrancy Act of 1822 rather than that of 1824, the phrase "intending thereby to insult or offend any female" had not formed part of the description of this offence. This phrase therefore appears for the first time, with the difference that the words "any female" are broadened to "any person," in keeping with the suggestion in the EDC.

It was objected during Committee Debate in the House of Commons, that the phrase "indecent act" left a large discretion in the hands of the court, especially in the hands of justices of the peace, who were not trained men and might not appreciate the niceties of the English language. It was also suggested that the term "grossly" which had been used previously be retained, but the change was not accepted, and no

17 *Ibid.*, p. 681.
19 This phrase is not in the EDC.
18 EDC, s. 146, p. 95.
20 S.C. 1892, c. 29, s. 177.

further discussion occurred at any other point in the bill's passage through the Commons.[21]

What had been set out originally in descriptive terms, "indecent exposure of the person," in the process of evolving into a separate offence took on the less explicit expression, "indecent act." Specificity was sacrificed in favour of the more abstract construction.

The only significant change which was made in 1953–54 was that in subsection (a); the phrase "in any place to which the public have or are permitted to have access" was changed simply to "public place." However, in the interpretation section (s. 130(b)), "public place" is defined as "any place to which the public have access as of right or by invitation, express or implied." Section 177(b) provides that an indecent act may be committed "in any place" where there is intent to insult or offend any person.

In committee debate in the House of Commons, there was but one short discussion on this section. Mr. Cameron raised the instance of a number of Doukhobors who were charged with contributing to juvenile delinquency under section 33 of the Juvenile Delinquents Act and later under section 205 (indecent act) for nude parading and were sentenced to three years. Mr. Garson, in correcting him, pointed out that the charges were probably laid under section 205(a), now covered by section 159, which prohibits nude parades. Although Mr. Cameron was in error, his complaint against the "distortion of the actual intent of the legislation," and the fact that he would raise it in discussion of the section on indecent act, points to a very serious problem. Is there not something radically wanting in the expression of the law when a section intended to cover a sexually deviant act could conjure up in the mind of a legislator, or anyone else, the image of an unusual public political protest?[22]

The question which arises is whether in our haste to provide a simple code we have not led ourselves into using a uniform terminology in both subsections (a) and (b), thus obliterating what might be very useful distinctions. Framing the concept of public indecency in terms of "indecent act in a public place" tends to focus our attention on whether the act itself is indecent, rather than on whether the public display of the act imparts an indecent quality to it. To take a simple example, intercourse between consenting married partners is not in itself indecent, but

21 Debates, H.C., Canada, 1892, II, 2968. In the Senate, the particular sections of the bill were discussed in committee of the whole, but the debate is not reported.
22 Debates, H.C., Canada, 1953–54, II, 2057–58.

if it occurs in public it takes on an indecent character. It is not only the *place* where it occurs, but the extent to which members of the public actually see or might see the act, which can give it an offensive character. The emphasis in the section should force us to consider whether the degree of publicity is such as to make sexual acts indecent. At present, "public place" is so widely defined that the publicity of the act is no longer at issue.

While this very serviceable and valuable notion of "public indecency" was becoming obscured in the expansion of "indecent act," the fairly concrete entity of "indecent exposure" lost its particular identity in the same phrase. The early terminology was much more specific as to what was prohibited, so that cases which fell within it were more likely to be of the same kind. To make the terms used more abstract is to extend the range of acts which it is possible to include under the offence. As one diversifies the range of cases falling under the subsection, it becomes necessary once again to sort out the "species" *before* one can study or discuss in any meaningful way the cases which fall under that section. Exposure of the genitals is a phenomenon which occurs frequently enough and which can be so easily specified that there are good grounds for providing a separate section for it in statute. In this instance, a return to the mode of setting out the offence in simple descriptive terms, as was the case in the early enactments, is to be preferred over the less precise phrase used over the last seventy-four years.

In freeing these subsections from their common terminology of "indecent act," it may be possible to restore and reinvigorate the notion of public indecency and also to re-establish the clarity of the earlier category of indecent exposure.

The punishment initially proposed for this offence was fifty dollars or six months, but the Hon. Mr. Campbell reported to the Senate (sitting as a Committee of the Whole on May 11, 1896) that "several eminent judges of Ontario [suggested] that the time of imprisonment should be limited to two months, instead of six as provided under the present Bill."[23] This amendment was adopted. Five years later, in 1874, an amendment was passed which increased the period of imprisonment to six months. Sir John A. Macdonald objected to the increase on the grounds that "this was a measure which was in interference with the

---

23 *Canadian Parliamentary Debates 1866–1870*, an account of the debates as taken from the *Ottawa Times*, the *Toronto Globe* and the *Toronto Mail*. Microfilm copy, produced by the Canadian Library Association (Newspaper Microfilming Project). Original in Parliamentary Library, Ottawa. The official record of the parliamentary debates did not begin until 1875.

liberty of the subject," and, "Vagrancy was no great sin and the term of imprisonment was long enough already." No other discussion is reported in either the Commons or the Senate.

In 1881 an amendment was passed to make it clear that punishment could be imposed "with or without hard labour in the discretion of the convicting magistrate or justices."[24] Apparently these words had been removed in the amendment of 1874 and one of the judges, in administering the act, held that without these words hard labour could not be imposed.[25] Although the EDC from which the new section was copied in 1892 provided for a penalty of two years' imprisonment, this was not followed and the provision of fifty dollars or six months was retained.

In 1953–54, the punishment was no longer set out as part of the section and the offence was made punishable on summary conviction. The effect of this change brings the offence under the operation of section 694(1), which provides for a five hundred dollar fine or six months' imprisonment, or both. No discussion can be found in any of the deliberations in either the House of Commons, the Senate, or the various committees which considered the bill, as to the necessity or the desirability of the increased penalty. Only a short notation marks the change in the Report of the Royal Commission on Revision of the Criminal Code: "In keeping with our desire for simplification, the draft bill provides one general penalty for all summary convictions, namely, a fine of $500 or six months' imprisonment, or both."

It is difficult to accept the single expressed criterion of "simplification" as giving adequate justification for increasing a fine tenfold. Was an increase necessary? Would five hundred dollars be a more effective deterrent than fifty dollars? How effective were fines of fifty dollars or less? Were fines effective at all? Was the six-month period of imprisonment effective? Did shorter periods work as well? How effective was probation? In short, what information did the commissioners call for before recommending such a change? They certainly did not publish any evidence in the way of either statistics or petitions which suggested that a change was advisable, nor did they discuss any principles of punishment, so that the change gives every appearance of being nothing more than an arbitrary action carried out for the sake of "simplification." It seems to bear no relationship to the offence or the offenders or society, which are surely the vital considerations that ought to determine any alteration in the law. The desire for simplification is understandable,

24 S.C. 1881, c. 31.
25 Debates, H.C., Canada, 1880–81, II, 1403. See Mr. MacDonald's comments on moving second reading of the bill.

even laudable, but it must never be allowed to become *the* criterion for revisions of this nature. Such uninformed changes lack meaning and raise the suspicion that they may typify the quality of the consideration given to other changes in this area.

Almost a century has elapsed since the first vagrancy act was passed in Canada. During that time none of the other sections we have been considering has evolved as far as the offence of "indecent act." It is peculiar that while the offence formed part of the clutter which fell under the broad concept of vagrancy, it had a rather clear identity. Yet when it emerged as a distinct offence, it also lost some of its clarity. The attempt to fuse the somewhat broader notion of public indecency with the specific phenomenon of indecent exposure under a common terminology may well have handicapped the development of the law in this area. The concept of public indecency is a broad one, and indecent exposure may well be one of the identifiable species, just as at one time it fell under the even broader concept of vagrancy. Taken separately, each act of exhibitionism is not regarded as a serious offence, but the frequency of its occurrence raises its importance as a chronic social problem and merits its continuance as a separate identity, but in more clearly defined terms, in the Criminal Code. It is impossible to say which other species of public indecency are at present falling under that notion as expressed in its present terms, but a phenomenological analysis would enable one to identify various groups of similar cases. Whether these in turn could or should be spelled out separately might well depend on their numbers and their importance for other reasons. It may also be found that acts which are at present covered by other sections of the code could be more clearly identified and more meaningfully covered as species falling under the concept of public indecency. An example is homosexual acts between consenting adults committed in public, now charged under the ill-conceived offence of gross indecency.

The value of an evolutionary consideration of our present offences is that it enables us to re-assess the path which has been taken. What suggests itself in this process may not necessarily be the plotting of a new path, but perhaps, as here, the rediscovery of an older one to which we may return.

Pedophilic Offences

One of the most frequent sex charges which are brought before the courts arises out of sexual contacts between male adults or adolescents and children. This kind of behaviour is particularly disturbing not only to the parents of the child or children involved but to the community as well. The question which arises is how adequately and appropriately these kinds of acts are covered by the existing legislation. Before proceeding to this inquiry, it is of course necessary to know more about what is meant by a "pedophilic" act. Pedophilia is a term which is not found in the Criminal Code. As a result of studies conducted at the former Forensic Clinic of the Toronto Psychiatric Hospital the term has been defined as "the expressed desire for immature sexual gratification with a prepubertal child."[1] According to the sex of the child, a distinction is made between heterosexual pedophilia and homosexual pedophilia.

Heterosexual Pedophilia

As the definition indicates, the kind of sexual act involved is of an immature type, principally fondling, showing, looking, and excludes those cases where there is any attempt at coitus or penetration as the final aim. The majority of sexual acts involving female children are of this type, and instances of rape and sexual intercourse are rare. The majority of victims fall between the ages of 6 and 11, with a sharp decrease after the peak, which falls between the ages of 8 and 10. In a study of male sex offenders in Metropolitan Toronto, a preliminary breakdown of the victims in cases of indecent assault on a female shows that a little more than twenty-eight per cent are between the ages of 5 and 9 and that almost half of the known victims are under 12.[2] As for the offender, contrary to the popular stereotype of the "dirty old man," the age distribution of offenders shows clearly that there are three groups: "the adolescent group, with a peak in puberty; the middle-aged group culminating in the mid-to-late thirties; and a senescent one in the late fifties and early sixties."[3] There are cases where an accused is charged under gross indecency or indecent act when the behaviour is pedophilic, but the occurrence is rare. As yet there is no statistical picture of the number of heterosexual pedophilic acts which are charged under "Contributing to Juvenile Delinquency" under the Juvenile Act.

1 J. W. Mohr, R. E. Turner, and M. B. Jerry, *Pedophilia and Exhibitionism* (Toronto, 1964), p. 20.
2 J. W. Mohr, "Sexual Behaviour and the Criminal Law," Part IV, "Indecent Assault on a Female," Section I – Introduction, Study Population and Age Factors (Forensic Clinic, Toronto Psychiatric Hospital, February, 1966), mimeographed.
3 Mohr *et al., Pedophilia*, p. 41.

Attention is here directed to the Criminal Code offence of indecent assault on a female, the one most commonly employed to cover heterosexual pedophilic acts.[4]

Homosexual Pedophilia

In cases involving male children, the sexual act is more aggressive and more often orgastic than that encountered in heterosexual pedophilia;[5] it involves fondling, masturbation, and fellatio, and less frequently anal or intercrural intercourse. The age of the victim and the nature of the act do not provide as clear a basis for the definition of homosexual pedophilia as is the case with heterosexual pedophilia. While with the increase in age of the female there is a development of the sexual behaviour in heterosexual relations into intercourse, there does not seem to be a corresponding development between homosexual partners; thus "homosexual pedophilic acts seem to be generally the same as those of adult partners." The age of the victim is somewhat higher than one finds it in heterosexual pedophilia, and the peak in the age of victims falls between 12 and 15, thus coinciding more closely with puberty. Relating this to the definition of the act as occurring with prepubertal children, it should be borne in mind that the onset of puberty is later for boys than for girls and also that the "development of secondary sexual characteristics is not as dramatic in boys as it is with girls."[6] In the preliminary analysis of male sex offenders charged in Metropolitan Toronto in the course of a year with the offence of indecent assault on a male, about 9 out of 10 cases involved male victims under the age of 15. Although at face value the section appears to be an adult homosexual offence, in practice one finds it is used predominantly to cover cases of homosexual pedophilia. As the evolution of this offence has already been discussed under the heading of Homosexual Offences, it will not be repeated here.

4 The number of female sex offenders is extremely small. The Cambridge study shows that over a five-year period (1947 to 1951) only 0.6 per cent of the indictable sex offences proceeded with involved female offenders. For more specifics see L. Radzinowicz, ed., *English Studies in Criminal Science*, vol. IX, *Sexual Offences* (London, 1957), p. 6. Under the Canadian Criminal Code, although females may be charged with indecent assault on a female they cannot be charged with indecent assault on a male. The term heterosexual pedophilia, then, as used here applies to cases involving a male offender and a female child.
5 Mohr *et al.*, *Pedophilia*, p. 32. "Orgasm was sought by only about 6 per cent of the offenders in the *P.het.* [heterosexual pedophile] group, but by over 50 per cent in the *P.ho.* [homosexual pedophile] group."
6 *Ibid.*, p. 26.

Indecent Assault Female

History of Classification

Introduced in 1869,[7] the offence of indecent assault female followed the English section of 1861,[8] but added a provision for whipping. Originally classified under a section covering "Rape, Abduction and Defilement of Women," this offence shared the same section as attempt carnal knowledge of a girl under 12. The classification suggests that this offence was conceived of as one of those having intercourse as the ultimate aim. Although no age limit was included in the offence, the fact that it was grouped with attempt carnal knowledge of a girl under 12 suggests that it was originally seen as a similar kind of offence, that is, that it was in some ways related to the protection of young girls. Because of the kinds of acts involved – looking, touching, fondling – it is understandable that these acts were regarded as preliminary steps to intercourse, and from that point of view the classification was not inappropriate. It is only when one understands that in the large majority of cases, where young female children are involved, these acts are not preliminary steps in a chain leading to intercourse, but are the final aim in themselves, that the classification can be seen to be inappropriate.

No change was made in 1886[9] but in 1890 the penalty was changed from any time less than two years to two years, and the offence of indecent assault was separated from the offence of carnal knowledge of a girl under 12.[10] At the same time, a new section was introduced which took away the defence of consent in cases of indecent assault where the young person assaulted was under the age of 14.[11] In order to understand better the significance of this particular change, it is necessary to consider it within a wider context. In 1886 an act passed "to punish Seduction and like offences, and to make further provision for the protection of Women and Girls" made it an offence for anyone to "seduce and have illicit connection" with a girl of previously chaste character between the ages of 12 and 16.[12] This age group had not been covered previously. In the general revision in the same year, this new offence was included not under "Offences against the Person," as were

7 S.C. 1869, c. 20, s. 53.
8 Offences against the Person Act, 1861, 24–25 Vict., c. 100, s. 52.
9 R.S.C. 1886, c. 162, s. 41.
10 S.C. 1890, c. 37, s. 12.
11 *Ibid.*, s. 7.
12 S.C. 1886, c. 52, s. 1(1).

earlier offences, but under the "Offences against Public Morals and Convenience."[13] In 1890 these offences were reformulated along more stringent lines, the age of absolute protection against acts of carnal knowledge was raised from under 10 years of age to under 14, and limited protection was given to girls between the ages of 14 and 16.[14]

The increased protection afforded girls under 14 in cases of indecent assault paralleled and was consistent with the philosophy expressed in the newly reformulated offences against chastity. At the same time that the change was made to give absolute protection to girls between 10 and 14 in cases involving intercourse, the change affecting the indecent assault section meant that even in cases where a girl under 14 consented to sexual involvement short of intercourse the male person was now liable to a charge of indecent assault.

Although indecent assault was physically separated from its relationship with one of the offences against the chastity of young girls and given a section by itself, it was not altogether conceptually freed from its earlier association. That indecent assault was still regarded as a preliminary step towards further sexual acts is indicated in a remark made by Sir John Thompson when the section was discussed in the House of Commons: "[Indecent assault] is an assault made in persuance of an attempt to commit a graver offence."[15] Although there was no age distinction made in the section of indecent assault itself, the effect of the new provision was to draw a clear demarcation between cases involving girls under 14 and those involving girls and women over that age.

In 1892 there was a marked shift in the classification of the offence, from "Abduction and Defilement of Women" to "Assaults." It was an unsatisfactory reduction, in that the emphasis was placed on the element of assault rather than the sexual content of the act. The effect was to separate this offence from the other sexual offences. The classification, with the addition of a section covering the obtaining of consent by false and fraudulent representations,[16] followed that set out in the EDC, and the section was the same except that the EDC did not provide for whipping and included a subsection covering attempted carnal knowledge of a girl under 12.[17] The same classification had previously been made in Stephen's *Digest*.[18]

13 R.S.C. 1886, c. 157, s. 3(a).
14 S.C. 1890, c. 37, s. 12, 3.
15 Debates, H.C., Canada, 1890, II, 3181.
16 S.C. 1892, c. 29, s. 250.
17 Report of the Royal Commission Appointed to Consider the Law Relating to Indictable Offences, Appendix, Second Schedule, p. 205.
18 Sir James Fitzjames Stephen, *A Digest of the Criminal Law* (St. Louis, 1878), Article 245(d), p. 183.

The characterization of this offence as an "assault" eventually brought about a further development in the same direction. In 1909 a subsection was added which covered anyone who assaulted or beat his wife or any other female, thereby occasioning actual bodily harm.[19] The confusion of the various kinds of acts included under the section at this point was at its greatest, for it covered consenting sexual acts with children, forcible acts with children, forcible sexual acts with women and girls over 14, fraudulent sexual acts, and forcible acts, either sexual or non-sexual in nature, which caused actual harm to a wife or any other female. The linking together of child-molesting on the one hand and wife-beating on the other demonstrates a singular lack of ability to understand and make meaningful distinctions within the subject matter at issue.

This state of affairs was endured until 1953–54, when the section was reclassified as a sexual offence and the penalty increased to five years.[20] The form of the section was changed so that there is now but one offence of indecent assault, while subsection 2 sets out that indecent assault includes acts where consent was obtained by fraudulent representation as to the nature and quality of the act. The subsection which referred to occasioning bodily harm to a female was removed from this section and now forms part of the general assault section (s. 231). The only discussion which is reported with respect to this section in Hansard centred around a point raised by Mr. Diefenbaker as to whether the provision of section 134 regarding corroboration should also be made to apply to this section.[21] When the Commons returned to consider the clause, Mr. Garson pointed out that in Cullen v. The King [(1949), 94 C.C.C. 337 (S.C.C.)] it was said that corroboration was not necessary in cases of indecent assault. However, he agreed that the Canadian law should conform with that of the United Kingdom, and section 134 was amended to apply to section 141 as well.[22] No other discussion of this section was reported at any stage in its passage through parliament.

The present classification of this section under "Sexual Offence" is an appropriate one in that it identifies the content of the act and brings together all of the sexual offences into one part of the Code. The section itself fails in one major respect, however, in that it does not distinguish between consenting acts and forcible acts where children under 14 are concerned. It may be argued that both kinds of acts are offensive and ought to be punished, and therefore the distinction is irrelevant. But if

19 S.C. 1909, c. 9, s. 2 (Schedule, re s. 292).
20 S.C. 1954, c. 51, s. 141(1)(2).
21 Debates, H.C., Canada, 1953–54, I, 2050.
22 Ibid., III, 3559.

criminological and clinical data about pedophilic acts and the people who commit these acts is to be meaningful and useful to the courts, it is necessary either to train magistrates and judges to identify pedophilic acts among the array of indecent assault cases which they see, or to define an offence in a way which distinguishes the pedophilic act from other kinds of sexual acts presently charged under the one broad category of indecent assault female. Information surrounding recidivism rates and the appropriateness and efficacy of various forms of punishment and treatment is most significant when related to a specific homogeneous group. Before this information is useful for any case which presents itself, it is essential to define clearly the criteria or parameters which permit a specific classification. If the definition of the offence is so constructed that it admits of only one kind of offence, the homogeneity of the group convicted under that offence is already established. At present, the pedophile, the frotteurist, and the hostile and aggressive offender all fall together under the common offence of indecent assault and cannot be regarded for any clinical or criminological purpose as comprising a homogeneous group.

Punishment

The provision of maximum penalties in a criminal code is no indication of what sentences are in fact being imposed by magistrates and judges. The factual data of actual sentences comprise a vital piece of information about the courts' reaction to particular crimes, and reflect perhaps more clearly than anything else society's reaction to the kinds of offensive events which occur in it. The legislators, in reviewing a code, periodically have an opportunity to express their reaction through the maximum sentences which are set out in the legislation. Maximum sentences must of course allow for the extreme cases which might occur, and one would expect these to be substantially higher than the normal sentences which are imposed. They nevertheless can be looked at as a generalized response made by the elected representatives at various times, and they give an overall impression of the changing tenor of society's attitudes towards certain crimes.

The offence of indecent assault female was punishable in 1869 with a maximum of any term less than two years, and whipping. In 1890 the prison term was raised to two years (a penitentiary sentence) and remained unchanged until the amendment in 1953–54, when the penalty was raised to five years and the provision for whipping retained.

Whipping was not provided for in the English statute from which the Canadian legislation was taken. On June 1, 1869, the Senate, while sitting as a Committee of the Whole, held a long and spirited debate with respect to the provision for whipping in numerous sections.[23] As first proposed, the provision for whipping was to apply only "if such offender be under the age of 16." The Hon. Mr. Sanborn, the principal opponent, contended, "It is not the spirit of the criminal law to try to deaden feelings of self respect, and to crush in man all that makes him noble and honourable. It is contrary to the spirit of the age." The Hon. Mr. Campbell, in reply, said, "If it was not the spirit of the age, it was the spirit we should endeavour to foster and make the spirit of the age." He was of the opinion that if a boy under 16 was led away by momentary excitement to commit a crime, "and if it was thought that in considering his youth to deal leniently with him, would he not be better dealt with by flogging and sending him about his business, than by sending him to a reformatory prison or to a penitentiary?" Later, on a motion by Hon. Mr. Campbell, the section was amended, leaving out the words, "if such offender be under the age of 16 years." The effect of the change was to make the provision for whipping apply to anyone who committed the offence. It has remained unchanged since that time and in the debates on the most recent revision no mention was made of it.

The increase in the length of the maximum prison term from two to five years is in keeping with the increases which have been made over the years with respect to "the offence against chastity." Although the death penalty for carnal knowledge of a girl under 10 was abolished in 1877 and a life sentence with a minimum of five years substituted, the raising of the age limit from under 10 to under 14 years in 1890 considerably increased the number of cases to which this penalty might apply. At that time, a provision for whipping was added to that offence as well. In 1920, the punishment for the offence of seduction of a girl between 14 and 16 was raised from two years to five, and a further seduction section added to cover girls between the ages of 16 and 18. In the most recent amendment to the code, the maximum punishment for attempted carnal knowledge of a girl under 14 was raised from two years to fourteen years. It can be seen that not only has the length of

---

23 *Canadian Parliamentary Debates 1866–1870*, an account of the debates taken from the *Ottawa Times*, the *Toronto Globe* and the *Toronto Mail*. Microfilm copy, produced by the Canadian Library Association (Newspaper Microfilming Project). The debate in full is far too long to reproduce here but it bears study. As originally proposed the previous year, the punishment for whipping was attached to some 40 to 50 offences, but had since been reduced to a very few. Equally interesting debates on the same topic occurred in the House of Commons, April 27, May 4, and May 21, 1869.

maximum terms been increased but also the ages for which protection is provided have followed an upward trend.

If one looked no further than the increased penalty, one might fairly come to the conclusion that society's attitude towards these offences has become more punitive than it was almost a century ago. Immediately this strikes one as contrary to the general social attitudes and changing sexual mores, as society has moved further away from the more restricting sexual code of the Victorian era. Can it be that these changes have brought with them a reaction in the opposite direction as far as sexual offences are concerned? Before any such meaning is ascribed to the changes, it would be helpful if one could learn more about why the increase was necessary, what justification there was for it, who called for it and what was said about it.

In 1952, the royal commissioners who recommended the most recent increases made the following statements with respect to sentencing in their report.

The sentences provided in the present Code follow no apparent pattern or principle and in our view are frequently not consonant with the gravity of the offences to which they relate.

Your Commissioners are of the opinion that there should be a few general divisions of punishment by imprisonment, each offence being assigned to one of the divisions. Accordingly, apart from the cases where the sentence of death may be imposed, maximum sentences of imprisonment are provided as follows.

(a) Life.
(b) 14
(c) 10
(d) 5
(e) 2[24]

The Commissioners did not report what basis they used to determine the "gravity" of an offence, nor is it known why a five-point scale was used rather than some other. They may have provided the code with "a pattern" of sentences, but it is unclear to what, besides their own judgments, it relates. Are indecent assaults on females to be viewed twice as seriously as before? Is attempted carnal knowledge to be treated as seven times as serious? Is indecent assault on a male twice as "grave" an offence as indecent assault on a female? The simple and obvious approach of rating each offence in relation to others does yield a kind of order, but the Commissioners' own objection to the preceding scheme, that it lacks an "apparent principle," can just as easily be applied to

24 Report of Royal Commission on the Revision of Criminal Code (Ottawa, 1954), p. 10; Debates, Sen., Canada, 1952, p. 233.

this one. It would seem that the newer provisions were less a reaction to the particular offences under consideration than an abstracted quest for an external order. When these offences were first legislated, the penalties which were established indicated at least a clear legislative reaction to the offence under consideration. But what was the legislators' reaction on this last occasion? A search of Hansard on this point discloses no reported discussion concerning the increased penalty in either the House of Commons or the Senate, or in the various committees which considered the bills. One can only take it that the recommendations of the commission were accepted uncritically.

Society expects that some solid evidence will be provided before changes of this order are even recommended, much less adopted. Maximum sentences are taken by the courts as a guide, and they do reflect a policy. The policy which the changes indicate in the instant case is one which passes to the courts an even wider discretion than was available previously. But in moving in this direction, it was incumbent on those responsible for the changes to at least give an accounting of how in fact the courts had been using their discretion. This would have permitted the Commissioners to use the previous policy of the courts as a starting point. But they did not give an accounting. Nor did they apparently make an appeal for an evaluation to determine how the various kinds of sentences had worked out in practice.

To ask these empirical questions – what has been done? how has it worked? – does not of itself commit one to any particular policy, but it at least enables one to move with some conscious aim or purpose in mind. The expressed aims which prompted the most recent changes seem to be somehow extraneous to the offences themselves and suggest more a reaction to the words expressing the offences than to the substance of the events they were used to cover.

Apart from the offence of carnal knowledge of a girl under 14, the Criminal Code does not set out any specific sex offence against children as such. And the question arises whether, because of their numerical importance and the special concern which arises about child molesting, separate and special offences ought not to be framed to cover these acts. The wording of the present section, using the elements of "indecency," "assault," and "female" or "male," admits a diversity of acts within the same offence. The elimination of the defence of consent in cases where young children are involved expands the original meaning of the term assault, with the unfortunate result that it is no longer possible to determine what proportion of the cases actually involved force of some kind.

The severe cases of child molesting are not conceptually or legally isolated from the more common and relatively less harmful forms of sexual involvement with children. With respect to the less severe or pedophilic type of offence, there is already a great deal known about recidivism which has important implications for the courts in terms both of disposition and of other correctional facilities such as parole.

One of the conceptual obstacles which has perhaps retarded the development of the law in this area was the notion that all sexual acts involving females were coital in aim or in fact. It is now known that in the large majority of sexual cases involving females, the sexual relationship is non-coital in character.[25] This is certainly true in most cases in which children are involved and also with respect to another large group, the frotteurists. The separation of the various kinds of acts according to the involvement of children, adolescents, or adults, the presence or absence of force, and the coital or non-coital character of the intentionality shows clearly that several distinct kinds of behaviour are at issue. The translation of this material into legal forms or offences will also call for a re-examination of the maximum sentence and the provision for whipping which do not appear to be appropriate for all the kinds of offences they cover at present.

The evolution of indecent assault female reveals society's central concern to protect children from sexual contact with adults. Those who implemented this concern as legislation misunderstood pedophilia, seeing it on the one hand as a threat to chastity and on the other as a forceful attack on the child. A major advance was made when the law undertook to punish consenting acts when young children were involved. The main emphasis was lost, however, when the concept of assault was selected as the characterizing feature of the offence. The reclassification of this offence with other sexual offences marks an appropriate return to the earlier conception of the problem.

It is now known that pedophilic acts represent by far the greater proportion of offences involving children. Taken collectively, these acts form the bulk of the cases which prompt society's general concern for the protection of the young. It is now possible to isolate them not only clinically but in the law as well. The provision of a more specific offence to cover them will enable the courts to identify them more clearly. Moreover, it will also make it possible to bring to the courts' attention

25 Evidence for this is contained in numerous sub-studies by Dr. J. W. Mohr in the major study of "Sexual Behaviour, Society, and the Criminal Law" referred to above, n. 2. In particular, reference may be made to his study of indecent assault on a female, in four sections. This and other relevant studies await future publication.

information with respect to recidivism and the efficacy of certain forms of dispositions and treatment which will better enable them to cope with one of society's chronic problems.

The 1949-54 Revisions of the Criminal Code

In the preceding pages, the sexual offences under discussion have been examined from the point of view of their own particular evolution. It is necessary at this point to change to a new focus so that broader and somewhat more important aspects of the problem can be seen. The treatment afforded the sex offences in the most recent revision has been criticized from the point of view of the end-product of the process of revision. In this chapter the process itself will be examined to see in what ways the attitudes and the means taken towards the revision contributed to the rather limited results achieved and to learn what we can about the defects of the process so that the approach which is taken in the future may be an improvement over the last attempt.

It is of course true that a full understanding of the legislative process would have to consider the two other periods of importance in Canadian law: the first framing of the national criminal law in 1869 following transfer of criminal jurisdiction to the federal government, and the adoption of the Criminal Code in 1892. The problems faced in those two instances were different from that which confronts us today. In 1869 the country required some uniform criminal law, and the easiest, quickest, and most reasonable way to provide it was to borrow wholesale from what had already been achieved in England. Some twenty years later, when the time had come for a reconsideration of the criminal law, the same pattern was followed, except that on that occasion the Minister of Justice had available to him a full ready-made criminal code which required but minor adjustments for its adaptation to Canada.

In moving the second reading of Bill No. 7, as the act was then called, Sir John Thompson had this to say, in part, about the origins and the purpose of the codification of the criminal law:

The objects of the bill are very tersely expressed in one passage of the report of the Royal Commission which investigated the subject of the Criminal Law in England, in defining the effect of that codification in a similar bill in Great Britain in these words: "It is a reduction of the existing law to an orderly written system, freed from needless technicalities, obscurities and other defects which the experience of its administration has disclosed. It aims at the reduction of a system of that kind of substantive law relating to crimes and the law of procedure, both as to indictable offences and as to summary convictions."[1]

The idea of codification did not erupt into the great controversy which had raged in England for so many years, and in fact the debate on the second reading centred principally on the question of the abolition of the grand jury system. A select committee of the House of Commons and the Senate was set up on April 12 (1319). On May 17, announcing that the select committee had reported, Sir John Thompson said, "Amendments made were not at all numerous and they were principally of a verbal character" (2701). The bill was read a third time in the Commons on June 28 and on July 6 the second reading was given in the Senate.[2] The only voice raised in opposition to codification was that of the Hon. Mr. Scott who objected to it on the grounds that "the law as it stood was well understood and the magistrates would have to unlearn what they knew and take up the code" (465). He regarded the new code as a great misfortune and said he believed it would be a great mistake, unless there was a defect in the present system, to change it. He called the limited time available to review the code as it stood, "at the least of it, a parliamentary farce." Others joined him in this: the Hon. Mr. Vidal, the Hon. Mr. Wark, and the Hon. Mr. Kaulback, who said, "Almost everyone has packed up his trunk and prepared to start for home." In fact the debate on second reading centred primarily on whether to consider the bill then or to let it lie over to the next session. The Hon. Mr. Read pressed for the debate to go forward, saying, "Magistrates throughout the country require a measure of this kind. The public looks for it, the judges look for it" (472). The bill was read the second time on July 6, and the Senate agreed to go into committee of the whole. Two days later, on July 8, the Senate passed the third reading of the bill. The theory of the slow, calm, dispassionate review of legislation by the upper house crumbled under the members' desire to return to their homes, and Canada thus gave birth to her first Criminal Code.[3]

1 Debates, H.C., Canada, 1892, p. 1312. Further references to the same source will be made parenthetically, by column number only, in the text.
2 Debates, Sen., Canada, 1892, p. 464.
3 The tribute paid to Sir John Thompson and the credit given to his adaptation of the English Draft Code for Canadian use was apparently boundless: "It is as true as a proposition in Euclid, that the criminal law of Canada is above that of any nation or State on the face of the earth. It embodies most of the suggestions of Bentham, Becarri [sic], Livingston, MacKintosh and Romily [sic], and hundreds of others which never occurred to them, and is the first attempt on a national

For the next half century, the Code was amended on a piecemeal basis, so that inevitably it deteriorated finally into a bulky, confusing, and complicated statute. In 1942, in the criminal law section of the Canadian Bar Association, under the chairmanship of J. C. McRuer, K.C., it was proposed that a Criminal Law Section be added to the Conference of Commissioners on Uniformity which had been formed in 1918. It had been pointed out that "no body existed in Canada with proper personnel to study and prepare recommendations for amendments to the Criminal Code and relevant statutes in finished form for submission to the Minister of Justice."[4] This proposal was adopted by the Uniformity Commissioners, and a Criminal Law Section was added in 1944. An examination of the work of the Section between 1944 and 1948 indicates a struggle with partial revision of the Code, particularly with respect to the procedural provisions. Questions which required substantive changes were avoided. In 1947, the formidable task facing the commissioners was apparent; it was acknowledged by a formal resolution calling for a royal commission to undertake a complete recodification of the criminal law and a revision of the Criminal Code.

At this point, the recognition of the need for revision had reached such a stage that it could no longer be avoided. In what follows, I will trace the various stages of the process leading to the final acceptance of the revision when royal assent was given on June 26, 1954. It will not be possible, of course, to detail the scope of the debate on all offences, but by selecting once again the offences which concern us I intend to mark the various phases and at the same time specifically note what if anything occurred at each stage.

Preceding the Appointment of the Commission

A question was raised in the House of Commons on February 27, 1948, by Mr. Hackett, who asked Mr. Ilsley, the then Minister of Justice, if there was any hope that the revision of the Criminal Code might be initiated that year. Mr. Ilsley replied,

---

scale to make criminal law synonymous with justice, and substitute civilization and Christianity for barbarism." This passage is quoted in A. J. MacLeod and J. C. Martin, The Revision of the Criminal Code, Can. Bar Rev., xxxiii, 6. The original citation given there is J. Castell Hopkins, *Life and Work of Sir John Thompson* (1895), p. 382.

4 Proceedings of the Conference of Commissioners on Uniformity of Legislation in Canada, 1944, p. 12.

I expect to make an announcement later in the session as to the appointment
of a commission or body of some kind to undertake a revision of the Criminal Code, but a question arises as to what powers these commissioners should
be given. In all probability their duties should be different from those Commissioners who are appointed to revise statutes. That also is a matter to
which consideration is being given.[5]

During a supply debate with respect to the Department of Justice on
June 9 of the same year, Mr. John G. Diefenbaker asked the following
question:

In view of the numerous amendments to the Criminal Code, what, if anything, has been done to mobilize the support of the law schools as well as
of judges and magistrates who have retired, looking to a revision of the
Criminal Code and bringing it up to date by removing obsolete sections and
changing others to conform to the penological, psychological, and physiolo-
gical advances which have been made?[6]

Mr. Ilsley's reply provides some insight into the direction of the government's thought at the time:

The Criminal Code certainly needs revision. The Commissioners on Uniformity have been working on it year after year. They advised me last August
that they did not think that they were the proper body to revise the Criminal
Code.[7] They are not remunerated for their work and they do not have much
time to devote to it. Certain provinces review certain parts of the code, and
a great deal of work has been done. We have been rather hoping that a
piecemeal revision of the code could be made by that method, and we have
not completely given up the idea. The difficulty about revision is to get the
proper persons to take charge of it, persons in whose judgment one has confidence and who are in every respect competent . . . the work has not ceased;
and it is being done all the time by the commissioners, and these important
amendments are being introduced year by year and are continually cutting
down the amount of work that is left.
    There is a view that we should try to prevail upon the commissioners on
uniformity of law to do the whole thing, part by part, and section by section,
but I do not think they are quite disposed to accept that view. (4940)

Mr. Ilsley's reply did not answer several issues raised by Mr. Diefenbaker's question, such as participation by law schools and magistrates,
and the scope of the work of the commission in terms of not only
"pruning" the code but also making substantive changes to conform

5 Debates, H.C., Canada, 1948, II, 1674.
6 Ibid., IV, 4939.
7 No mention of this is made in the Minutes of the Proceedings of the Criminal
Law Section of the Uniformity Commissioners. The Commissioners passed a
resolution asking that the Criminal Code be revised. Mr. Ilsley visited the Committee but the minutes only show that a resolution with respect to section 242 of
the Code was discussed.

with certain "scientific" advances. These issues which seem important are not subsequently discussed in any of the reported debates.

On June 19, Mr. John Hackett again asked about recodification of the Criminal Law, but he was told that no provision had been made.

Appointment of the Commission

Some seven months later, on January 31, 1949, in reply to a question raised by Mr. John G. Diefenbaker, the Hon. Stuart S. Garson, the new Minister of Justice, announced that a commission had been set up, the commissioners named, and a legal committee appointed to assist them.[8] No further information was given nor was the matter discussed. The Criminal Code Revision Commission and its committee were formally appointed on February 3, 1949, to examine and study the Criminal Code. Three commissioners were appointed: the Hon. W. M. Martin, Chief Justice of Saskatchewan, chairman, Mr. J. H. G. Fauteux, Q.C., then of the Quebec Bar, and Mr. F. P. Varcoe, Q.C., Deputy Minister of Justice.[9] Mr. Arthur Slaught, Q.C., of Toronto was appointed counsel to the commission. The committee appointed to assist the commission consisted of Mr. Robert Forsythe, Q.C., then of the Department of Justice, Mr. Fernand Choquette, Q.C., Bar of Quebec, Mr. H. J. Wilson, Q.C., Deputy Attorney General of Alberta, Mr. J. Sedgwick, Q.C., Bar of Ontario, Mr. J. J. Robinette, Q.C., Bar of Ontario (added later), Mr. W. C. Dunlop, Q.C., Bar of Nova Scotia, Mr. H. P. Carter, Director of Public Prosecution, Newfoundland, and Mr. T. D. MacDonald, Q.C., Department of Justice, formerly Attorney General of Nova Scotia.

The committee, under the direction of the commission, held twelve meetings, each of which occupied approximately a week. Owing to other commitments and duties occupying the attention of some of the appointees, the work on the revision of the code was given over to a smaller committee appointed on September 26, 1950. This committee consisted of the Hon. W. M. Martin, Chief Justice of Saskatchewan, chairman, the Hon. Mr. Justice Fernand Choquette, Quebec, formerly of the Bar of Quebec, His Honour Judge Robert Forsythe, Toronto, formerly of the Department of Justice, Mr. H. J. Wilson, Q.C., Edmonton, Mr. Joseph Sedgwick, Q.C., Toronto, and Mr. A. A. Moffat, Q.C., Ottawa.

8 Debates, H.C., Canada, 1949, I, 73.
9 Report of Royal Commission on the Revision of Criminal Code (Ottawa, 1954); also Debates, Sen., Canada, 1952, p. 226.

In terms of personnel, there was a close relationship between this committee and the Uniformity Commissioners. The chairman, the Hon. W. M. Martin, Premier of Saskatchewan from 1916 to 1922, was a member of the Uniformity Commissioners in 1921. His Honour Judge Forsythe, formerly Senior Counsel of the Department of Justice, Canada, had been a member of the Criminal Law Section from 1944 to 1949. Mr. Wilson, Deputy Attorney General of Alberta, joined the Uniformity Commissioners in 1943 and attended the Criminal Law Section from 1944 to 1953 and beyond. Mr. Sedgwick (who had been a solicitor with the Ontario Attorney General's Department, 1929–1937), attended the Criminal Law Section from 1944 to 1948. Mr. A. A. Moffat, Deputy Attorney General of Manitoba, attended meetings in 1945, 1946, and 1949 and was a member of the Commissioners throughout this period. There is no record of Mr. Justice Choquette's having been a member of the Uniformity Commissioners. It can be seen that although Mr. Ilsley as Minister of Justice was not able to prevail on the Uniformity Commissioners to undertake the revision of the Code, his successor, the Hon. Stuart S. Garson, was successful in drawing heavily from its membership.

On May 10, 1951, the committee was appointed as a commission authorized and directed to prepare a draft bill to revise the Criminal Code. The terms of reference were as follows:

(a) revise ambiguous and unclear provisions;
(b) adopt uniform language throughout;
(c) eliminate inconsistencies, legal anomalies, or defects;
(d) rearrange provisions and Parts;
(e) seek to simplify by omitting and combining provisions;
(f) with the approval of the Statute Revisions Commission, omit provisions which should be transferred to other statutes;
(g) endeavour to make the Code exhaustive of the criminal law; and
(h) effect such procedural amendments as are deemed necessary for the speedy and fair enforcement of the criminal law.

The report of the royal commission shows that there were meetings with the Criminal Law Section of the Conference of Commissioners on Uniformity of Legislation in August 1949 and September 1951.[10] Although the report does not make reference to it, the committee in 1950 asked the Uniformity Commissioners to consider certain procedural parts of the Code, and their views were communicated through Mr. H. J.

10 *Ibid.*, p. 227.

Wilson, a member of both bodies.[11] The commission held four meetings, each of which extended over about a week. There is no report of a meeting with any body other than the Uniformity Commissioners.

The report of the royal commission was completed on January 22, 1952, and sent to the Minister of Justice on February 27, 1952. The report and the draft bill were tabled in the House of Commons and the Senate on April 7, 1952.[12]

Six Phases of Parliamentary Consideration

(1) As Bill H-8 in the Senate

Bill H-8, ". . . a redraft of the Commission's Draft containing changes in some minor respects made by the Department of Justice, under instructions of the Government," was introduced in the Senate on May 13, 1952. The Hon. Stuart S. Garson, on addressing the senators on second reading of the bill, said:

Hon. Senators will note that under the terms of reference the purpose of the revision was not to effect changes in broad principle, but was to evolve as simple a Code as possible by the elimination of unnecessary or obsolete provisions, the correction of errors and the removal of inconsistencies, and to effect such consolidation and rearrangement as was deemed necessary to facilitate reference.[13]

On May 15, 1952, the bill was referred to the Standing Committee on Banking and Commerce of the Senate (275).[14] The Standing Committee considered a report of its own subcommittee on June 11, 1952.[15] The

11 Proceedings of the Conference of Commissioners on Uniformity of Legislation in Canada, 1950, p. 31.
12 For a more detailed account of the steps outlined above and for background information on the need for revision, see an address given by the Hon. Stuart S. Garson to the Senate on second reading of the bill. Debates, Sen., Canada, 1952, p. 207.
13 Debates, Sen., Canada, 1952, p. 208.
14 Nothing is available from the public record which gives an answer as to why the Standing Committee on Banking and Commerce was selected, but consider some remarks made by the Hon. Stuart S. Garson in his Senate address: "One of the quite important reasons why we in the Department of Justice and in the Government decided to avail ourselves of the services of your honourable chamber on this occasion was the magnificent work which you did for us in considering the Bankruptcy Bill of 1949. . . ." Could the reasoning have been that since the Banking and Commerce Committee had coped so well with the problems of bankruptcy, they could do as well with the criminal law? It may well have been that this committee had among its members the most competent legally-trained Senators, but to accept the appropriateness of the choice still requires, it seems to me, a little leap of faith.
15 Standing Committee on Banking and Commerce, Senate, Canada, 1952.

subcommittee reported that "the lack of satisfactory explanatory notes appended to the bill made the task of the subcommittee tedious and difficult and delayed the Committee's progress" (6). Some explanatory memoranda were received from the Department of Justice, and appendices denoting changes or no changes were prepared by the subcommittee and are attached to the printed proceedings (33–35). Sections 141, 147, 148, and 158 were not discussed by the Standing Committee. Section 149, the gross indecency section, was discussed, as reported on p. 49 (18).

In the appendices prepared by the subcommittee, it is noted that Section 141, Indecent Assault Female, is a "change in form only" from previous Code no. 292(a) (b); section 147, Buggery, is a "change in form only" from previous Code no. 202; section 158, Indecent Act, is "unchanged" from the Code no. 205 (34).

Under that part of the appendices dealing with sections in which there are substantive changes is a notation regarding section 149, Gross Indecency, previous Code no. 206, as follows: "Widened to include all acts of gross indecency irrespective of sex" (39). Nowhere in the report of the proceedings of the Standing Committee or in the appendices prepared by the subcommittee is reference made to section 148, Indecent Assault on a Male or Assault with Intent to Commit Buggery. On June 20, the committee reported to the Senate recommending that the bill not be further proceeded with at that session.[16]

(2) As Bill "O" in the Senate

On November 24, 1952, the bill, substantially the same as when presented at the previous session (21), was re-introduced in the Senate as Bill "O."[17] On November 25 it was read a second time and referred to the Standing Committee on Banking and Commerce (23). A subcommittee of the Standing Committee considered Bill "O" at fifteen sessions and reported to the main committee on December 16, 1952.[18] None of the amendments suggested by the subcommittee was in relation to sections 141, 147, 148, 149 (89), or 158 (87). The report of the subcommittee is available as Appendix "A" to the report of the Standing Committee.

The subcommittee's report was considered by the main committee on the day it was submitted. The committee considered the provisions of the bill clause by clause, but no discussion was held with respect to

16 Debates, Sen., Canada, 1952, p. 479.
17 Debates, Sen., Canada, 1952–53, p. 6.
18 Standing Committee on Banking and Commerce, Senate, Canada, 1952–53.

sections 141, 147, 148, 149, or 158 (58–60). The Standing Committee recommended 116 amendments to Bill "O,"[19] none of which affected any of those sections, and the Senate adopted the report on December 17, 1952, likewise without reference to them.

Bill "O" as amended and adopted by the Senate was checked, and in it sections 141, 147, 148, and 158 appeared exactly as they do at present in the Criminal Code.

(3) As Bill 93 in the House of Commons

The Hon. Mr. Stuart S. Garson, Minister of Justice, moved first reading of Bill 93 (which had been bill "O" in the Senate) in the House of Commons on January 13, 1953.[20] On January 23, 1953, the Minister reviewed the steps which had been taken with respect to the bill prior to its presentation to the House of Commons (1274). In the general discussion on second reading, there was no reference to the sections we are concerned with here, and it was agreed that the bill be referred to a special committee appointed to consider it (1303).[21]

The Special Committee formed on February 2, 1953, was comprised of 17 members (1518). The minutes of the committee's proceedings and evidence have been published in seven parts, including its three reports to the Commons.[22]

The bill was considered clause by clause, and on February 11, 1953, clauses 130 to 160 (containing the sections in which we are interested) were allowed to stand (7). One of the witnesses appearing before the Committee on March 10 was Mr. Norman Borins, Q.C., who presented a brief on behalf of the Canadian Welfare Council. In the course of his presentation, Mr. Borins quoted a report of Mr. McGrath, the then Secretary of the Delinquency and Crime Division of the Canadian Welfare Council, as follows:

The whole question of sex behaviour has been clouded by a lack of factual information. Within the past few years the social scientists have carried on a number of studies in this area, and if our criminal law is to reflect a realistic understanding of the situation the findings of these studies should be taken into consideration when our laws are framed.

However, despite the work already done, the picture is far from clear, and

---

19 *Ibid.*, Appendix B.
20 Debates, H.C., Canada, 1952–53, I, 931.
21 Several members expressed the opinion that it was regrettable that the House of Commons did not have a standing committee on justice, particularly when they "have one on a restaurant," referring to the members' dining room. See the remarks by Mr. G. C. Nolan at p. 1293 and Mr. D. Fulton at p. 1303.
22 Journals, H.C., Canada, XCVII, Appendix 15, Criminal Law.

a comprehensive and thorough study by a government commission is advocated. It should not be a superficial one. It should be as extensive and as complete as possible. All disciplines should be involved. These should include anthropology, education, law, medicine, psychiatry, psychology, religion, social work and sociology. (155)

The brief of the Canadian Welfare Council also deals with the sex offences, in part, as follows:

7. In our opinion the section of Bill H-8 [the original designation of the bill before it was introduced in parliament] that deals with sex offences was framed without sufficient consideration being given to the knowledge of human sexual behaviour collected by the social scientists over the past few years. These scientific studies have uncovered information regarding the causalities and frequency of certain sexual habits presently defined as criminal offences which raises questions as to the wisdom of the laws governing these matters. (170)

Most of the discussion of the committee with Mr. Borins centred on section 661 dealing with criminal sexual psychopaths, and the broader questions raised in this brief were not discussed. A check was made of the other published briefs presented to the committee (some were not published) but none of these dealt with the sex offences.

On April 15, 1953, the committee resumed a clause-by-clause consideration of those portions stood over at former meetings. The following notation appears: "The Committee then heard Dr. Louis Phillipe Gendreau, Assistant Director and Deputy Commissioner of Penitentiary and Psychiatry, Dept. of Justice, in regard to Part IV of Bill 93, respecting Sex Offences, Public Morals and Disorderly Conduct" (244).[23] On April 20, 1953, clauses 130 to 149 and 151 to 160 were severally considered and passed (246). No discussion is recorded.

The second report of the special committee to the House of Commons showed no amendments affecting the section we are considering (281–293). The report of the special committee was tabled in the House of Commons on May 1, 1953.[24]

(4) As Bill 7 in the House of Commons
Bill 7 was introduced in the House of Commons, again by the Hon. Mr. Stuart S. Garson, Minister of Justice, on November 16, 1953.[25] On

23 Dr. Gendreau was contacted about this meeting. I was informed that by some mischance no stenographer was present and therefore there is no transcription of what took place. To the best of his recollection the substance of the discussion centred on the necessity of defining what is meant by the term "psychopath" in the section dealing with sexual psychopaths.
24 Debates, H.C., Canada, 1952–53, V, 4641.
25 Debates, H.C., Canada, 1953–54, I, 32.

second reading on December 15, 1953, the Minister noted that Bill 7 was the same bill as passed by the Senate in December 1952 (Bill "O") as amended and reported by the Special Committee of the Commons (Bill 93), except for six small matters involving only eleven sections, none of which touched on the matters we are considering (940).

The House of Commons sitting as a committee of the whole began consideration of Bill 7, clause by clause, on January 19, 1953.[26] With respect to section 141, Mr. Diefenbaker raised the issue that the provisions of section 134, regarding corroboration, should also apply to section 141, and that section was stood aside (2050). On the same day, February 12, 1954, sections 144 to 149 inclusive were agreed to without discussion (2057).

With respect to section 158, the Indecent Act section, Mr. Cameron (Nanaimo) raised the instance of a number of Doukhabors who were charged under Section 33 of the Juvenile Delinquents Act with contributing to juvenile delinquency for parading in the nude; this objection was discussed earlier, when the offence of Indecent Act was considered (2057–58).

On April 1, 1954, the Commons reconsidered section 141 in the light of the point raised by Mr. Diefenbaker previously. Mr. Garson pointed out that in *Cullen* v. *The King* [(1949), 94 C.C.C. 337 (S.C.C.)] it was said that corroboration was not necessary in cases of indecent assault. However he agreed that the Canadian law should conform with that of the United Kingdom and moved an amendment to section 134, adding the words "or subsection (1) of section 141."[27] Following this amendment, the clause was passed without further discussion. Bill 7 was read the third time and passed on April 8, 1954 (3927).

(5) As Bill 7 in the Senate

The bill was referred to the Senate on May 4, 1954, for a first reading there.[28] On May 11 it was referred to the Senate's Standing Committee on Banking and Commerce (464) which decided to consider only the clauses that it had not already approved when bill "O" was under consideration at the previous session of parliament.[29] The effect of this decision was to exclude discussion on the sections with which we are concerned, all of which had received prior approval.

Senator Salter A. Hayden, chairman of the Standing Committee,

26 *Ibid.*, II, 1249.
27 *Ibid.*, III, 3559.
28 Debates, Sen., Canada, 1953–54, p. 437.
29 Standing Committee on Banking and Commerce, Senate, Canada, 1953–54, p. 5.

presented the report of the committee to the Senate on June 10, 1954.[30] The amendments proposed were concurred in, and the bill received third reading the same day.

(6) Bill 7, Reconsidered by the House of Commons

On June 15, 1964, in the House of Commons, the Hon. Stuart Garson moved second reading and concurrence in the amendments made by the Senate.[31] The motion was carried without further amendments. Royal assent was given to the act on June 26, 1954, and the new Code was brought into effect, perhaps innocently, on April 1, 1955.

Comments

Although the revision was necessary, its purpose was narrowly conceived, and the composition of the body in whose hands the work was placed was equally restrictive. The Hon. Mr. Ilsley made the hopeful comment that "in all probability their duties should be different from those Commissioners who are appointed to revise statutes," but the terms that were eventually given to the commission were in effect not very different. The revision was not undertaken to make substantive changes in the law (although some in fact were made); the aim was rather to achieve as simple a code as possible: to eliminate unnecessary or obsolete provisions, to simplify, to correct errors and remove inconsistencies, to effect consolidation, and to facilitate reference by arranging provisions and parts. To begin with, then, the type of work which was necessary was grossly misconceived.

The work of the commission was begun at the end of January, 1949, and completed in January of 1952, a period of three years. One learns from the commission's report, however, that the committee it appointed held twelve meetings, each of which occupied approximately a week, and that the smaller committee which was appointed as a commission in May of 1951 met on another four occasions, each of which lasted about a week. This part of the work constitutes at best a total period of four months, which seems on the surface, at least, an impossibly short period. There is no indication in the report that anyone other than the Uniformity Commissioners met with the members of the royal commission. There is no mention made of any law school having been invited to play any part, nor were judges and magistrates or informed

30 Debates, Sen., Canada, 1953–54, p. 584.
31 Debates, H.C., Canada, 1953–54, VI, 5973.

laymen apparently asked to participate. The impression remains that the whole work was done in a hurried way by a small group, albeit well qualified, with almost no assistance from those in the community who could have made a contribution.

In the narrow field of sex offences, the major effort of the commissioners was to bring all of the sexual offences under one part of the code, but the offences themselves remained virtually unchanged, with the single exception of gross indecency, which was expanded in a way which has been open to much criticism. On this point, as on others, the commission neglected to provide explanatory notes in its report. Many of the broader, more difficult issues of fundamental importance were left untouched. With respect to the revision as a whole, it has been said that "a close examination of the work performed by the members of the Royal Commission does not justify the conclusion that a substantial or worthwhile revision was effected in 1953–54."[32]

During the legislative process, including passage of the bills through both the Senate and the House of Commons and the several committees, as outlined above, one can only come to the conclusion that in so far as the sex offences are concerned the debate was sparse, and on those rare occasions on which any was reported, it was inadequate and unsatisfactory in the extreme. In both houses and in committee the legislators were obviously uninformed of the issues involved, and where the spark of curiosity or criticism did flicker, they were poorly advised. The passage of this part of the bill was a smooth and almost a silent one.

Looking back at the period immediately before the revision, one can see that there was a swell of informed opinion calling for a much needed reform after more than half a century of patchwork and neglect. It seemed to promise the beginning of a thorough-going period of penal reform. Now, after a decade in which there has been ample time to evaluate what occurred, it is plain that what resulted was little more than a neater repackaging of an essentially nineteenth-century product. The magnitude of the work that should have been done was underestimated, the guidelines set down for the commissioners were restrictive and misconceived, the plan lacked courage and imagination, the available resources and manpower, though not great, were not utilized, the amount of information sought from outside sources was negligible, and the depth to which the issues were pursued was shallow.

Having failed to take full advantage of the opportunity to effect the reform or revision of the substantive criminal law during the last

32 J. Ll. J. Edwards, "Penal Reform and the Machinery of Criminal Justice in Canada," 8 Crim. L.Q. 408 at 413 (1966).

reconsideration, we will again have to face up to the prospect of undertaking the task. The illusion that we have just completed a reform is
beginning to fade. Now comes the task of mounting a new effort by an
approach very different from that employed in 1949. Doubtless part of
the failure at that time was attributable to the mistake of attempting a
revision of the whole Code at one time. It is unrealistic to suppose that
in the foreseeable future we will have sufficient manpower available to
mount a massive assault on the scale undertaken by the American Law
Institute, for example, in their effort toward the Model Penal Code. And
yet, that the Criminal Code as a whole must be revised is without
question, for many of the problems which arise in connection with one
part are interrelated with problems in other parts. This inevitably involves a planned, co-ordinated, and sustained effort over a number of
years. The men qualified to undertake this kind of effort are dispersed
across the country, thus further complicating the matter. Nothing short
of a permanent body to plan penal reform, assign problems, establish
priorities, and co-ordinate an undertaking of this scope can hope to
achieve the aim. There is nothing in the history of Canadian penal
reform to suggest that what appears to me to be a rational approach
will be taken. We are more likely to be faced with a series of royal
commissions or special committees set up by the Department of Justice,
such as the present Canadian Committee on Corrections (the Hon. Mr.
Justice Ouimet, chairman), or the Fauteux Committee before that.
Although these studies have necessarily touched on ancillary and related
questions which arise out of the core area of the substantive and procedural parts of the criminal law, and although they will continue to do
so, that is not their area of central concern. It is doubtful whether this
core area will be grappled with for some decades to come. The prospect
is not necessarily a gloomy one, for the time can well be spent in
preparation for the inevitable periodic decision to reform the criminal
law.

Homosexual Offences in England: 1954-1967: The Wolfenden Report

In contrast to the legislative process just described it will be useful to
take a look at the development of the law in England in relation to
homosexual offences. It may be argued that this is not a parallel

problem, but nevertheless it reveals a process which provides an extremely valuable example from which we can profit. If we must continue to copy and follow English law as we have in the past, it would at least be of some merit if we chose our models with care. I do not suggest that this is a model we can follow for the total revision of the Code – that is folly – but its selective and appropriate use in relation to controversial areas of the Code can be of specific help with those problems and at the same time kindle the fires for penal reform generally. The following is a brief résumé of that process.

Following two notorious cases of homosexuality in 1954, Lord Winterton, supported by Lord Vansittart, introduced a debate in the House of Lords calling for an appointment of a committee on the "nauseating subject" of homosexuality. He was offended by what he regarded as a propaganda campaign in the weekly press, waged by those he termed "pansies," and indicated that he would be largely influenced by any recommendation that such a committee might put forward. A fifteen-member committee was appointed by the then Home Secretary (Sir David Maxwell Fyfe, who later became Lord Chancellor, Viscount, Lord Kilmuir) on August 24, 1954, under the chairmanship of Sir John Wolfenden. The terms of reference given the committee are set out in what has come to be known as the Wolfenden Report,[1] and from this point on my remarks will be limited to the aspects dealing with homosexuality as they are more directly related to the subject at hand. The committee was asked to consider not only the law but also the practice of it relating to homosexual offences, as well as the treatment of persons convicted of such offences by the courts.[2] The construction of the terms of reference is important, for it directs attention to the substantive criminal law, the administration and enforcement of the law, and the treatment of the offender, which the committee did not hesitate to interpret in its widest sense to cover the various ways in which convicted offenders are dealt with by the courts.[3]

The committee met for 62 days (32 of which were taken up for oral evidence), a figure which compares most favourably with the reported 80 days (approximately) spent together by both the committee and the

1 Report of the Committee on Homosexual Offences and Prostitution (London, H.M. Stationery Office, 1957).
2 Ibid., p. 7.
3 Ibid., para. 148, p. 54. This latter aspect has been traditionally regarded as the field of "corrections." Have we started off our most recent Canadian Committee on Corrections by a confusing use of that term? See J. Ll. J. Edwards, "Penal Reform and the Machinery of Criminal Justice in Canada," 8 Crim. L.Q. 408 at 411 (1966).

commission during the latest revision of the entire Canadian Criminal Code. Written and oral evidence was received from 35 professional and public bodies who were represented by 123 witnesses, 6 government departments represented by another 20 witnesses, and 20 individual witnesses. Oral evidence was received from 11 other professional and public bodies and government departments, and from 15 other individuals.[4] This is described by the committee as a "representative list," the other witnesses being too numerous to mention by name.

The committee also had available to it access to data on sexual offences prepared by the Cambridge University Department of Criminal Science,[5] and a study of medical treatment given sex offenders on probation prepared by the Oxford University Department of Criminal Science.

I have gone into this aspect in some detail to point up the attention given and the use made of the available resources, groups, individuals, universities, and government departments, which stands in marked contrast to the effort made here in 1953–54.

I do not propose to discuss the contents of the report itself, which is readily available, apart from noting that before stating its major recommendations it took pains to spell out its approach to the problem and to define the position the committee took on the other various implied questions dealt with (moral, theological, sociological, and psychological) and particularly on the question of the relationship between private morality and the law.[6] The report, written by Sir John Wolfenden, is a masterly example of form and style, argument and counter-argument, detailed opinion considered, accepted, or rejected. One can find not only the decisions reached, but the reasons and arguments for and against them clearly spelled out, and, in all, a most helpful procedure which one might hope would find ready acceptance by our future, unlike our past, commissioners. The report was signed by the committee on August 12, 1957, and presented to parliament in September of that year.

Three months later on December 4, 1957, Lord Pakenham rose in the House of Lords to call attention to the report.[7] It is impossible to give anything like a detailed account of this fascinating, often brilliant

4 *Ibid.*, Appendix IV, pp. 152–55. All of the oral evidence was by invitation.
5 With an impeccable sense of timing, the Cambridge Department published its study in the same year as the Wolfenden Report, 1957.
6 Report of the Committee on Homosexual Offences and Prostitution, para. 62, p. 24.
7 206 Parl. Deb., H.L. (5th ser.) 733 (1957). Further references to this source will be made by column number only in the text.

debate, and I am conscious of the disservice I do those who took part by presenting a brief sketch. Lord Pakenham praised the report as a "social document of first importance" and proceeded to review in detail the position taken towards the report by the three leading church councils in the country (733). Lord Moynihan, like Lord Pakenham before him, supported the suggested amendments, but before doing so eloquently stated the position of the considerable number in the country who took a conservative attitude to the report, "[those] who would prefer to leave things as they are, even though they are most unsatisfactory, rather than make a change, the result of which might be difficult to envisage." He was followed by the Lord Archbishop of Canterbury, who, surprisingly, expressed the view that in his judgment the threat to general public moral standards was less from homosexual acts done in private than the damage done to public morality and domestic health by fornication and adultery (754). He agreed with the main recommendation of the report but favoured the retention of the offence of buggery. Lord Brabazon of Tara strongly condemned the manner in which the Labouchere Amendment (which established the offence of gross indecency) had been passed, and although he was doubtful that the government would accept the main recommendation of the report, he called for the early acceptance of some of the lesser recommendations (762). The Lord Bishop of St. Albans pointed out that the report followed almost exactly the proposals recommended by the Church of England's Moral Welfare Council, of which he was the chairman, and he too gave it his support (766).

The moment which the whole House had been waiting for arrived when the Lord Chancellor (Viscount Kilmuir) rose to speak (769). He expressed the government's position that the general sense of the community was not with the recommendation of the committee and the problem required further study and consideration, and he held out no prospect for early legislation on the subject. He outlined specific areas of difficulty, in particular the removal of sanctions, which might be seen as tantamount to approval, the definitions to be given terms such as "consent" and "private," and the problems which would arise in the Armed Forces. In retrospect, his most telling remark was his last sentence in which he seems to have revealed the strategy of the government. "I am sure that in the sphere of the education of the community this report will be a great landmark."

The Earl of Winterton, who had indicated before the committee was appointed that he would be guided by its decision, found himself unmoved by the report and could not accept its recommendations. (His reasons, in print, seem somewhat forced: Wolfenden had not made a good defence of his case over the wireless; Mrs. Lovibonds, a committee member, made an unjustified attack on the nursing profession and shook his confidence in the committee; a doctor friend of his told him the evidence received was weighted in favour of psychiatric opinion; and the minority report submitted by Mr. Adair, a member of the committee, seemed more tenable.) He reiterated the oft-proclaimed theory that homosexuality was one of the causes of the downfall of many ancient civilizations (787).[8] The Lord Bishop of Rochester (795) spoke of the "horror of these offences," the dangers of contagion, and the need to be guided by the Scriptures rather than academic discussion which was in his opinion divorced from reality. He urged that homosexuals should be "kept on a leash." The Earl of Huntington (803) reviewed the statistics showing the prevalence of this behaviour in countries which had less restrictive laws. Lord Denning took the position that the law must either condemn or condone and that in cases such as this it must condemn even though convictions were rare (810). In his view the law should condemn this evil for the evil that it is, but judges should be discreet in their punishment of it. Lord Jessel (811) emphasized the need for parliament to lead public opinion, but the Lord Bishop of Carlisle followed the lead given by Lord Denning and expressed a fear concerning the effect a change would have on the attitude and opinion of people at large. He stressed the view not previously raised that the law exists more to defend society than to punish evildoers (813).

Lord Lawson sounded a more dire warning that to follow the recommendations made would be to "strike at something that is finest in the life of the people of this nation (i.e., the abhorrence in which homosexuality is held), with consequences from which the nation would probably never recover" (820). Lord Mathers (821) stressed the help which spiritual guidance could give those afflicted, and Lord Darwen (823) urged the hope which medical help could offer. Lord Strabolgi reviewed the essential positions taken by speakers on both sides of the question. The Minister of State, Scottish Office (Lord Strathclyde) assured the House that the government would consider the arguments raised in debate with care. Lord Pakenham, who had initiated the debate, closed on a prophetic note, "There will be opportunities of discussing these great questions again and again until they have been much further advanced" (831).

A year was allowed to pass before the Wolfenden Report was taken

8 For a refutation of this argument see Lord Annan's remarks: 274 Parl. Deb., H.L. (5th ser.) 622 (1966).

up for debate in the House of Commons.[9] The government's position was presented by the Secretary of State for the Home Department and Lord Privy Seal, Mr. R. A. Butler, who gave two main reasons for not implementing the recommendations of the report. First, the government was concerned that a change in the law would be interpreted by the community at large as encouraging and legalizing the practice, and second, on the basis of opinions expressed to that point, the government did not consider itself justified in proposing legislation. He stressed the theme that education and time were needed to bring people to understand that the removal of the offence from law was not to condone the practice. He urged members to express their own opinions in the debate to assist in the formation of public opinion, and to educate opinion towards the type of reform which may be accepted.

It is not necessary to review the opposing points of view raised in the House, which on the whole followed the tenor of the debate in the House of Lords, but it is important to point out that the members of the House were very well informed, which was by no means a happy accident. In the period following the publication of the report, the matter had become one of widespread public interest. One speaker pointed out that there had hardly been a week since the publication of the report when its author had not been appearing either in the press or at public functions or on the BBC (454). Another cited the extensive support given to the recommendation by the press, specifically referring to the *Sunday Times*, the *Observer*, the *Times*, and the *Manchester Guardian* (390). A copy of Peter Wildeblood's book, *Against the Law*, had been sent to every member of parliament, and parts of it were introduced into the debate (418). Many of the churches had taken public positions on the issue, and these were reviewed, with one speaker stressing those in favour (389), and another those opposed (461).

Before leaving this debate, we should note one other matter which seems of particular importance. Two of the members of the committee, Sir Hugh Linstead and Mr. William T. Wells, were also members of parliament. Both were present when the matter was debated in the House, and both helped to correct errors and misconceptions about the report and to impart some information directly to the House. For example, Sir Hugh Linstead told the House of the substantial cross section of the judiciary – including magistrates, chairmen of quarter

9 596 Parl. Deb., H.C. (5th ser.) 365 (1958). Norman St. John–Stevas is in error when he says in *Life, Death and the Law* (London, 1961), at p. 210, that the recommendations in the report were not considered by the House of Commons until three years later.

sessions, recorders, and High Court judges – who had given evidence, and of the widespread divergence among them as to how seriously these offences should be taken (412). This tactic of having members of parliament serve on the committee, so that they can later participate actively in the debate, is a procedure which has much to recommend it.[10]

The issues the report dealt with continued to evoke comment, not the least of which was the Hart-Devlin controversy, which took up the old jurisprudential question of the relationship between law and morals. Much more important than the subject matter itself, important though that be, was the fact that a member of the bench and a jurisprudent from the academic world became involved in a public debate over a current social issue.

On June 29, 1960, Mr. Kenneth Robinson, a Labour member, moved a motion calling on the government to implement the relevant sections of the report, but the motion was defeated by a vote of 213 to 99.

Five years later, on May 12, 1965, the fires were once again kindled in the House of Lords, when the Earl of Arran made a motion calling attention to the recommendations of the Wolfenden Committee, and moved for Papers.[11] Twenty-two members spoke on the motion, the overwhelming majority of whom (17 of the 22) expressed themselves in favour of the recommendations. The motion was withdrawn without a vote being taken, largely because the procedure used and the terms of the motion itself would not give a meaningful reflection of the opinion of the House. The Earl of Arran served notice that he would introduce a Private Member's Bill.

The following day, on May 13, he did just that, moving the first reading of a bill to amend the law of England and Wales relating to homosexual acts in private (268). On May 24, the House of Lords moved into debate on second reading of the bill (631),[12] which provided simply that: "Notwithstanding any statutory or common law provision,

10 The Marquess of Lothian, also on the Committee, was a Member of the House of Lords.
11 266 Parl. Deb., H.L. (5th ser.) 71 (1965). The Earl of Arran had employed a little used procedural measure for re-introducing debate on this topic. There was a great deal of doubt and controversy over the use of this procedure and whether or not there should be a division on a motion of this kind. The Earl, finding his intention thwarted by procedural difficulties, helplessly announced to the House, "I do not want Papers."
12 The Earl of Arran was aware that a Private Member's bill was pending debate in the House of Commons two days later, and having sounded the favourable reaction in the House of Lords on the 13th, was anxious that they give the lead in the reform.

a homosexual act in private shall not be an offence provided that the parties consent thereto and have attained the age of 21 years."

The Earl of Arran was well aware that the bill in this straightforward form could not pass as it was into the law, and he willingly invited amendments to it. It was an effective tactical move calculated so that the House did not become embroiled in detail and also to give the House the impression that they were collectively to draft the bill. "Would they not themselves like to draft the Amendments that would put the matter right?" (634) He particularly invited the Lords Spiritual to make amendments to insure that the bill would be strengthened by their active participation in its provisions.

Particular attention should be paid to the position taken by the government as expressed by the Joint Parliamentary Under-Secretary of State, Home Office, Lord Stonham. "I have to say that it is entirely for your Lordships to decide the issue, and we want you to decide it" (638). Here again, as the bill had potentially serious political implications, the government wisely withdrew from overtly taking a position. Lord Stonham agreed with the view of the Wolfenden Committee that if a line was to be drawn it should be drawn between private offences and offences committed either in public or against minors. There was no compromise, he suggested (obviously referring to the suggestion made by the Lord Primate in the previous debate that buggery in private be continued as an offence) which would not make nonsense of the moral and logical issues involved, as well as making the enforcement of the law impossible. He offered statistics for consideration suggesting that if the figure of 500,000 which represented the best minimum estimate of the number of adult homosexual males in the country were accepted, even allowing that a large number remained continent, "the remainder may well constitute the largest class of criminals (except motoring offenders) in the country" (641). It would have to be accepted also, he said, that medical science could not materially change that condition.

He reported that the conviction rate was but a fraction of one per cent of the offences committed, a situation which he found manifestly unsatisfactory. A vote away from the proposed amendment would be tantamount to a vote that the law as it stood should be enforced, which would mean that more policemen should spend their time prying into the lives of individual citizens, for there was no other way of catching those who committed the acts in private. He expressed the opinion that police time might better be spent pursuing those homosexuals who interfered with boys. This is a remarkable statement, for it expresses, from the police view, a preferred policy for the deployment of its limited resources. He strongly emphasized that neither society nor the police were united or wholehearted about enforcing the present all-embracing criminal law. He believed that if the scope of the law was restricted to that area of vice involving young boys, and relentlessly attacked, it might contribute to the strengthening of morality in general (642).

Lord Kilmuir, one of the major speakers opposed to the bill, stressed the need for the use of the criminal law to preserve minimum standards of decency in the community and asked the House to consider whether this was the right moment to extend the "permissive world" at a time when crime was increasing and personal standards were low (659). Lord Goddard, also opposed to the bill, reviewed the history of the offence of buggery, and regarded the proposal to remove the offence from the law when the act was committed in private as "a most undesirable revolution in criminal law" (666).

One of the strongest speeches made contained the following remarks: "My Lords, it is the opinion of many of us on this Bench that the law as it stands is one of the most misguided, the most vicious and the most evil in its consequences of any law upon our Statute Book" (694). The speaker was the Lord Bishop of Southwark, and he pointed out that this was the view of all three Houses of the Church (of England) Assembly, and included the opinion held by the bishops, the priests, and the laity.

Thirteen speakers were in favour of the bill and eight opposed it. On division, the House voted 94 in favour and 49 opposed (712).

Two days later, on May 26, 1965, Mr. Leo Abse in the House of Commons moved for leave to bring in a bill to amend the law relating to homosexuality.[13] Permission was refused on division, the House voting 178 to 159.

On June 21 the House of Lords began consideration of the bill in committee.[14] In spirited, sometimes angry debate, amendments were put forward. A motion to exclude the offence of buggery from the exemption was defeated 86 to 42 (316). Amendments which would have changed the age levels up to 25, down to 18, or up to 80 years (the latter put forward by Viscount Montgomery of Alamein) were withdrawn (332, 349, 346). An amendment which would have made it an offence to obtain "consent" by gifts of money was also defeated 37 to 18 (383). An amendment did succeed (41 to 26) which provided that "Commission of such acts when more than two are present shall not be deemed to be in private," aimed at so-called "buggers' clubs."

The House met again on June 28 (677), and a motion with respect

13 713 Parl. Deb., H.C. (5th ser.) 611 (1965).
14 267 Parl. Deb., H.L. (5th ser.) 287 (1965).

to homosexual brothels was withdrawn (685); another with respect to homosexual prostitution was also withdrawn (691). Further amendments affecting procedure, allowing persons charged with soliciting for immoral purposes to be tried by indictment, and allowing persons charged with gross indecency to be tried summarily if they so wished, were agreed to without division (695). An amendment seeking to make it an offence for third parties to procure, even though the act itself was not an offence, was withdrawn (702). The question of defining what was a "private place" was set over to the report stage of the bill (709).

On July 16 the House considered the amendments received.[15] The amendment excluding cases "where more than two persons are present" was expanded to "in the presence of persons other than the parties to the act," which of course has a very different meaning (and a much wider one) but was nevertheless accepted, defeating, I think, the purpose of the original clause (432). An amendment was introduced which had the effect of excluding the operation of the bill from the Armed Forces, and it was accepted without objection (436). A further series of amendments touching on mental incapacity to give consent (437), revised punishments for homosexual acts (438), procuring others to commit homosexual acts (440), living on earnings of male prostitution (440), time limit of prosecution (443), restrictions on prosecution (443), choice of mode of trial for certain offences (443), and a change in the citation and interpretive section (445) were agreed to with little or no debate.

The third reading of the bill was moved in the House of Lords on October 25, 1965,[16] after three months had elapsed and served to "arouse the public conscience once again" (680). The earlier debates had taken some twenty-seven hours and included some eighty-two speeches, and now the aim of the proponents of the bill was to come to a final decision and press the government for action in the House of Commons. Of the eighteen speeches made at the third reading, fifteen were in favour and three opposed. Lord Stonham could offer little hope for early passage of the bill in the House of Commons, and none for the support of the government, but he noted that if the public opinion poll published that morning was accepted, then it could no longer be argued that the public was against the measure (726). It will be recalled

15 268 Parl. Deb., H.L. (5th ser.) 403 (1965).
16 269 Parl. Deb., H.L. (5th ser.) 677 (1965). One amendment was made and carried at this stage, changing the word "persons" to "any person" in clause 1(a) of the bill, so that if the act was committed in the presence of one person other than the "parties to the act" it would be an offence. See Lord Arran's comments, at 679.

that this was the major reason given by Viscount Kilmuir, then Lord Chancellor, when the matter was first raised in the House of Lords in 1957. The vote was taken and the bill carried, 96 to 31. But the session ended without the matter being taken up in the House of Commons, and the bill, as the expression goes, "died."

In the following session of parliament on February 11, 1966, Mr. Humphrey Berkeley in the House of Commons moved second reading of his Private Member's Bill, which was word for word and comma for comma the bill which had been passed in the earlier session by the House of Lords.[17] It was met with considerably more opposition than in the House of Lords, but the motion for second reading was carried on division, 164 to 107. The time appeared ripe for further passage of the bill, but a general election intervened, and once again the bill passed into limbo.

The bill was once more resurrected following the election, and on May 10, 1966, the Earl of Arran moved second reading. There was little said that had not been said in earlier debates, and the second reading was carried by a vote of 70 to 29.[18] The House took up debate again on May 23, 1966 (1170). Amendments proposed followed much the same lines as in the earlier debate in the same place, with the same results, and the bill was reported without amendments. On third reading, which followed on June 16, 1966,[19] the controversial clause which had previously read, "in the presence of any person other than the parties to the act" was amended to read "when more than two persons take part or are present," thus meeting all objections which had been raised on the grounds that the bill was an open license for "buggers' clubs" (148). Provision was made for dealing with offenders who had been charged but whose trials had not been held prior to passage of the bill (152). Although the bill was almost identical to that debated earlier, the mood of the House had changed, and instead of the three-to-one majority recorded before, the bill was carried by a vote of 78 to 60 (176).

Mr. Leo Abse (member for Pontypool) obtained leave on July 5, 1966,[20] by a vote of 244 to 100, to introduce a bill in the House of Commons, but the matter was not brought forward for debate on second reading until December 19 of that year.[21] The controversy was once again revived; the references to the community's reaction increased, and the bill was sent to a standing committee for detailed study without a

17 724 Parl. Deb., H.C. (5th ser.) 782 (1966).
18 274 Parl. Deb., H.L. (5th ser.) 605 (1966).
19 275 Parl. Deb., H.L. (5th ser.) 146 (1966).
20 731 Parl. Deb., H.C. (5th ser.) 259 (1966).
21 738 Parl. Deb., H.C. (5th ser.) 1068–1148 (1966).

vote being taken. Six months later, on June 23, 1967,[22] the bill was again taken up, the amendments of the standing committee considered, and the debate adjourned once more. Second and third reading of the bill were completed on July 3, 1967, and the bill passed on an over- whelming vote of 99 ayes and 14 noes.[23] Ten days later, on July 13,[24] the House of Lords, without amendment, gave second reading to the bill which carried on division: "Contents, 111; Not-Contents, 48." On third reading a week later on July 21, 1967,[25] thirteen years after the debate which led to the appointment of the Wolfenden Committee, the bill was passed, without controversy and without a recorded vote.

Many more comments could have been made on specific arguments raised in debate, but I have been more concerned here with attempting to contrast the process of consideration with the rather lamentable pro- cedure followed in the last revision of the Canadian Code. I do not suggest, as I have already explained, that this is a procedure which can be followed where large areas of the Code are concerned. But there are a few areas where it has direct application; for example, there are homo- sexual offences, abortion, the sale of contraceptives, and other legal- moral issues which have for some time been left untouched in the criminal law. It also has wider application than this, for the principles which the process follows can be adapted to other areas of the sub- stantive law.

Just as in any other research, the initial step is the crucial one. The areas to be considered must be clearly demarcated, the problem to be answered must be spelled out. In this instance, the debate was concerned with a limited number of offences which were to be examined in depth. The questions were, What is the substantive law on the subject? How is it administered? How do the courts deal with it? The three aspects of the one problem were clearly set out and the relationship between them acknowledged without question at the outset. It was, in short, a directive to consider basic information on the problem, that is, the law and its operation.

The next phase, as in any research, was the task of gathering informa- tion. This meant to the appointed committee the marshalling and tapping of resources to obtain the information it required on what the law provided, the views and opinions about the law and the problems emanating from it, empirical and statistical data about its operation, and

22 748 Parl. Deb., H.C. (5th ser.) 2115–2200 (1967).
23 749 Parl. Deb., H.C. (5th ser.) 1403–1524 (1967).
24 284 Parl. Deb., H.L. (5th ser.) 1283–1322 (1967).
25 285 Parl. Deb., H.L. (5th ser.) 522–526 (1967).

views and opinions on possible changes. This research was carried out using a large cross section of the community: laymen and specialists, policemen and psychiatrists, judges and ministers, government departments and voluntary groups. Contrast this to the last revision of the Canadian Code, where the record shows that the only persons consulted by the commissioners were by and large their former colleagues who formed the Criminal Law Section of the Uniformity Commission. That body at the time represented nothing more than a thin slice of senior administrative government officials. It is to be noted also that this stage of the operation in England, sensibly enough, was conducted by the committee itself, *before* it made its report. In the latest Canadian revision, the community's views were received by parliamentary committee *after* the commission's report.

Time was needed and taken for purposes of allowing publicity on the subject and recommendations of the report. The publicity was widespread in many media, and time was given for public opinion to form and express itself not only through the newspapers and television but through the social institutions such as the churches and professional organizations. (At the time of the last Canadian revision, the work of the commission and its report – all that there was of it – raised little public attention considering the scope and importance of the task involved.[26]) A full year was wisely allowed to elapse before the matter was even debated in the House of Commons. Following this, time again was taken for public opinion to catch up to the advanced views of the report before it was proceeded with as legislation.

There are lessons here for everyone concerned in this area: the government might learn from the whole strategy that was used; in particular it might learn the necessity of fashioning simple and workable terms of reference, the merit of appointing members of the House and the Senate to committees, the tactics of using the Senate where political accountability is not an issue to serve as a forum for controversial social problems. Legislators might recognize not only their responsibility to call for law reform but also the role they can play earlier in the process; future commissioners or committee men may be sensitized to seek widespread involvement from many levels in the community in their work; and researchers in and out of law schools and other centres may become alert to their role in preparing the legal and empirical studies which are essential for committee consideration.

---

26 The reader will, I hope, forgive a personal recollection. During the last revision of the Code in Canada, the writer was at law school, and apart from a mention that the Code was being revised, nothing more was heard about it.

Central to all of this should be the awareness that the making of criminal laws can be a form of education of the community through a thorough, open review of the community's social problems. What is achieved through this process is more important than the specific points at issue. Although particular criminal laws are applied to particular persons in the community, the repeated application of them over a period of years results in an accumulation of "criminals" in our midst, the sheer number of which has economic and social effects on the community as a whole. It is not only the offender and his family who are affected by our criminal laws; we must communally become more aware of the nature and extent of the repercussions which affect all of us, individually and as a society. The realization of the importance of this social dimension, the concern about it, and the responsibility for the decisions which need to be made in light of it must be more widely shared.

After considering the approach taken in England with this problem, and comparing it with the effort that was made in Canada during the last revision, I am forced to conclude that in matters of criminal law reform we are still groping in the dark. One hears on occasion of the need for reform of the Code, but exactly what is meant by that term, or what is involved, or the process we should follow, is with few exceptions never spelled out. At this time, when effort is being made across a widening front of law reform in general, one can lead oneself to believe that there is also a rising wave of opinion in favour of criminal law reform, but the signs are erratic and barely discernible. There seems to be much more agreement about or uneasiness over our progress in the field of corrections.

What we have not yet grasped is that what we do or do not do in the area of criminal law reform has a direct and powerful impact on the field of corrections. When we approach the complex problems in this area, we seem to become fascinated by the wagging of the correctional tail, and we return to it again and again. We keep trying to brush and preen it while the beast which propels it lies aged and neglected. We do try to take the burrs out of its coat from time to time but we are not yet convinced that what we really need and should invest in is a new dog.

3

The Case Law as a Basis for
Criminal Law Reform

When a defence counsel is faced with a point of law arising from one of his cases, whether the problem is one of procedure, evidence, or substance, by habit bred of training he reaches for the case law. A crown attorney, magistrate, or judge reacts in the same way. It would not be surprising to find that those legally trained persons who from time to time are charged with the responsibility of revising or reforming the criminal law react in a similar fashion.

It goes almost without saying that the case law does not represent anything like a complete picture of the decisions reached by the courts. In fact, only a very few cases are ever reported. It is not surprising that few of the decisions made at the trial level are reported, since most do not involve disputed issues of law. Only a small percentage of cases are appealed and even of these not all are or can be or need be reported. A selection of appellate cases is made by the editors of various series of reports on the basis of what appears to them to be important. What remains at the end of this process is the case law, representing the only readily available, permanent record of decisions which is kept within the legal system.

There is no question that it is invaluable for the bench and the bar alike, whatever its limitations may be for other purposes. It is also a guide for the lawmaker, for the case law reveals many issues which call for legislative action. The legislation that results is better termed revision, taken in a narrow sense; undoubtedly it is necessary and will always be so.

The concern here is directed towards a different level of the problem, that of criminal law reform, in an attempt to show how the case law considered alone does not provide an adequate and a sufficient source of information to serve as *the* basis of criminal law reform. There is other cogent information and evidence which must be taken into consideration, and where appropriate I have tried to bring some of this information forward to demonstrate its usefulness, not only for the purpose of reassessing our present provisions but also to assist in the task of reformulating the offences with which we are concerned.

Buggery and Bestiality

147. Every one who commits buggery or bestiality is guilty of an indictable offence and is liable to imprisonment for fourteen years.

Buggery

The crime consists of sexual intercourse, or carnal knowledge, (a) by man with man per anum, or (b) man with woman per anum.[1] Sexual intercourse and carnal knowledge has the same meaning as in rape, except that the act must be committed *in ano*, and the offence is complete on penetration even if there is no emission [R v. *Reekspear* 168 Eng. Rep. 1296 (Cr. Cas. Res., 1832)]. It is also clear that penetration of the mouth does not constitute the crime [R v. *Jacobs*, 168 Eng. Rep. 830 (Cr. Cas. Res., 1817)]. The offence has not been defined in any of the Canadian cases.

In R v. *Hartlen* [(1898), 2 C.C.C. 12 (N.S. App. D.)] an 11-year-old boy was convicted of an "unnatural act" with a 7-year-old boy. The facts show the act was fully consummated and that there was considerable penetration and force. On appeal, by a unanimous decision of five judges, the conviction was quashed on the basis that "the accused under 14 years of age is by the common law of England assumed to be *physically* incompetent to commit the crime with which he is charged." It has also been said that where an offence has been committed on a boy under 14, it is not an offence in the boy but only in the agent [R v. *Wiseman*, 92 Eng. Rep. 774 (K.B., 1718)]. Where, however, an adult induced a boy of 12 to have carnal knowledge of his person, it was not open to the accused, who was the pathic in the offence, to argue that the youth was *physically* incapable of committing the act [R v. *Allen*, 169 Eng. Rep. 282 (Cent. Crim. Ct., 1848)]. Section 139 of the Code provides that persons under 14 shall be deemed not to commit the offence of rape, attempted rape, carnal knowledge of a girl under 14 and between 14

1 L. Radzinowicz, ed., *English Studies in Criminal Science*, vol. IX, *Sexual Offences* (London, 1957), p. 345; and *Report of the Committee on Homosexual Offences and Prostitution*, H.M.S.O., (London, 1957), notes to paragraph 77.

and 16, and incest, but no such legislative provision is made respecting buggery. It is obvious from the facts in both the *Hartlen* and *Allen* cases that a boy under 14 can perform the act and there is little reason why the legal myth of "physical incapability" should be maintained when it is obvious that it was used as a policy decision to spare prosecution of young boys. The remedy is an amendment to include the offence of buggery under the provision of section 139.

On the question of the evidence of accomplices and the need for corroboration, the position taken by the courts is that a trial judge who hears a case without a jury may convict on the uncorroborated evidence of an accomplice, having due regard to the rule of the danger of so doing, if he entertains no reasonable doubt as to the guilt of the accused. In two cases decided by the Appellate Division of the Supreme Court of Alberta, the court ordered new trials where the only evidence available was that of accomplices (ages not given) and the trial judge had been of the opinion that he had no right in law to make a conviction on the evidence of an accomplice without corroboration.

For while the rules in question are intended as a safeguard in favour of a person charged with crime, to avoid the risk of conviction of an innocent person, it must also be kept in mind that society is also entitled to be safeguarded against crime, and it would be unfortunate if it could be thought that crimes of this character, which can only be committed by the participation of two persons and are committed almost always in secret, could be so committed with impunity and without fear of punishment, which appears to be the most effective way to prevent their repetition, simply because there could be no conviction on the evidence of one of them without any further possibility of it being corroborated.

> [*R* v. *Ragna* and *R* v. *Dick* (1942), 78 C.C.C. 342 (Alta. App. D.)]

As to who are accomplices, Lord Alverstone, in *R* v. *Tate* [(1908), 21 Cox C.C. 693 (Ct. Crim. App.)] said that a "boy over 16 years of age who consents to acts of this kind is an accomplice." In *R* v. *Hughes* [(1949), 33 Cr. App. R. 59)] the court would not convict on the uncorroborated testimony of a 19-year-old mentally deficient boy who admitted to the act and was regarded as an accomplice. In *R* v. *Tatam* [(1921), 15 Cr. App. R. 132], where the accused had committed the offence with three boys under 14, Mr. Justice Salter was of the opinion that the boys could not be accomplices because they were unable at law to commit the offence. Since they were not accomplices, corroboration was not necessary; however, the court did find that there was corroboration in respect to some gifts of money. In *R* v. *Cratchley* [(1913), 9 Cr. App. R. 233] the court held that a 10-year-old boy who had acted as a look-out in a case involving an assault with intent to commit buggery on a 13-year-old was not an accomplice. To establish that a person is an accomplice, "it must be proven that he had guilty knowledge," which is a question for the jury to decide. In any event, the court was of the opinion that "In such cases it is generally desirable, apart from any rule of law, and whether the witnesses are accomplices or not, that a warning should be given to the jury as to acting on the evidence of boys of this age (12 and under 10) who are concerned with this offence." The offence is not one which is included in section 131 as requiring corroborative evidence; however, the courts apply the rule requiring corroboration of the evidence of an accomplice.[2] In the *Tate* case, Lord Alverstone quotes with approval Taylor on *Evidence* (10th ed., vol. I, p. 688): "But no positive rule of law exists on the subject, and the jury may, if they please, act upon the evidence of the accomplice, even in a capital case, without confirmation of his statement. Judges, however, in their discretion generally advise a jury not to convict a prisoner upon testimony of an accomplice." He also quotes Russel on *Crimes* (6th ed., vol. 3, p. 646): "But it may be observed that the practice in question [conviction on corroboration of an accomplice] has obtained so much sanction from legal authority that it deserves all the reverence of the law, and a deviation from it in any particular case would be justly considered of questionable propriety."

In *R* v. *Hartley* [(1940), 31 Cox C.C. 456 (Ct. Crim. App.)] the accused was convicted of an "unnatural offence" with a boy aged 10. The boy's evidence with respect to that offence was uncorroborated, but he also testified to an earlier offence against him by the accused man. Two independent witnesses, young boys, testified that on that earlier occasion they waited outside an office where the door was locked and curtains drawn while the accused and the boy were inside. The trial judge directed the jury that they were entitled to treat that evidence as corroboration of the boy's evidence with regard to the offence charged. The Court of Appeal agreed with the direction and cited *R* v. *Baskerville* [(1916), 25 Cox C.C. 524 (Ct. Crim. App.)] in which Lord Reading C.J. said (at pp. 529, 530), "Confirmation does not mean that

---

2 *R* v. *Tate* (1908), 21 Cox C.C. 693 (Ct. Crim. App.); *R* v. *Brown* (1928), 49 C.C.C. 334 (N.S. App. D.); *R* v. *Cutt* (1936), 67 C.C.C. 240 (Ont. C.A.). See also *R* v. *McBean* (1953), 107 C.C.C. 28 (B.C.S.C.), where it was held that the rule as to the danger of convicting a person on uncorroborated evidence should be applied not only to charges laid under the Criminal Code but also to all judicial enquiries involving sexual offences. In this case the charge had been laid under the Juvenile Delinquent's Act but the nature of the charged behaviour was not specified.

there should be independent evidence of that which the accomplice relates. . . . what is required is some additional evidence rendering it probable that the story of the accomplice is true and it is reasonably safe to act upon it."

With respect to the offence of attempted buggery, there are two cases which show that a conviction for this offence may lie when there is not enough evidence to prove the full offence of buggery. In *R* v. *Tom Ging* [(1924), 57 N.S.R. 196 (N.S.C.A.)] the accused was originally charged with buggery and convicted of the attempt and the issue on appeal was whether the acts disclosed were sufficient to go to the jury on the charge of attempt or whether they constituted only preparation for the commission of the offence. The court of appeal decided it was the former, but regrettably no facts were given so that it is not known on what basis its decision was reached. In *R* v. *Cutt* [(1936), 67 C.C.C. 240 (Ont. C.A.)] the magistrate, after deciding there was not sufficient corroboration to convict on a charge of buggery, considered the facts *de novo* in relation to the charge of attempted buggery, and convicted. The court of appeal upheld the conviction but again the facts on which it relied are not given.

In *R* v. *Yee Jam Hong* [(1928), 50 C.C.C. 117 (Sask. App. D.)] the issue was whether the accused could be tried and convicted on the offence of "counselling A and B to commit the offence of buggery" when he had been committed for trial on attempt to commit buggery. The conviction was upheld on the grounds that the prosecuting officer was empowered by chapter 38, section 21 (3), to prefer "any other charge founded on the facts or evidence disclosed in the disposition."

In another Canadian case, *R* v. *Elliott* [(1928), 49 C.C.C. 302 (Ont. C.A.)], a conviction on a charge of attempted buggery was quashed on the grounds that the complaint made by the boy (age not given) was not made until one month after the event in question and was not admissible. "A complaint therefore is admissible only where it is made immediately after the offence or at the first convenient or reasonable opportunity thereafter." On the question of whether or not the rule with respect to the admissibility of complaints which applies in cases involving females can also be used in cases involving males, the court of appeal in England in the case of *R* v. *Camelleri* [(1922), 16 Cr. App. R. 163] held that it did. In that case, the charges were sodomy and indecent assault and the boys involved were 15 and 12 respectively. In coming to its decision the court cited with approval the decision of four judges of the New Zealand court of appeal in *R* v. *McNamara* [(1917), 36 N.Z.R. 382 (N.Z.C.A.)] and held that the principles laid

down in *R* v. *Lillyman* [(1896), 18 Cox C.C. 346 (Cr. Cas. Res.)]
and *R* v. *Osborne* [[1905] 1 K.B. 551 (Cr. Cas. Res.)] also applied to
cases of indecent assault on male persons.[3]

In all of these cases involving attempted buggery there is only one,
R v. *Delip Singh* [(1918), 26 B.C.R. 390 (B.C.C.A.)] which provides
a careful review of the facts of the case. A police trap was laid after a
15-year-old boy became suspicious of the accused's purpose in inviting
him so often to ride with him. The boy met the accused, who proposed
the commission of the offence and gave him fifteen cents. The two went
to a stable where they removed their coats, the accused man laid a
blanket on the floor, unbottoned his trousers and told the boy what to
do. He then grabbed the boy and was going to lay him on the blanket
when the police intervened. The issue in the appeal was whether the
evidence disclosed an attempt to commit, or merely preparation for the
commission of, the offence. The court unanimously held that it was an
attempt, Macdonald C.J.A. stating: "It would hardly be possible to
imagine a clearer case, a case where the act was more approximate to
the crime which was about to be committed than this evidence shows."
The case is exceptional and avoids many of the evidentiary problems
which arise on the question of accomplices and corroboration, because
of the fact that the police were present, saw the events, and could give
direct third party testimony.

There is but one case which pays much attention to the question of
sentencing, *R* v. *Belt* [(1944), 84 C.C.C. 403 (B.C.C.A.)], where the
appellant, who had "a long and continued record of unnatural offences
involving many small boys and youths," appealed a life sentence imposed after he had pleaded guilty on a charge of buggery with a boy
(age unspecified). The accused had told a psychiatrist that he was
willing to undergo a surgical operation (the nature of which was unspecified, but presumably it referred to castration) so that his unnatural
propensities might thereby be cured. The appeal was rejected with Sloan
C.J.B.C., at p. 403, saying:

The suggestion is one which we cannot take into account in reaching our
decision upon the question of the reduction of sentence. It must be borne in
mind that the proposal to submit to the said operation emanated from the
appellant himself. Should we now in turn express our willingness to reduce
the sentence in the light of the proposed physical change in the appellant we
would be placed in the position of attempting to strike a bargain with him
in that regard. We consider such a position highly improper and one in which
the Court must in consequence refuse to be placed. There are other authori-

---

3 Also followed in *R* v. *Coulthread* (1933), 24 Cr. App. R. 44, a case of indecent
assault by a scoutmaster on a 13-year-old boy.

ties who may, if the occasion arises, review the sentence on that basis with propriety, but we cannot do so.

From all the circumstances of the case we feel that, drastic as the sentence is, the only way to protect society from the continued criminal activity of this man is to remove him from the scene until such time as the Minister of Justice is satisfied he is no longer a menace to the community.

Although all of the cases cited above refer to male persons in relationship with other males, it is also possible, where the offence is committed on a female person with her consent, to hold the female liable as the patient [R v. *Wiseman*, 92 Eng. Rep. 774 (K.B., 1718)]. The crime may be committed by a husband against his wife [R v. *Jellyman*, 173 Eng. Rep. 637 (Gloucester Assizes, 1838)], in which case the wife is a competent witness against the husband [R v. *Blanchard* [1952] 1 All E.R. 114 (Leeds Assizes); also, R v. *Leary* (unreported), Leeds Assizes, Birkett J., March 1942], in one of the exceptions to the well-established general principle at common law that one is not a competent witness against one's spouse, a wife is considered a competent witness against her husband in cases of personal injury to her. (In the *Blanchard* case, the defendant was found not guilty and discharged; the case is reported on the sole question of the competence of the wife to give evidence.)

Bestiality

The term "bestiality" was employed in the case law well before that term was incorporated in the legislation. There are two parallel cases, R v. *Bourne* [(1952), 36 Cr. App. R. 125] in England and R v. *Wishart* [(1954), 110 C.C.C. 129 (B.C.C.A.)] in Canada, which involve instances in which a husband forced his wife to have carnal connection with a dog. In neither case were the exact circumstances or the nature of the force used reported. In the *Bourne* case, the accused had been charged and convicted as an aider and abettor and the case was argued on the basis that had the wife also been charged she would have been entitled to an acquittal on the grounds of duress. The Lord Chief Justice Goddard was of the opinion that if she raised the plea of duress, not as showing that no offence had been committed but as showing that she had no *mens rea* because her will was overborne by threats of violence, such a plea would mean that she admits she committed the crime but prays to be excused from punishment, and in the circumstances of the case the law would allow a verdict of Not Guilty to be entered. This view has been seriously criticized on many grounds: that where a defence of duress has been successfully raised, the verdict of

Not Guilty is not a discretionary but a mandatory one; that the defence of duress affects liability and is not merely an excuse from punishment; that it is contrary to the position taken in other cases (for example where the defence has been "infancy" and "mistake") to hold in the face of a successful defence on the grounds of duress and a verdict of Not Guilty that the offence charged has still, in fact, been committed; that applying the principles used in other cases, an acquittal of the wife on the grounds of duress would mean that no offence had been committed and consequently no offence for aiding and abetting could properly stand.[4] The criticisms made of the judgment in the *Bourne* case were not to suggest that the accused should escape liability, for he could quite properly be convicted of inciting, on which charge he was, in fact, also convicted. The Canadian case of *R* v. *Wishart* avoided the controversy raised in *Bourne* by charging the accused with the full offence of buggery "by causing his wife to have connection with a dog." In *R* v. *Bensette* [[1958] O.W.N. 223 (Ont. C.A.)] it was held by reference to section 21(1) of the code that a person who aids and abets is in the same position as the principal offender.[5] In the *Wishart* case, a new trial was ordered on the ground that although the Criminal Code does not require it, there must be independent evidence corroborating that of the complainant in this type of case. In that case the only evidence which might have been corroborative was brought forward not by an independent witness but by the complainant herself.

Cases involving bestiality are not at all common in the law reports; in fact the *Wishart* case above is the only reported Canadian decision; but the older English decisions show the offence to have been committed with a wide variety of domestic animals. It is general in these cases that the male is the agent and the animal or other living creature is the patient.[6] It has been said that the offence cannot be committed when the parts of a fowl are so small that they will not admit those of the offender and are torn away in the attempt.[7] In the unreported case of

4 For full discussion of the problems raised by the statements of Lord Goddard, C.J., see J. Ll. J. Edwards, "Duress and Aiding and Abetting," 69 L.Q.R. 226. See also, criticism by Glanville Williams, "Secondary Parties to Non-existent Crime," 16 M.L.R., 384. For a contrary opinion in support of the position taken by Lord Goddard, see a reply by Rupert Cross, 69 L.Q.R. 354.

5 See also *R* v. *Kravenia* (1955), 112 C.C.C. 81 (S.C.C.), where Estery J. said at p. 82, "While at common law aiding and abetting was a separate and distinct offence, under the Criminal Code, by virtue of section 69, one who aids and abets is a party to the principal offence." Section 69 is now covered by section 21.

6 L. Radzinowicz, ed., *Sexual Offences*, p. 346, refers to an unnamed case, where the opposite was the case, i.e., the male was the patient and a dog the agent.

7 *Russell on Crime* (10th ed.), p. 357, citing *R* v. *Multreaty*, Hil.T 1812; MS. Bayley J.

R v. *Dodd*, it was held that the accused could not be convicted of an attempt to commit the offence with a duck where it would be impossible for him to be convicted of the whole offence because the parts of the fowl would not admit of penetration. In coming to this decision, the court relied on *R* v. *Collins* [(1864), 9 Cox C.C. 497 (Ct. Crim. App.)] where it was held that the accused, a pickpocket, could not be convicted of attempted theft if there was nothing in the pocket to steal. The question was reconsidered in *R* v. *Brown* [(1889), 16 Cox C.C. 715 (Cr. Cas. Res.)], where the act involved certain unspecified domestic fowls, and the decision in the *Dodd* case was rejected on the grounds that "an animal which could extrude a thing so large as an egg could receive the male organ of the prisoner." The accused's conviction for attempt was affirmed, as was the sentence of twelve months.[8]

The foregoing review of the case law in relation to the offences of buggery and bestiality reveals various aspects of the problem which presents itself to the courts. Generally, these can be seen as the liability of boys under 14, the long-standing rule with respect to the danger of convicting on the uncorroborated evidence of an accomplice, the rules for determining who are regarded as accomplices, the use of the offence of attempt buggery where proof of the full offence is not forthcoming, the acceptance of the rules with respect to the admissibility of complaints in cases involving females and their application to cases involving males, and the admissibility of the evidence of a wife against her husband. In the cases on bestiality, the most recent problem involved the issue of the proper legal charge to be laid in cases where a husband coerces a wife to enter into sexual relationship with an animal, and the need for independent corroborative evidence, while a line of older cases coped with the problem of whether or not it was possible to commit the act with certain domestic fowls.

There are very few reported cases in this area, and the number of Canadian decisions is too small to be of much guidance. Nevertheless, the cases taken as a whole do reveal certain basic attitudes of the courts. On the one hand, the courts have allowed the defence based on physical incapacity to be established in cases involving boys under the age of 14. Although the rationale for the defence is patently a myth, there is good reason for it, and more than anything else it reveals the compassionate

---

8 In *R* v. *Lockhurst* (1853), 6 Cox C.C. 243 (Ct. Crim. App.) the sentence of *death* was imposed for buggery with a mare. The conviction was reversed on appeal on the grounds that the confession made by the accused was inadmissible, for it had been made under a threat of the police being called.

attitude of the courts for the protection of the young from convictions of this sort. (It is unfortunate that the legislators have not reacted in a similar way by providing a bar to actions against boys under 14, as they have in analogous circumstances. Although the Code specifically excludes boys under 14 from committing such offences as rape, sexual intercourse, and incest, the same legislative provision does not cover buggery. The common law defence based on physical incapacity in these cases is possible through the operation of section 7(2) which leaves open to an accused the possibility of setting up any common law defence which was open to him prior to the passing of the act.)

The courts also appear to lean over backwards to ensure that no one is easily convicted of this offence. The legislation does not require corroborative evidence to be given in these cases (s. 131(1)), nor is the offence covered by the special provisions of section 134 which require a judge to instruct a jury that it is not safe to find the accused guilty in the absence of corroboration. Nevertheless, the courts have gone a long way towards applying the same rules in these cases as well. Although appeal courts repeatedly emphasize that corroboration is not necessary, they are at great pains to point out to judges, whether in deciding cases alone without a jury or in instructing a jury, the danger of convicting on the uncorroborated evidence of an accomplice. Though a rule of practice, it is a strong one, and as Lord Alverstone was moved to re-emphasize, "a deviation from it in any particular case would be justly considered of questionable propriety." In this strong position taken by the courts, one can detect reverberations from some cautions sounded by Blackstone over two hundred years ago, calling for strict proof in these cases: "A crime, which ought to be strictly and impartially proved, . . . an offence so easily charged, and the negative so difficult to be proved, that the accusation should be clearly made out. . . ."[9]

On the other hand, one finds a movement in the opposite direction where the various courts of appeal clearly indicate that they wish to uphold convictions if they can. For example, in the *Tate* case, Lord Alverstone C.J. said that even though the trial judge did not warn the jury of the danger of convicting on the uncorroborated testimony of an accomplice, the appeal court nevertheless would have upheld the conviction if it could have found any corroborative evidence even though it was convinced in that case that in a particular instance the accomplice had not told the truth. Where corroboration was not available, the trial

9 William Blackstone, *Commentaries on the Laws of England*, vol. IV, *Of Public Wrongs* (Oxford, 1769), 215.

courts in *R* v. *Tom Ging* and *R* v. *Cutt* substituted convictions for attempted buggery, and both convictions were upheld by the court of appeal. In the *Tatam* case, the court of appeal held that three boys under 14 were not accomplices because they were unable at law to commit the offence, thus obviating the necessity for corroboration on that ground, even though they were consenting parties to the act and had guilty knowledge of it. In the *Bourne* case, Lord Goddard was moved to overturn some long-standing principles of criminal law to enable the court to uphold a conviction of aiding and abetting.

This attitude of the courts, particularly evident where young children or women have been involved, is most understandable, for the facts presented to the court are greatly distressing and evoke a strong reaction in them. On occasion this reaction breaks through to the surface in the reports. For example, in the *Bourne* case Lord Goddard commented: "The circumstances were such that nobody could approach this case without feeling the utmost repulsion." And again, "That such a man should be at large is almost intolerable and dreadful." In the face of such powerful emotions as expressed here, one need not be surprised to find that even a most disciplined intellect can be bent to absurdities to achieve a desired end.

It is not at all unlikely that it is the very nature of the subject matter which accounts for a large measure of the failure of the courts to provide even the basic factual data from which the case arises. This may also explain why so little attention has been paid to these offences over the centuries. But the very fact that the subject is one which most people find nauseating, and to which emotional reaction runs high, signals the necessity for the introduction of as much rationality and dispassionate study as can be brought to bear on the problem.

But how can a greater degree of rationality be introduced when so little information on the problem is systematically gathered and analysed? The courts deal of necessity with individual instances and strive in endeavouring to solve the particular problem before them to establish or clarify or apply principles which will be useful in determining how future cases should be dealt with. But the kind of information which is necessary can never be extracted from the case law. How large is the problem? Who are the offenders? Who are the victims? And, fundamentally, how can we begin to understand and evaluate our rules of law unless we can see them in their social context?

In terms of the number of convictions for this offence annually, the problem is really very small. For example, in the Cambridge Study, out of 1,985 cases considered, only 1.4 per cent involved buggery and .2 per cent involved bestiality, which together account for 31 cases.[10] In comparison, in a study made at the Forensic Clinic of the Toronto Psychiatric Hospital, out of a total of 597 cases considered only 11 cases of buggery (1.8%) were reported, none of which involved bestiality.[11] When it is considered that sex offences, taken together, represent approximately 5 per cent of all indictable offences, the size of the problem, relatively, is minute.

Regrettably, the *Sexual Offenders* study conducted by the Institute for Sex Research founded by Alfred C. Kinsey, which is the most elaborate study of its kind, does not treat these offences as separate problems.[12] Of the 1,356 sex offenders considered, only 5, or .4 per cent, had been "legally punished for sexual behaviour with animals" and the group was too small to be included in the extensive analysis (420).[13] The "homosexual offenders" were classified into three groups: Against Adults (over age 16), Against Minors (ages 12 to 15 inclusive), and Against Children (under age 12) (38).[14] Anal intercourse was involved in 6 per cent of the cases involving adults and played a part in 3.5 per cent more (353); it was involved in 11–12 per cent of cases involving minors (320), and in 4 per cent of cases where children were concerned (293). It occurred in only one heterosexual case in which a minor female was involved (785). While it was concomitant behaviour in three other cases, it did not form the basis of the final charge. Although the use of force and the threat of force were reported in the three homosexual categories, in only one case was the force used in relation to anal intercourse and that offence took place in a jail cell (491).[15]

10 L. Radzinowicz, ed., *Sexual Offences*, p. 528. The total number of cases considered (1,985) would represent about one-third of all sexual cases in the whole of England and Wales if 1947 is taken as the base year, or about one-fifth if comparison is made to 1954. See Preface, p. xiii.
11 J. W. Mohr and A. K. Gigeroff, "A Study of Male Sexual Offenders Charged in Court Over a Twelve Month Period: Report on the Development of the Study with an Inventory of the Data Collected and a Basic Analysis" (Forensic Clinic, Toronto Psychiatric Hospital, May 1964, mimeographed), Appendix 1, p. 13.
12 Paul H. Gebhard, John H. Gagnon, Wardell B. Pomeroy, and Corneila V. Christenson, *Sex Offenders: An Analysis of Types* (New York, 1965). Further references to this source will be given in the text by page number only.
13 A brief summary of these five cases is provided; see *ibid.*, p. 420. The animals involved in the five cases include dogs, cows, chickens, and a mare. The ages of the males at the time of offence were 16, 16, "in youth," 26, and about 38.
14 The numbers of cases in each group were 199, 136, and 96 respectively.
15 The study goes into a rather elaborate examination of prepubertal sexual activity of the various offenders and compares these with a control (non-offender) group and a prison (non-sexual) group. For example, in regard to their early homosexual contact with other children, 20–25 per cent of homosexual offenders

Studies such as these begin to throw a glimmer of light on the extent of the various kinds of these offences being prosecuted in the community. For example, we begin to see in this study that the offences of buggery occurred more frequently with boys between 12 and 15 than with boys under 12, that the incidence of such offences involving females was very much less, that use of force was rarely a factor, and that the incidence of bestiality as an offence appears to be low, an observation corroborated by reports from other jurisdictions.

But if one restricts one's inquiry to *offences* and *offenders* alone, one obtains only a very limited concept of the problem. It is necessary at least to be aware of the extent of the behaviour as it occurs in the community before one can decide how to cope with it. For example, the Kinsey study on *Sexual Behavior in the Human Male* reports that somewhere between 40 and 50 per cent of all rural males in the population have animal sexual contact in their pre-adolescent, adolescent, or post-adolescent histories.[16] About 17 per cent of these contacts occur after the onset of adolescence. Not all of these contacts involve intercourse, but vaginal coitus is the most frequent technique used.[17] Kinsey holds the view that the reported instances are low because of the reticence of the subjects to talk of these experiences. The social significance of these reports is startling.

In the light of these social facts, we are forced to the realization that our existing legislation and case law are a limited resource for study and can at best serve as a springboard for our inquiries.

---

had such contact and in about 37 per cent of these there was anal-genital contact. Although this was considerably higher than the control group, the incidence for the control group was higher than that found among heterosexual offenders *v.* minors and children. See Gebhard *et al.*, Tables 23 and 25 at pp. 463 and 465, and discussion at p. 453.

16 Alfred C. Kinsey, Wardell B. Pomeroy, and Clyde E. Martin, *Sexual Behavior in the Human Male* (Philadelphia and London, 1948), p. 671. The study suggests that the incidence is as high as 65 per cent and higher in some places.

17 *Ibid.*, p. 675.

Gross Indecency

149. Every one who commits an act of gross indecency with another person is guilty of an indictable offence and is liable to imprisonment for five years.

In the case of *R* v. *K. and H.* [(1957), 118 C.C.C. 317 (Alta.)], the Supreme Court of Alberta gave consideration to this offence in relation to the actions of two men in a car who had been observed by a policeman. The headnote refers to the acts as buggery, and Judge Egbert refers to "buggery, and acts akin thereto," but the specific act is not made mention of in the case. The decision in part reads as follows:

An act not inherently indecent may become so by reason of the circumstances surrounding its performance, but an act which is inherently grossly indecent, according to the concepts and morals of our times, cannot be decent by reason of the circumstances surrounding its performance. I cannot believe that buggery, or acts akin thereto, can ever be anything but grossly indecent, whatever the circumstances under which they are performed.

In such a case the indecency depends upon the nature of the act, and not upon the circumstances under which it is performed.

If the act in question was buggery or attempted buggery, the question arises as to why those offences were not charged. Can it be that the act of buggery can also be charged as gross indecency? In *R* v. *Landlow* [(1922), 38 C.C.C. 54 (N.S. Mag. Ct.)] the magistrate refused to convict the accused who had been charged with gross indecency and attempted gross indecency with a boy of twelve. "The offence of gross indecency and attempt thereof in my opinion deals with a *set of circumstances of facts entirely different* from those dealt with by section 202 [buggery] which deals with an offence at common law. The evidence establishes an offence under section 202, either that or nothing." (Italics are mine.) Similarly, in the case of *R* v. *Barron* [(1914), 10 Cr. App. R. 81)] it was stated that neither the act of penetration nor the intention to penetrate is an essential element in the offence of gross indecency and that the offence was neither the same nor substantially the same as buggery. On a charge of buggery alone it was not open to the jury to convict on gross indecency, and an acquittal on buggery was no bar to a subsequent indictment for gross indecency.[1]

The difficulty which the courts have had in attempting to clarify what gross indecency means can be seen in the passage quoted from the decision in *R* v. *K and H*, which raises more questions than it answers. Can an act "not inherently indecent" become merely "indecent" because of the circumstances? If so, what elements in the circumstances would it be necessary to find before it became "gross indecency"? Is there a distinction to be made between acts which are "inherently indecent"

---

1 In *R* v. *Tatam* (1921), 15 Cr. App. R. 132, four convictions for gross indecency were quashed on the grounds that "the acts of gross indecency are the same as the acts of sodomy for which penal servitude has been passed."

and those which are "inherently grossly indecent," and on what grounds is this to be done? Would it make any difference to a finding of gross indecency? The case refers to "buggery and acts akin thereto" as "grossly indecent": what acts are "akin" to buggery? In cases where such an act occurs it is said that the "indecency depends on the nature of the act, and not upon the circumstances under which it is performed."[2] But does the "grossness" also depend on the "nature of the act" or can it be found in the circumstances? For what it may be worth, the decision can be given some structure in this way: that acts which are "inherently indecent," "inherently grossly indecent," and "grossly indecent" are included under the offence of gross indecency without any reference to the surrounding circumstances. It was set out earlier in the judgment that the standard to be applied in assessing these cases was that of "any right-thinking member of the public" after consideration is given to the act, the circumstances, and the customs and morals of our times. (Presumably the circumstances would not need to be taken into account if a consideration of the act and the customs and morals of our times was sufficient to determine that the act was grossly indecent.) In applying this standard to the facts before him the judge concluded that it was "inconceivable that in these times the act performed by the accused could be considered otherwise than grossly indecent." As the reported decisions in this area are so few it can be imagined that lawyers and judges in many an unreported case in the future will attempt to arrive at a meaning to be given to this decision, and arguments will be raised as to whether it should or should not be applied to the set of facts they have before them. All of this endeavour will not of course remedy the initial deficiency: we do not know what the act was which gave rise to this decision in the first place.

In the English case of *R* v. *Hornby and Peale* [[1946] 2 All E.R. 487 (Ct. Crim. App.)] two men who were found in a lavatory, both in positions suggesting that an act of buggery was about to occur, were acquitted on a charge of attempted buggery but found guilty of gross indecency. Each of them denied being a consenting party in the act and blamed the other. Lynskey J., in allowing the appeals, stated, "The jury

---

2 Compare this statement with the judge's address to the jury in the *A.B.* case quoted in full in Appendix I, at p. 202. The act was one of fellatio between two men in a car, in a parking lot, late at night. In that case the judge said, "Of course, gross indecency, probably if such an act was committed in private, committed in the privacy of their own homes you might not consider it grossly indecent, whereas you might consider the act grossly indecent if committed in public or where it was committed in this case but I say that is a question for you as jurymen representing the citizens of this country to decide. . . ."

ought to have been directed that the act of gross indecency must be by one prisoner with the other and that, to be guilty of the charge, they must be acting in concert." Although it was not necessary to decide the point in that case, in reply to argument he was of the opinion that "if two people are acting in concert to act in an indecent manner, there may be gross indecency by one person with the other even though there is no actual physical contact taking place."

In the case of *R* v. *Hunt and Badsey* [(1950), 34 Cr. App. R. 135], also decided in England, two grown men were found in a shed by a policeman, in positions which "can only be described as constituting filthy exhibitions by the one to the other." It was decided that it was not necessary to show that there had been any physical contact between them. "If two men put themselves in such a position that it can be said there is a grossly indecent exhibition going on, they can be found guilty of committing an act of gross indecency."

In *R* v. *Horn* [(1923), 40 C.C.C. 117 (Alta. App. D.)] a 4-year-old boy was taken for a ride by one of his father's employees, and the accused was found guilty of both indecent assault and gross indecency. The boy's evidence was not admissible because of his tender years, but there was some evidence that the accused had emitted into the boy's mouth. (The court was of the opinion that the facts in this case were precisely the same as those in *R* v. *Jacobs* [168 Eng. Rep. 830 (Cr. Cas. Res., 1817)], where it was held that where a man had forced open the mouth of a 7-year-old boy and emitted, it was not buggery.) Consideration was given to the statement made by the accused to the police, the details of which are not given, to determine whether it disclosed evidence coming within this section, but Stuart J. stated (at p. 125): "In view of the history and purpose of the section, I do not think we ought to extend the meaning of the section. Such acts are sufficiently covered by section 293." It was held that it was not essential to a charge of gross indecency that the other male person (in the instant case, aged 4) must also be legally capable of committing the offence.

There are two Canadian cases reported which refer to acts which occur between heterosexual partners. In *R* v. *B. and S.* [(1957), 119 C.C.C. 296 (Alta.)] the Crown attempted to prove that a man and woman who were in a car late on a midsummer night had engaged in cunnilingus and fellatio, and contended that the mere contact of the male mouth with the female genital organs would constitute the offence of gross indecency. Edgar J., who tried the case, stated,

If during the course of preliminary love-making leading to intercourse the male implanted a kiss on the outward genital organs of the female, I would not consider that an act of gross indecency; there must be something more proven, but once that something more is proven then I am of the opinion that regardless of the time or place or circumstances under which the act takes place, it is gross indecency.

In the instant case there was only a brief glimpse of twenty seconds by the police, the other evidence being circumstantial and consistent with the accused's denial, and the accused was discharged.

In the second case, *R* v. *J.* [(1957), 118 C.C.C. 30 (Alta. App. D.)], the accused was charged with this offence, the facts disclosing that his fiancee, a girl of 16, had engaged in fellatio on him. The court heard expert evidence from doctors to the effect that this behaviour was natural and normal.[3] The magistrate stated, "Being unable to find any other case to help me interpret this section, either in Canada or as far as I can trace any other Commonwealth country, I do not feel justified on the evidence of the doctors and on the circumstances of the case in finding the accused guilty of the offence of which he is charged." The Court of Appeal dismissed the crown's appeal on the narrow ground that it involved something more than a question of law and therefore not open to the crown under section 584 (1)(a) of the Code. The court, without having to decide so, was "doubtful that the evidence supports the charge as limited by the particulars."

In the case of *White* v. *R* [(1965) 44 C.R. 75 (N.B. App. D.)] a police recorder and his wife had testified that while driving down a well-lit main street they had observed "an act of indecency" being committed by two sailors on the sidewalk in front of a restaurant. The specific indecent acts are not stated in the case (McNair C.J.N.B.: "I feel no purpose can be served by any attempt to summarize the evidence"; Ritchie J.A.: "I do not deem it necessary to discuss their evidence in detail"; West J.A.: "The facts are fully stated by my brother Ritchie"). The conviction was quashed, Ritchie J. stating, "I cannot picture the act of gross indecency described by the Garners being committed on the sidewalk of a busy street in full view of anyone passing by. That just does not happen."

The remaining reported cases deal mainly with problems of evidence and are noted here briefly. A new trial was ordered in *R* v. *Boynton* [(1934), 63 C.C.C. 95 (Ont. C.A.)] on the grounds that evidence showing that the accused had committed previous offences of the same kind was not properly admitted. The case involved no question of identity, nor was the act (facts not stated) one which might be innocent

3 Egbert J., in *R* v. *K. and H.* cited above, in distinguishing *R* v. *J.*, stated that he would be skeptical of such expert evidence.

or guilty according to the intent of the accused: consequently, evidence of similar offences was not relevant to any issue before the court.

A conviction was confirmed in *R* v. *Williams* [(1914), 23 C.C.C. 339 (Ont. C.A.)], where it was held that corroboration of the evidence of accomplices was not essential to the validity of the conviction. (The offence was committed against two brothers; the ages, acts, and place of commission were not given.)

The respondent in *R* v. *O'Leary* [(1943), 80 C.C.C. 327 (B.C.C.A.)] was acquitted, even though the trial judge in his reasons had said he "could" not convict without corroboration, thereby misdirecting himself. The trial judge had made it clear in his report that he found it unsafe to convict without corroboration because the youth, the accomplice, "was admittedly a pervert." Even if he had misdirected himself, he must have reached the same conclusions as he did and there was no substantial wrong or miscarriage of justice.

In *R* v. *McDonald* [(1948), 91 C.C.C. 30 (Alta. App. D.)] the accused was acquitted when the only evidence before the court was the accused's own confession, which had been obtained without warning after a statement by the accomplice was read to him. The trial judge had said he would not have convicted on the basis of the accomplice's statement, and the accused's confession was not admissible.

In *R* v. *Laplante* [(1954) 18 C.R. 237 (Que. App. D.)] there are no facts given as to the acts, the parties, or the circumstances. The evidence was that of an accomplice corroborated partly by a third person, and was "more than sufficient to prove the offence."

In *R* v. *Hayward* [(1955) 22 C.R. 17 (Ont. C.A.)] the charge of "procure or attempt to procure the commission of an act of gross indecency" (under s. 206, R.S.C. 1927, c. 36) was not invalid for duplicity, because the procuring of which the accused was convicted also involved the attempt to procure. The facts showed the offence had taken place with two boys, ages not given, who spent the night with the appellant.

A new trial was ordered in *Sylvestre* v. *R* [(1964) 42 C.R. 355 (Que. App. D.)], where police had given evidence that the accused had committed five acts of gross indecency with different persons, but the accused was only charged with one offence and there was no way of knowing from the record on what evidence the trial judge had relied in coming to his verdict. Nothing appears in the report to show the ages of the accused or the accomplices, the acts, or the place.

In *R* v. *Jones* [(1895), 18 Cox C.C. 207 (Cr. Cas. Res.)] it was held that it was not necessary that both offenders should be before the court before there could be a conviction for this offence. In *R* v. *Pearce* [[1951] 1 All E.R. 493 (Cr. Crim. App.)] the court followed the *Jones* case.[4] "The offence is one which, if two persons are to be convicted of it, must be proved to have been committed with the consent of both of them. They must be proved to have been acting in concert together. There is nothing to support the proposition that where two persons are jointly indicted for such an offence, one cannot be convicted and the other acquitted." In this latter case, one of the accused gave evidence for the prosecution that he did not consent to the act.

In *Ponton* v. *R* [(1960), 127 C.C.C. 325 (Que. App. D.)] the accused appealed his twelve-year sentence, following convictions of one charge under section 138 (sexual intercourse with a girl under 14), two charges of indecent assault female, one charge under section 150 (obscene matter) and one charge under section 149 (gross indecency). There is nothing to indicate whether the offence of gross indecency also involved a female person as was the case under the first two charges. The court confirmed the sentence and was of the opinion that this was not the appropriate kind of case for a hearing under the Criminal Sexual Psychopath provision (s. 661). "It is sufficient to recall the appropriate and carefully selected environment in which he carried out his crimes and with what skill he succeeded, by means of special mechanism, in photographing simultaneously, in studied poses, both himself and his victims and associates."

In *R* v. *Marion* [(1956), 118 C.C.C. 388 (Ont. C.A.)] a case involving rape and indecent assault on a female, where the question was one of consent, Laidlaw J.A. stated, "undoubtedly the learned judge considered as we consider, that this crime was committed after use of much violence. It was a crime of gross indecency." Presumably, the learned judge did not use the expression with any precise legal meaning; but does this not merely emphasize the problem the expression creates? If he did mean the offence in the Code, the term has an even greater expanded meaning.

Although the offence of gross indecency has been on the statute books for 78 years the number of reported cases in the law reports is extremely small. In an article in the Criminal Law Quarterly, D. E. Saunders reports on twelve unreported cases between the years 1961–67 involving 24 male persons and in particular directs his attention to

---

4 In *R* v. *Edwards* (1924), 18 Cr. App. R. 140, where the accused persons were charged with "gross indecency with one another," the court held that, based on the particular way the case was put to the jury, it was impossible to uphold the conviction of the one side by side with the acquittal of the other.

the sentencing of homosexual offenders by the courts.[5] In one instance five persons were jointly charged; in eight other cases two parties were jointly charged; and in three cases only one person was charged. There were three cases in which a male person was dressed as a woman, a fact which was not known to the other male in two of the cases and in both of these cases the unsuspecting party was not charged.[6] Half of the persons involved committed the acts in public places (eight in public washrooms in Stanley Park and four others in parked cars). In one case it was argued that the offence occurred in private, but precisely where is not mentioned, and one of the cases involving a male dressed as a female occurred in a room, presumably not public. In the remaining cases the place where the act occurred is not reported. The range of sentences is extreme. One party, a senior civil servant, was fined $750.00 while nine others were fined between $100 and $250.00. Two sentences of three months were reduced to two years' probation by the British Columbia Court of Appeal. Six of the offenders received suspended sentences with probation, most frequently for a term of two years. Sentences of imprisonment included a sentence of one day (and a fine of $100.00), one month (plus a year on recognizance), three months, and three years concurrent on three [sic] counts of the same offence.

The latter sentence was handed down in the case of R v. Klippert by Magistrate Parker on August 24, 1965. (At this stage the case, like most magistrates' court decisions, was not reported, and had it not been for subsequent developments, it probably would have gone unnoticed.) On application under section 661, before Sisson J., the accused was declared a dangerous sexual offender under section 659(b) of the Code, which reads: " 'dangerous sexual offender' means a person who, by his conduct in any sexual matter, has shown a failure to control his sexual impulses, and who is likely to cause injury, pain or other evil to any person, through failure in the future to control his sexual impulses, or is likely to commit a further sexual offence. . . ." He was sentenced on March 9, 1966, to preventive detention for an indeterminate period, in lieu of the three-year sentence previously imposed. On October 26,

5 D. E. Saunders, "Sentencing of Homosexual Offenders," 10 Crim. L.Q. 25.
6 In one of these cases the male person who was dressed as a woman was paid ten dollars for an act of fellatio on the other male. If the essential ingredient of the offence is the "inherent indecency" of the act, as the case of R v. K. and H. proposes, then there is no strictly legal reason why the male impersonating a female was convicted and the other male was not charged. This of course is a matter of police discretion, and it may well have been that the police decided not to prosecute the "innocent" male in return for testimony against the impersonator at trial.

1966, the Court of Appeal for the Northwest Territories dismissed an appeal without written reason and a further appeal was launched in the Supreme Court of Canada. In a three-to-two decision handed down on November 7, 1967, the appeal was dismissed [*Klippert* v. *R* [1967] S.C.R. 822]. The point at issue in the case was the meaning to be given to the phrase "or is likely to commit a further sexual offence" in section 659(b) of the Code. The majority of the court was of the opinion that the phrase referred to any offence mentioned in section 661, which includes rape, sexual intercourse with a girl under 14 or between 14 and 16, indecent assault female, buggery or bestiality, indecent assault male, and gross indecency, or an attempt to commit any of these. In the majority view, since this list includes offences in which there is an element of violence as well as offences in which there is none, it is not necessary to show that a future offence would be a source of danger of injury to other persons. The minority disagreed and held that the phrase should be interpreted within the whole context of the dangerous sexual provisions and should be given the meaning "or is likely to commit a further sexual offence involving an element of danger to another person." It can be seen that the majority view places a much broader interpretation on the words of the statute and that it is no longer necessary to introduce any evidence as to actual injury, pain, or other evil to another person with respect to either the original offence charged or to a sexual offence likely to be committed in the future.

What is astonishing is that the phrase "or is likely to commit a further sexual offence" did not form part of the recommendations of the royal commission which gave detailed study to our earlier criminal sexual psychopath laws.[7] In reply to a question by Miss Judy LaMarsh as to the purpose of the addition to the definition as recommended by the commission, the Hon. E. D. Fulton, then Minister of Justice, said: "This idea was suggested by the uniformity commissioners as being a further test available to the court on the basis of which it could reach a conclusion as to whether or not a person should be adjudged a dangerous sexual offender. I think the hon. lady will agree that this creates a second and alternative test as a basis on which to form a judgment, and we felt it was a proper proposal."[8] However, in his opening address on second reading Mr. Fulton was more explicit: "We felt it was not essential to the determination of the matter to enter into an analysis of whether or

7 *Report of the Royal Commission on The Criminal Law Relating to Criminal Sexual Psychopaths*, Hon. J. C. McRuer, chairman (Ottawa, 1958), p. 128.
8 Debates, H.C., Canada, 1961, p. 6570.

not a person, in respect of whom an application has been made to have him declared a dangerous sex offender, may cause the damage in the future by physical coercion or by mere persuasion and temptation. It does not seem to make much difference what method is resorted to, but it is again the possibility of evil and damage which must be borne in mind here, as well as the elimination of the possibility of that evil or damage."[9] He said that it is in connection with this particular point that the further words were added. It was intended then that the words form a second or alternative test but in relation to the possibility of evil or damage. But is this not the old difficulty of defining these sex offences in terms of Offences against Morality or Offences against the Person? Did we not in our new code skirt that difficulty by grouping these together as Sexual Offences? Was the Supreme Court in the *Klippert* case not using a similar approach in passing over the difficult problem of examining what the moral harm or the physical harm of the past and likely future conduct might be and resting the decision solely on the phrase "further sexual offence"?

What was the conduct of the accused in the four charges of gross indecency on which the application was made to declare him a dangerous sexual offender? What were the acts; who were the parties involved? The mere words "gross indecency" do not tell us. Without knowing what the facts were it is impossible to decide whether that behaviour was or could be physically or morally harmful. Cartwright J. in his dissenting opinion pointed out that "No evidence was adduced as to *the nature of the acts* committed by the appellant in respect of either the four substantive charges to which he pleaded guilty before Magistrate Parker or the eighteen other charges upon which he had been convicted in 1960 [also for offences of gross indecency, and to which he had been sentenced to serve four years on each charge concurrently]." (Italics are mine.) He was convinced that from the evidence of the psychiatrists there was no danger of the appellant's using violence or coercion on anyone, nor was there a suggestion that he sought out youthful partners for his misconduct. In his closing remarks Cartwright J. indicated that if the interpretation of the lower courts was allowed to stand, it would mean that every man who "indulges in sexual misconduct of the sort forbidden by section 149" with another adult male person and is likely, if at liberty, to continue to do so should be incarcerated for life. He concluded: "However loathsome conduct of the sort mentioned may appear to all normal persons, I think it improbable that Parliament should have

9 *Ibid.*, p. 6538.

intended such a result. It may be that we cannot take judicial notice of the probable effect which such an interpretation would have on the numbers of those confined to penitentiaries; no one, I think, would quarrel with the suggestion that it would bring about serious over-crowding." With respect to homosexual offenders the royal commission which proposed the changes creating the dangerous sexual offender provisions had this to say (at p. 27): "We do not think that mere conviction for a homosexual act warrants an indeterminate sentence."

This case has received widespread publicity and most important because it undoubtedly played a part in prompting some of the proposed amendments to the Criminal Code.[10] It has been popularly assumed that the convicted man had been sentenced to an indeterminate term as a dangerous sexual offender because of homosexual acts with consenting adults in private. There is some doubt that the facts would support that assumption. There is indication in the psychiatric evidence considered by the court that some teen-agers, at times, were involved with the accused man. It would be highly unlikely, though not impossible, that all 18 of the previous convictions for gross indecency involved only homosexual acts with other adult males in private. Even granted that there was no physical violence or coercion present in any of the previous cases, the judgment to be made on the issue of "other evil" or moral harm might be very different depending on whether the other male parties involved were early adolescents, late adolescents, or adults. The simple knowledge that there was proof of convictions for gross in-decency did not and cannot yield that crucial information. Nor could it have provided that information to Mr. Justice Sisson, who heard the initial application, or to the Court of Appeal of the Northwest Terri-tories, or to the five justices of the Supreme Court of Canada. It is not without significance that none of them considered the real situations which were represented by the words "gross indecency," or at least they did not do so in written opinion.

Appendix I at the end of this volume is a complete copy of a trans-cript of evidence of the trial of A.B. before a county court judge sitting with a jury. It is given here not necessarily because it is a typical case, although the facts do not appear to be extraordinary, but because it demonstrates the difficulty which a judge, a jury, and a crown attorney face in a case of gross indecency. Attention is directed to the address

10 Clause 70 of Bill C-195 in the Second Session, Twenty-seventh Parliament (16 Elizabeth II, 1967) proposed that the phrase "or is likely to commit a further sexual offence" be deleted.

to the jury by the crown attorney on p. 196 and by the judge on p. 202.
Note the questions posed by the jury and the answers given by the court.

"[I]s there a definition in law as to what gross indecency is?"

"No."

"The law does not specifically define gross indecency. Secondly, are
there any precedents to this case and what role would a decision in this
case play as a precedent in other similar cases?"

"A certain act which is committed may under certain circumstances
be grossly indecent and in other circumstances it may not be grossly
indecent. That is for you to decide and adjudicate upon. You can
understand a certain act being performed under certain circumstances
where it might not be grossly indecent but the same act under other
circumstances might be grossly indecent."

"In your opinion are there precedents that would help us?"

"No."[11]

There are remarkably few reported cases involving gross indecency,
considering that this offence has been on the statute books for 78 years.
It is extremely difficult, if not impossible, on the basis of the case law
alone, to formulate any clear definition of what "gross indecency"
means, and indeed there is no case which gives a satisfactory definition.
Reviewing the situations in which the section has been successfully
prosecuted in Canada and the cases reported, one is confronted with a
rather bleak picture: two men were convicted for acts "akin to buggery"
and one adult male was convicted where the facts disclosed he had
emitted into the mouth of a 4-year-old boy. Although the section was
widened to include heterosexual acts (and female lesbian acts) in 1954,
the acquittals in both *R* v. *B. and S.* and *R* v. *J.* show the apparent
reluctance on the part of the courts to convict heterosexual partners
involved in non-coital behaviour. There are no reported cases of lesbian
behaviour either charged or convicted of this offence. The article by
D. E. Saunders (above, note 5) provides us with a slightly wider
glimpse of the operation of this section and shows primarily prosecu-
tions for homosexual acts in public places, particularly public lavatories.
He also shows the use of the section in particular instances where males
in the guise of females engage in homosexual acts, with an element of
prostitution present in at least one of the cases.

Even with this meagre information the spread of the different kinds
of events subsumed under the provisions in the Code begins to become
apparent. The difficulty the courts have experienced in constructing a

11 This case was appealed and the appeal dismissed without reasons given.

definition of gross indecency becomes more understandable. But the problem does not lie with the courts alone, for the legislators have failed to provide them with clear guidelines stating what specific behaviour is to be prohibited. The courts have been placed in the unfortunate and unfair position of having to fathom the intention of parliament when that intention has never been made clear. From all the evidence available it appears doubtful that the intention was ever clearly formulated in the minds of the legislators.

The acuteness of the problem of the absence of a clear statutory definition and the inability of the courts to fashion a working definition because of the wide application of the words used in the section is made painfully evident in the A.B. case presented in full in Appendix I. When the quandary of the judge, the crown attorney, and the jury is as deep as this case shows that it can be, there is an urgent need for reconsideration of the relevant statutory section.

The dangers inherent in this provision in the Code were already pointed out by experts more than a decade ago. R. E. Megarry, Lincoln's Inn, barrister at law, commented on the section as follows: "When a word as indefinite as 'gross' is coupled with a word as subjective and emotional as 'indecency' there can be little of that precision which is so desirable in criminal law. . . . The new Canadian Code has many substantial and welcome reforms to its credit, yet however much a broad sweep of the brush is to be admired, it may well be urged that unless section 149 is restrictively construed, its amplitude will, in harking back to Cromwellian England, be vice rather than virtue."[12] J. Sedgwick, Q.C., commenting on the expansion of the section to cover heterosexual as well as homosexual acts, says as follows: "I do not know what an act of gross indecency between a man and a woman is, but whatever it may be, it is now an offence. Nothing in the section requires that the act take place in public and thus what two lovers, or man and wife, may do in the privacy of their own apartment may turn out to be an offence. To some narrow minds all acts of sex are grossly indecent."[13]

The problem is, how do we collect the information which is necessary to enable us to fashion a more precise legal instrument? But first we must ask how the courts are using the present section. The courts referred to here are principally the magistrates' courts, where virtually all such cases are tried. We cannot rely on the case law alone because

12 R. E. Megarry, "Notes," 71 Law Quarterly Review, p. 463.
13 Joseph Sedgwick, "The New Criminal Code: Comments and Criticisms," 33 Can. Bar Rev. 62 at p. 70. See also Appendix II.

of what the reported cases *cannot* tell us. How many 4-year-olds, as in the *Horn* case, have there been, or more generally, how many children, are involved? How many adolescents? What are these "acts akin to buggery," or specifically what are the nature of the acts in the cases prosecuted? What proportion of the cases occur in washrooms and other public places? How many of the cases involve homosexual acts? How many involve heterosexual acts, and what are the relationships between the parties? How many involve lesbian acts? How many involve impersonation? How much prostitution is caught up by this law, and is it restricted to homosexual prostitution or does heterosexual prostitution also play a part, and how frequently?

Having endured the vagueness of this section for three-quarters of a century, having witnessed the obstacle the phrase "gross indecency" has put up to the development of the law in this area, should we not now invest something to unravel what we have been doing, to define what and whom we wish to prosecute?

Indecent Act

158. Every one who wilfully does an indecent act
    (a) in a public place in the presence of one or more persons, or
    (b) in any place, with intent thereby to insult or offend any person,
    is guilty of an offence punishable on summary conviction.
694. (1) Except where otherwise expressly provided by law, every one who is convicted of an offence punishable on summary conviction is liable to a fine of not more than five hundred dollars or to imprisonment for six months or to both.

The offence of indecent act is now generally regarded as covering those cases in which a male person indecently exposes his genitals – what in clinical terms would be called an act of exhibitionism. But in tracing the early cases on the common law misdemeanour of indecent exposure it was found that it in fact covered acts which would now fall into each of three categories used here: homosexuality, exhibitionism, and pedophilia. There is a question whether or not the earliest case which gave rise to many of the subsequent problems may not have been a case involving nudism among other things.

Sir Charles Sidley was indicted in 1663 for a misdemeanour in that he "monstre son nude corps" in a balcony in Covent Garden to the great multitude of people and there did certain things and spoke certain words the particulars of which the recorded case does not give.[1] Whether one sees this as a case of nudism or of exhibitionism depends to some extent on the meaning which is given to the Norman French quoted above. Literally, it means he "showed his nude body" but it may have meant "exposed his nude person," and although there appears to be no authority for it, "person" in this context is said to mean "genital organ."[2] I am more inclined to the view that the case was one of nudism on the grounds that the reported facts show that the act occurred in front of "a great multitude of people" and certainly from what is known of exhibitionism today it would be most atypical for an exhibitionist to expose in this way. The exhibitionistic act as we find it occurs either to adult women who are alone or to groups of two or three young girls or children. The reporter's use of the phrase "multitude of people" suggests that both men and women were present. Two elements which were present in this case, the public place and the presence of more than one person, gave rise to many of the disputed issues which were to recur later.[3]

There are two cases in which the facts disclose that homosexual acts formed the basis for the charge of indecent exposure. It will be remembered that at the time the following cases were decided (in 1809 and 1848 respectively), the offence of gross indecency had not been introduced into the legislation. In *R* v. *Bunyan and Morgan* [(1844), 1 Cox C.C. 74 (Cent. Crim. Ct.)] two men went into the parlour of a public house and locked the door but were seen engaged in homosexual acts (they exposed and touched each other) by a girl who, after observing them through a window which faced on to a corridor, called the police. The question arose whether this was a place where they were likely to

1 *R* v. *Sidley* (1663), 1 Sid. 168; 82 Eng. Rep. 1036 (K.B., 1663). The case is referred to in *R* v. *Read* [(1707), Fortescue 99; 92 Eng. Rep. 777 (K.B., 1707)], in which Powell J. comments that in the Sidley case the accused "pissed down upon the people's heads." In a short note on the punishment (which involved a combination of fine, one week's confinement in jail, and one year of binding over for good behaviour), it is reported that part of the offence involved "throwing down bottles (pist in) among the people in Convent [*sic*] Garden." See *R* v. *Sydlyes* (1663), 1 Keb. 620; 83 Eng. Rep. 1146 (K.B., 1663). The *Read* case reports the facts as "showing his naked body" while the latter notes describes the event as "shewing himself naked."
2 L. Radzinowicz, ed., *English Studies in Criminal Science*, vol. IX, *Sexual Offences* (London, 1957), p. 427.
3 For examples of the same offence used to cover acts in which no sexual motive is involved, such as undressing in preparation for a swim or nude bathing which can be seen by members of the public, see *R* v. *Crunden* (1809), 2 Camp 89; 170 Eng. Rep. 1091 (K.B., 1809); *R* v. *Reed* (1871), 12 Cox C.C. 1 (Sussex Assizes).

be observed by members of the public. It was held that it was not necessary to prove that the parties intended the public to see them and it was left to the jury as to whether this was a situation in which there was no reasonable probability of their being so discovered. The jury convicted. In *R* v. *Orchard and Thurtle* [(1848), 3 Cox C.C. 248 (Cent. Crim. Ct.)] the two accused men entered a urinal at Faringdon market where certain homosexual acts occurred which were observed by one other individual.[4] It was held that the urinal was not "an open and public place" for although open to the public for certain proper purposes, it was enclosed. The court also followed *R* v. *Watson* (discussed below) which decided that the exposure to one person was not sufficient to constitute the offence.

In *Reg.* v. *Wellard* [(1884), 15 Cox C.C. 559 (Cr. Cas. Res.)], a case of pedophilia in which the common law misdemeanour of indecent exposure was charged, the accused man invited seven or eight girls aged from 8 to 11 to go with him to a marsh, for which he would give them a half-penny. They followed him along a footpath, then on to the marsh some 170 paces from the path and out of sight of it. He laid down by a log, "exposed his person indecently," to all seven or eight girls, who were close to him, and invited them to touch "his person."[5] The issue in this case was whether or not this was a public place. Technically, all were trespassers with no legal right to be there, but on the other hand the place was not in any way enclosed and members of the public could go there freely and did so without complaint from anyone. It was decided that it was not necessary to prove that the public had a legal right to be there. Lord Coleridge C.J. went further when he said, "It is my opinion the offence is complete if it is committed *in any place* where an assembly of the public is collected." (Italics are mine.) Huddleston J., in agreeing with the Chief Justice, opened the door with more caution when he said (at p. 563), ". . . it is not clear that an act of indecency is not an offence if it is committed before a number of persons, even if the place in which it is committed is *a private place*." (Italics are mine.)

The other cases involve acts of exhibitionism. In 1847 the accused in *R* v. *Watson* [(1847), 2 Cox C.C. 376 (Q.B.)] exposed to Lydia Crickmore, aged 12, in a Paddington Churchyard, was convicted, and obtained a rule *nisi* against the conviction. The objection raised to the

4 For a more recent treatment of the same situation over 100 years later, cf. *R* v. *Mayling* [[1963] 2 W.L.R. 709 (Ct. Crim. App.)], where the charge was "committing an act outraging public decency," and the conviction was sustained on appeal.
5 The proximity of the exposure and the invitation to touch, indicating a desire for closer contact, is what marks this case as pedophilia rather than exhibitionism.

indictment was that although the act charged was "one of gross indecency," yet, because only one person was present, it was no offence in law.[6] Lord Denman C.J., in giving the opinion for the court, held, in making the rule *nisi* absolute, "The general rule is, that a nuisance must be public; that is, to the injury or offence of several. There is no precedent of such an indictment as the present, and we are not inclined to make one."[7]

In *R* v. *Webb* [(1848), 3 Cox C.C. 183 (Cr. Cas. Res.)] the accused exposed to a woman who was taking care of a public house, whereupon she ran and told her husband. The prisoner was found guilty by a jury and the case was heard by five judges as a Crown Case Reserved. Pollock C.B. held that the case was governed by *R* v. *Watson* (above), and as only one person was present when the act occurred, there was no offence and the accused was acquitted. (The four other judges concurred.)

In *R* v. *Holmes* [(1852), 6 Cox C.C. 216 (Ct. Crim. App.)] the accused exposed "for a long space of time, to wit for the space of half-an-hour" in a public omnibus in the presence of three or four females. The issue was whether a public bus for hire could be considered a "public place." Lord Campbell C.J. dismissed the appeal on the grounds that it was a public omnibus going along a public road, and as the exposure was to three or four females, there was no element wanting. He was moved to say, "This would not be a country to live in if such an abominable outrage could go unpunished."

In *R* v. *Thallman* [(1863), 9 Cox C.C. 388 (Ct. Crim. App.)] the accused exposed from the roof of a private home to windows opposite where two females, and later five other females, and a waiter and a policeman saw him. Thallman could not be seen from the street. Once again, the issue was whether or not this was a public place. Chief Justice Erle upheld the conviction on appeal, on the grounds that it was not necessary to show that the man exposed in a public highway. It was sufficient to show that it was in a place where a number of the Queen's subjects could and did see the exposure.

In *R* v. *Farrell* [(1862), 9 Cox C.C. 446 (Ct. Crim. App.)], decided a year earlier, Monahan C.J. quashed a conviction because the facts

6 Notice the use of the phrase "gross indecency" in relation to this offence. The following chapter reports on a case of exhibitionism wherein the present-day offence of "gross indecency" was charged and a conviction registered.

7 In passing, it is of interest to note that Coleridge J., in argument, passed this opinion: "But if this indictment is good – every exposure to a female in a public place would be indictable. There are numerous offences against morality which the law cannot reach." How reminiscent is this same argument in another context?

disclosed merely that the accused exposed from the side of a highway in such a way that he was capable of being seen by one person, and in fact was only seen by one person. In *obiter*, however, he went on to say that if there had been others in such a situation as they could have seen the prisoner, there would be a criminal offence.

It is surprising that in all of these cases involving exhibitionism, with the exception of the *Thallman* case, the charge was not laid under the Vagrancy Act which had been passed in 1824 before any of these cases arose.[8] The definition of public place was a wide one in the statute, and covered "any street, road, or public highway, or in view thereof, or in any place of public resort." (The *Thallman* case occurred from the roof of a private house and the accused could not be seen from the street.) Also, the exposure under the statute covered an exposure to "any female" with intent to insult. The only explanation which seems likely is that under the Vagrancy Act the offence was punishable summarily by a term of not more than three months or a fine of £25, whereas a conviction for a common law misdemeanour is triable at Quarter Sessions and punishable by imprisonment in the discretion of the court.

In turning to the Canadian cases, it is important to note that all of them have arisen out of the statutory offence of Indecent Act, established in 1892. It is appropriate at the outset to demonstrate how the more abstract phrase "indecent act," already criticized in the previous chapter, has resulted in the prosecution of several kinds of acts which are significantly different from cases of exhibitionism.

In 1900, in the case of *R* v. *Jourdan* [(1900), 8 C.C.C. 337 (Que. Recorder's Ct.)], the accused was convicted on a charge of indecent act on the basis of the public performance of a song (the subject of which was the bosoms of women in St. Nazaire, Outremont, and Montreal), during which he made gestures which, "while natural in order to indicate breasts, not less naturally [were] of a nature to scandalize." The gestures were held to be "contrary to propriety, good behaviour and modesty and moreover indecent." This unlikely application of this section resulted in a new section being added to the Code in 1903 covering indecent performances (now s. 152).

In *Berman* v. *Kocurka* [(1915), 25 C.C.C. 44 (Que. Recorder's Ct.)], a private prosecution, a woman was convicted under subsection (b), the court deciding she "permitted herself, for no cause originating with the informant or the other persons in his company, on the occasion in question, to grossly and vilely insult and offend the informant and others while they were in the customary discharge of an exemplary religious duty." The accused had been charged under both subsections

8 (1824), 5 Geo. 4, c. 83, s. 4.

(a) and (b). The court drew the following distinction between the two: "The essence of a charge laid under subsection (b) is the intentional and wilful insult or offence offered to any person or persons in particular, whilst, under subsection (a) it is the public character of the place where the indecent act is committed which constitutes that aspect of the contravention to the law." There is nothing in the report to indicate that the woman had exposed herself, which would be unusual though possible. But even more puzzling is the fact that there is no mention made of *any* act. The court seized on and stressed the notion of the intentional insult to a particular person or persons but whether this consisted of words or of gestures is not known. Suffice it to say that the event which took place does not fall into the phenomenon of exhibitionism.

In the case of *R* v. *Clifford* [(1916), 26 C.C.C. 5 (Ont. H.C.J.)] the facts disclosed that the accused woman ran a massage parlour and committed "an abominable offence against morals" with a male customer. The conviction for indecent act was quashed on appeal on the grounds that the essence of the offence was that it should be committed "in the presence of one or more persons" and this was not satisfied by holding that the man who participated in the offence was "a person" contemplated by the statutes. "It is enough that one person should be shown to be present, but it must be a person other than those engaged in the offence." The case is significant for it indicates that it is open on the wording of the section to use this offence to cover indecent acts committed between two people. (The offence of gross indecency was not open to the crown because at that time the section was limited to male persons.) The case does not discuss why the arresting officer was not considered "a person" within the meaning of the statute.

The accused, in the case of *R* v. *Hastings* [(1947), 90 C.C.C. 150 (N.B. App. D.)], had been convicted of indecent act for urinating at the back of his car on a public street, where his companion, a girl, could not see him, but where he was seen by a policeman in a patrol car. He was acquitted on appeal, on the grounds that urinating was not an offence under the Code or at common law, and also that on the facts there was no exposure to any person in the presence of the accused.[9]

There is a short note in the Quebec Queen's Bench series of reports

9 Once again, it is curious that the policeman was not considered "a person" within the meaning of the statute. Cf. *R* v. *Mayling* [1963] 2 W.L.R. 709 (Ct. Crim. App.), an English case wherein it is decided in another context that policemen are "persons" who are also capable of being insulted. Consider the *Hastings* case in light of Judge Egbert's remarks in attempting to define gross indecency in *R* v. *K. and H.* [(1957), 118 C.C.C. 317 (Alta.)]: "Urinating in itself is not indecent, but becomes indecent because of the time, place, or circumstances of its performance. . . ."

on the case of *R* v. *Blackburn* [[1952] Que. Q.B. 796m.] covering an appeal against sentence by an accused who had pleaded guilty to a charge of "indecent act *on the person of a girl* of nine years of age." (Italics are mine.) No other facts except those set out in the charge are provided, but the wording of it suggests that a pedophilic rather than an exhibitionistic act had occurred.

Some *obiter dicta* in the civil case of *Denning* v. *Denning* [(1922) 23 O.W.N. 302 (Ont. H.C.D.)] will serve as the closing example of how the legislation has been confusing. A 60-year-old man married a woman in her fifties and shortly thereafter the husband "exhibited marked aberration and perversion in sexual relations" in that he was a confirmed "foeminarum fellator," as a result of which the wife developed a nervous and neurasthenic condition and sued for alimony. In granting alimony the judge noted, "These practices, though vicious, are not necessarily criminal. Section 205 of the Criminal Code covers only the commission of such acts in public or when intending an insult."

In all five of the criminal cases cited above, there was a criminal conviction and in two of them the appeal court reversed the decision. These cases covered instances of indecent songs, insults at a religious ceremony, pedophilic acts, urinating in a public street, and sexual acts involving heterosexual partners. Mr. Davies' criticism of the section in the House of Commons in 1892, on the grounds that "a very curious construction" might be put on the words used, has been proven by the course of time to be a valid one.[10] I have been able to point to five cases, the only *reported* ones which I have been able to find, but I cannot help wondering what a splendid range the offence may have covered in the unknown, unreported cases which flow through our lower courts.

The offence has of course been applied to cases of exhibitionism, but not one of the cases provides a definition of indecent act nor do any discuss all of the elements of the offence. In *R* v. *Keir* [(1919), 34 C.C.C. 164 (N.S. App. D.)] the accused exposed in a private road leading to a garage, the gate between the street and the road being twenty-two feet wide and open at the time. He was seen by several young girls on the street or sidewalk less than fifty feet away. The issue in that case was whether the place in question was a place to which the public have or are permitted to have access within the definition provided by the statute at that time.[11] It was argued that the place was private, that the public did not have the right of access and consequently there was no offence. It was objected that on this view a man might expose on his

10 Debates, H.C., Canada, 1892, II, 2968.
11 R.S.C. 1906, c. 146, s. 205.

own property within a few feet of the street, within plain view of the public and not be convicted. The court, in reviewing the authorities, came to the conclusion that a place was public for the purpose of this offence if it was so situated that it could be seen by the public or any considerable number. The central ingredient contemplated was the publicity, which has reference to the persons who may witness the act rather than the locality. In the *Kocurka* decision cited above, the court had said merely that it was the *public character of the place where the indecent act is committed* which is the essential element.

In the *Clifford* case it was decided that a massage parlour was a "public place" on the grounds that it was a place "where all comers were admitted" and therefore constituted a place to which the public "were permitted to have access" as the definition provided. The court recommended that parliament amend the statute looking to the English phraseology in 14 and 15 Vict., c. 100, s. 29, where the interpretation is given as "any place to which the public have access as of right or invitation or permission of the owner," a suggestion accepted and expanded thirty-eight years later in the revision of 1954.

The term "indecent" has not been considered in a case of exposure, but was considered in *R* v. *McAuliffe* [(1904), 8 C.C.C. 21 (N.S. Co. Ct.)] on a charge of "indecent acrobatic variety or vaudeville performance," specifically in relation to a song by a female member of a ballet company, which was performed at the Academy of Music in Halifax. Judge Wallace of the County Court discussed the term as follows:

There is no fixed legal meaning to the word "indecent" but counsel for the prosecution has quoted several dictionary definitions of the general meaning of the word. In popular language, however, such a word was used or misused according to the taste or training or point of view of the individual or the custom of the community. It was not a word of unvarying precision in definition. . . . Where words have no fixed legal meaning the prosecution must show that what was done constituted the offence mentioned in the statute, and in this case they have failed to do so and I therefore do not consider it necessary to hear any evidence offered by the defence, but will grant the motion dismissing the case and discharging the defendant.

There is a series of early cases considering whether the failure to include the word "wilfully" in an information or warrant of commitment is or is not a curable defect.[12] In the case of *Ex parte O'Shaughnessy* [(1904) 8 C.C.C. 136 (Que. K.B.)] where the accused was convicted

12 *R* v. *Barre* (1905), 11 C.C.C. 1 (Man. App. D.); *R* v. *Tupper* (1906), 11 C.C.C. 199, (N.S.S.C.); *R* v. *Gerald* (1916), 26 C.C.C. 7 (Ont. C.A.). *R* v. *Smothers* (1924), 57 N.S.R. 179 (N.S.C.A.).

of "unlawfully" committing an indecent act in the presence of a 19-year-old girl, a writ of *habeas corpus* was maintained on the grounds that the words "unlawful" and "wilful" were not synonymous. The court was of the opinion that "wilful," in relation to the offence of indecent act, indicates that the act must be done "wantonly, which is to wander from moral rectitude, and to do an act licentiously and dissolutely, unrestrained by law and morality, intentionally and without excuse."

What constitutes a wilful act in a case of exhibitionism has been examined in more concrete fashion in a more recent case, *R* v. *Parsons* [[1963] 3 C.C.C. 92 (B.C.S.C.)]. The accused had been convicted on this charge, the facts disclosing that on three occasions he had been observed masturbating behind the window of his room, accompanied by certain bodily movements and the flashing on and off of an electric light. On appeal by stated case, Wooton J. held that there was evidence to be considered on the question of wilfulness, and sufficient, if so found, to sustain a verdict on the following grounds: (*a*) the exposure of the body and private parts was deliberate and therefore wilful, (*b*) the flashing on and off of the electric light was a possible effort to attract attention, (*c*) the movement of the body, (*d*) the repetition of the act. The question was also raised by the magistrate whether there was any evidence on which to make a finding that the accused did the indecent act *with intent to insult or offend any person*. It was decided that the performance of the acts suggested by the evidence, if seen by any person, would raise a presumption of intent to perform the indecent act wilfully; that is, if the acts were seen by anyone it was sufficient to raise a *prima facie* case. There was no need, in the court's view, to name the person or persons who may have been insulted or may have been intended by the accused to be insulted. It was sufficient if someone passed by and was simply a viewer whom the accused may or may not have known was there.

Evidence of similar acts on other occasions ought not to be admitted unless and until the defence of accident or mistake has been raised, or absence of intention to insult is definitely put forward, and it must be shown that the other occasions are sufficiently proximate to the alleged offence to show a systematic course of conduct.[13] In *R* v. *Kozodoy* [(1957), 117 C.C.C. 315 (Ont. C.A.)] the accused had exposed on two occasions within a few hours to the same four girls, aged 15. It was held that on the facts the "first occurrence cannot properly be severed in time or occurrence from the subsequent occasion." But it was also said that repeated acts of misconduct were plainly relevant to prove intent on the part of the accused to "insult or offend."

13 *Perkins* v. *Jeffery* (1915), 25 Cox C.C. 59 (K.B.).

There are two other reported decisions arising out of cases involving indecent acts which involve ancillary matters. In *R* v. *Roach* [(1914), 23 C.C.C. 28 (Ont. C.A.)] a conviction was set aside on several grounds, one of which was that the evidence had been whispered to the trial magistrate out of hearing of the accused. In *Benning* v. *A.-G. for Saskatchewan* [(1963) 40 C.R. 37 (Sask. Q.B.)] it was held on an application for prohibition that a magistrate, in clearing the court room in a case involving small children, under the Code provisions of section 428 was not in contravention of the Canadian Bill of Rights.

A review of the case law discloses the wide spectrum of behaviour which falls within the present provisions of the offence of indecent act under the Code, and which earlier fell within the ambit of the common law misdemeanour of indecent exposure. One is accustomed to hear the expression "dark figures" of crime, applied to the unknown offences in the community, and yet in another sense the same expression can be applied to the known crimes and convictions revealed in our criminal statistics. While we know that the number of offences under a certain section have been counted, we are equally aware that the vast majority are never reported, and their actual content is equally unknown. It was a surprise to discover that five of the fifteen reported Canadian decisions on indecent act which I was able to find did not involve acts of exhibitionism. This is not to suggest that this ratio has any meaning at all in relation to the total number of cases which are tried in our courts, the bulk of which are undoubtedly in relation to exhibitionism, but how many of the convictions involve acts other than exhibition and what kind of acts these are is a mystery.

The problems posed by the *Sidley* case – the element of public place and the element of the number of persons who must see the act – have been met partly by interpretation by the court and partly by statute. Although the present statute continues to define public place in terms of "access to" (as of right or invitation express or implied), following the *Wellard* and *Thallman* cases in England, the *Keir* case finally enunciated the idea that the important element in this offence is the *publicity*, defined in terms of the people who see the act and not in terms of the locality where it occurs. "Access to," then, by interpretation, includes not only physical but visual access. The statute now provides that the offence may be committed even in the presence of one person who is present and sees. This removes what had been the main obstacle to conviction, resulting from the decisions in the *Watson* and *Webb* cases.

But the problem raised by the term "indecent exposure," which admitted cases involving homosexuality and pedophilia, has really not been overcome by the statutory phrase "indecent act," as has been shown. It is agreed that with the development of the offence of indecent theatrical performance, and the offence of gross indecency which originally applied to males and then extended to apply to heterosexual acts as well, some of the objections which could have been levelled against this offence have been removed. However, the central criticism is still valid: the offence as at present constituted does not sufficiently distinguish between acts of exhibitionism and other acts of public indecency.

Stephen must have been aware of this similarity between the common law offence of public indecency, which he described as involving "any grossly indecent act," and the statutory offence under the Vagrancy Act of exposure of the person with intent to insult females. The latter provision was clearly in relation to exhibitionistic acts. Undoubtedly Stephen's qualification of the new term "indecent act" with the old established phrase "with intent to insult" in subsection (b) was done in the expectation that "does an indecent act" in this context would have virtually the same meaning as the earlier phrase "exposes his person." It can be argued that he introduced the phrase "in any place" to overcome the problems which had arisen when the offence occurred in other than public places. What he did not sufficiently appreciate was that the wording in part (a) of the offence "indecent act in any place to which the public have or are permitted to have access," was framed so broadly that it too could be used to cover acts of exhibitionism when perpetrated in public places, where most of them in fact do occur. Thus the legal distinction between acts of public indecency and exhibitionistic acts has in practice become blurred through the use of the common term "indecent act."

The American Model Penal Code has attempted to rediscover and redefine these two offences.[14] The comments made in discussing the tentative Draft no. 13, in relation to these offences, are to the effect that "open lewdness amounts to gross flouting of community standards in respect to sexuality or nudity in public," while indecent exposure is a "special case of genital exposure for sexual gratification" and is punishable more severely than ordinary open lewdness, "since the behaviour amounts to, or at least is often taken as, threatening sexual aggression." On these same grounds, indecent exposure is classified under "Sexual Offences" while open lewdness is classified under "Public Indecency."

The offence of indecent exposure in the *Model Penal Code, Proposed*

14 The American Law Institute, *Model Penal Code: Tentative Draft No. 13* (Philadelphia, April 1961), sections 213.4 and 251.1, at p. 82.

Official Draft (July, 1962), is contained in section 213.5 at page 149, as follows: "A person commits a misdemeanour if, for the purpose of arousing or gratifying sexual desire of himself or of any person other than his spouse, he exposes his genitals under circumstances in which he knows his conduct is likely to cause affront or alarm." The provision in the section "for the purpose of arousing or gratifying sexual desire" is questionable, for it attempts to include in the definition the motive for the act which does not as yet have scientific validity. It is known that some cases involve an exposure of the erect penis, masturbation, and an experience of sexual satisfaction, but there are other cases at the opposite end of the scale where there is only partial exposure of the flaccid penis and no conscious experience of sexual satisfaction.[15] The role sexuality plays in the act and the extent of it is far from determined. The phrase "exposes his genitals" is a precise description of the act and a welcome clarification. The phrase "under circumstances in which he knows his conduct is likely to cause affront or alarm" meets the difficulty of defining the place where the offence occurs and correctly includes the factor of "alarm" as well as affront, in keeping with what is known about the reaction which exhibitionism evokes.[16]

Taken as a whole, the offence as proposed by the Model Code is in my opinion properly directed, for it follows more closely than previous formulations the exhibitionistic acts as one finds them occurring in the community. I would criticize it on the grounds that it is not limited to male persons,[17] that it makes an unjustified assumption regarding the motive or purpose of the act, and that it fails to direct the court where children under 12 are concerned to make special enquiry as to whether any invitation to further acts was involved (as exemplified in the *Wellard* and *Fairclough* cases); such an invitation would place the act in the

15 J. W. Mohr, R. E. Turner, and M. B. Jerry, *Pedophilia and Exhibitionism* (Toronto, 1964), p. 119. As to the arousing or gratifying of sexual desire in the person to whom the exposure is made, see p. 120: "It is very doubtful whether the expected reaction is one of pleasure."
16 *Ibid.*, p. 121. That this is the reaction which is intended can also be seen in the following passage, at p. 120: "In many cases there is an aggressive-defiant element in the act which seems to be intended to evoke fear and shock rather than pleasure from the victim."
17 It is this particular behaviour on the part of male persons that presents itself as the problem. Female exposure of this kind is virtually unheard of; however, should it ever become a problem, which I tend to doubt, then it should be dealt with separately in light of what may be learned about it. We should not leave the section in broad terms to cover unspecified but speculatively objectional behaviour which may or may not occur, for eventually this leads to bizarre interpretations and abuse. The expression of the criminal law is of necessity general in character, but it should never be framed more broadly than we intend or need to make it.

pedophilic rather than the exhibitionistic category.

The relatively few reported cases in this area reflect the minor concern of the courts in regard to the nature of the act. But in terms of the frequency with which it occurs, representing as it does about one-third of all sexual offences, it is important. I believe we are now at a point where it is necessary to separate this offence further from its historic entanglement with the notions surrounding public indecency and to give it a clearer identity than exists at present.

Indecent Assaults

Indecent Assault Female

141. (1) Every one who indecently assaults a female person is guilty of an indictable offence and is liable to imprisonment for five years and to be whipped.
(2) An accused who is charged with an offence under subsection (1) may be convicted if the evidence establishes that the accused did anything to the female person with her consent that, but for her consent, would have been an indecent assault, if her consent was obtained by false and fraudulent representations as to the nature and quality of the act.

132. Where an accused is charged with an offence under section . . . 141 . . . in respect of a person under the age of fourteen years, the fact that the person consented to the commission of the offence is not a defence to the charge.

In order to establish the offence of indecent assault, it is necessary to prove an assault accompanied by circumstances of indecency. It is not necessary to show that the act which constituted the assault was in itself indecent. For example, in *R* v. *Louie Chong* [(1914), 23 C.C.C. 250 (Ont. C.A.)], the accused seized a girl of 15 in a lonely spot and made an indecent proposal to her. Although the manner in which the girl was seized was not indecent, the indecency could be interpreted from the circumstances in which she was seized and also from the words spoken at the time. Similarly, in another case decided the same year, *R* v. *Fontaine* [(1914), 23 C.C.C. 159 (Ont. C.A.)], an "indecent suggestion" taken in connection with the accused's act (which was not specified) was sufficient to constitute the offence. Again, in *R* v. *Edgett* [(1947), 90 C.C.C. 274 (N.B. App. D.)], where the evidence shows the accused threw a coat over the complainant's head, the indecency was found in some "dirty remarks" and some indecent suggestive gestures made to the girl.[1]

The offence is dependent upon there having been an "assault" committed. Chief Justice Baxter, in *R* v. *Landry* [(1935), 64 C.C.C. 104 (N.B. App. D.)] was of the opinion that "to find the prisoner guilty on either [attempted rape or indecent assault], he must have *used some physical force* unaccompanied by consent on the part of the victim." (Italics are mine.) This case has been cited in two fairly recent cases as establishing the principle that "physical contact" is a necessary ingredient.[2] This attempt to limit the term "assault" to cases involving physical contact or to what would earlier have been known as "battery" is highly questionable. The issue is clearly dealt with in *R* v. *Rolfe* [(1952), 36 Cr. App. R. 4], where the appellant admitted in evidence that he had exposed himself to a woman, and had moved towards her while in that condition and invited her to have connection with him but denied that he actually touched her. In dismissing the appeal against conviction, Lord Chief Justice Goddard said (at p. 6),

. . . the offence of assault is often confused with battery. An assault can be committed *without touching a person*. One always thinks of an assault as the giving of a blow to somebody, but *that is not necessary*. An assault may be constituted by a threat or a hostile act committed towards a person . . . [Here the Chief Justice repeated the acts set out above] that, in the opinion of this court, can amount to an assault. [Italics are mine.]

As a result of two cases decided in England, a question has arisen, however, whether an assault has been committed where the accused merely invites another person to touch him. In *Fairclough* v. *Whipp* [(1951), 35 Cr. App. R. 138] the facts disclosed that a man was urinating at the side of a river where there were four girls, varying in age from six to nine. The accused with his penis exposed asked one of the girls, a 9-year-old, to "touch it," which she did. He then went away and was later charged with indecent assault. The charge was dismissed by the magistrates. Lord Goddard, on appeal by the prosecutor by way of stated case, said (at p. 139),

1 In *R* v. *Hay* [(1959), 125 C.C.C. 137 (Man. C.A.)] it is reported that a trial judge instructed the jury that "the commonest form is touching or attempting to touch the private parts of another or similar action." It is clear from the judge's remarks and from the cases cited above that although this may be the commonest form of the offence it is not the only form.
2 *R* v. *Fiset* (1953), 107 C.C.C. 248 (Que. Mag. Ct.), and *R* v. *Jones* [1964] 2 C.C.C. 123 (N.S. App. D.).

The question is whether the conduct amounts to an assault. . . . An assault can be committed, without there being a battery, for instance, by a threatening gesture or a threat to use violence against a person, but I do not know any authority which says that where one person invites another to touch him that can amount to an assault.

The problem as to what constitutes an assault has arisen in another way in *D.P.P.* v. *Rogers* [(1953), 37 Cr. App. R. 137 (Div. Ct. Cas.)]. In that case a father put his arm around the shoulders of his 11-year-old daughter and led her upstairs, on two separate occasions, where he exposed his genitals to her and told her to masturbate him. Lord Goddard C.J. said (at pp. 139, 140):

Before you can find a man has been guilty of indecent assault, you must find that he was guilty of an assault, for an indecent assault is an assault accompanied by indecency, and if it could be shown here that the respondent had done anything toward this child which, by any fair use of langauge could be called compulsion, or had acted . . . in a hostile manner towards her, that is with a threat or gesture which could be taken as a threat, or by pulling a reluctant child towards him, that would undoubtedly be an assault and, if it were accompanied by an act of indecency, it would be indecent assault.

The disturbing problems raised by these two cases have not yet been decided by a court in Canada. In the case of *R* v. *Fiset* (already noted in another connection above), a magistrate found the accused guilty of attempt indecent assault against two girls aged 13, on the grounds of his "invit[ing] the children into his house, his immediate indecent exhibition [details not given], his request to touch his privates, his offers of money to do wrong." Assuming the girls had accepted the invitation to touch the accused without his touching them, it would be ludicrous if he could be guilty of the attempt but not the full offence.[3] Undoubtedly in the majority of cases involving pedophilic acts, there will be evidence

3 An interesting technical argument might be raised in these cases. The present definition of assault (s. 230) is said to recognize but obviate the common law distinction between assault and battery. Hawkins, P.C., bk. 1, p. 107, says "every battery includes an assault . . . if the defendant is found guilty of battery, it is sufficient." A battery may be committed if the impact is occasioned by the movement of the victim himself against some stationary matter, provided the accused intentionally caused the impact, "as where a person intentionally digs a pitfall for another." (Abraham (1918), South Africa C.D., 520 at 597–598). In the cases of indecent assault which we are considering, it appears that the accused by his invitation causes and intends the indecent impact. Is this indecent impact a battery and therefore an assault? It would appear to be clear that no mere words can amount to an assault. Can mere words, in the form of an invitation to touch the accused's person, without any other physical act on his part, be construed as an attempt to cause an indecent impact, and therefore attempted indecent assault? See an unpublished article by John A. Patterson, "Legal Implications of Three Sexual Deviations," Osgoode Hall Law School, December 19, 1963.

of some touching of the child by the accused. However, there is some evidence to show that cases in which the adult is fondled are not infrequent.[4] If the courts decided to follow *D.P.P.* v. *Rogers* so that it becomes necessary to show elements of compulsion, or hostile manner exhibited by threat or gesture which could be taken as a threat, it could well prove an insuperable obstacle in most cases involving pedophilic acts. What these cases should alert us to is the realization that the concept of "assault" is unsatisfactory because it is too narrow to cover the kinds of situations which arise when children are involved.

Included Offences

There are a number of cases which show that indecent assault is an included offence in a number of more serious offences. It is apparent from the factual situations which present themselves in these cases that these are entirely different from cases involving pedophilic acts. A brief review of these cases will illustrate these points.

Rape

In *R* v. *Marr* [(1955), 114 C.C.C. 318 (N.B. App. D.)] the accused, a 19-year-old, was charged with raping a 30-year-old married woman he had previously known (the "sordid details" are not described) and convicted of indecent assault. In *R* v. *Marion* [(1956), 118 C.C.C. 388 (Ont. C.A.)] the accused, a 24-year-old, was charged with both rape and indecent assault where the facts disclosed that the crime was committed after much violence. The complainant had resisted his advances and had struck him with a beer bottle, and was subsequently dragged from the car and her clothes were badly torn. Laidlaw J. said, "It was a crime of gross indecency," hopefully not using that expression with any technical meaning.

Attempted Rape

In *R* v. *Landry* [(1935), 64 C.C.C. 104 (N.B. App. D.)] a jury found an accused guilty of both attempted rape and indecent assault (which involved a girl of barely 14), but a new trial was ordered on appeal, on a question of consent. This time, the court was of the opinion that working upon a girl's passions, so as to break down her resistance and induce consent, was not sufficient to constitute either offence.

In *R* v. *Ollech* [(1938), 70 C.C.C. 73 (Alta. App. D.)], where the facts in evidence showed an attempt by the accused to commit rape on

4 J. W. Mohr, R. E. Turner, and M. B. Jerry, *Pedophilia and Exhibitionism* (Toronto, 1964), Table IX, p. 32. In 34 cases of heterosexual pedophilia, four involved this type of behaviour.

his own daughter, a new trial was ordered on appeal on the grounds that the case was outside of the jurisdiction of the magistrate to try. The magistrate's conviction of indecent assault was set aside.

In *R* v. *Quinton* [(1947), 88 C.C.C. 231 (S.C.C.)] the Supreme Court held that indecent assault was an included offence under a charge of attempted rape, overruling in that regard an opinion expressed in the Ontario Court of Appeal. In this case, the jury had found the accused guilty of assault occasioning actual bodily harm, but the Ontario Court of Appeal substituted a conviction for common assault. The Supreme Court refused, on appeal by the crown, to substitute a conviction for indecent assault, on the grounds that the jury's decision, "in finding the accused not guilty on the count of attempted rape, negated the existence of the element of indecency, and, therefore, in effect found the accused not guilty of indecent assault."

In *Gauthier* v. *R* [(1950), 98 C.C.C. 39 (Que. App. D.)] the court of appeal confirmed a jury's verdict of guilty on a charge of indecent assault, where the original charge was attempted rape. In that case, the girl was 13, and the evidence showed "red patches, abrasions and signs of anterior irritation," but there was "no deflowering" and the "hymen was not torn." The age of the accused is not reported.

Sexual Intercourse with a Girl under 14[5]

This offence requires corroboration, while that of indecent assault does not, and there are a number of cases which show that the latter is substituted where the evidence of the complainant was not corroborated.

In *R* v. *Terrell* [(1947), 88 C.C.C. 369 (B.C.C.A.)] where the evidence of a medical doctor, offered as corroboration, was as consistent with penetration as with manual handling, the court was of the opinion that the doctor's evidence was corroboration of neither, and substituted a conviction for indecent assault for the jury's conviction of carnal knowledge. The girl was 12 years old.

In *R* v. *Jing Foo* [(1939), 73 C.C.C. 103 (B.C. Co. Ct.)] a trial judge substituted a verdict of indecent assault where there was no corroboration of the major offence. There are no facts given in this case. The same occurred in *R* v. *O'Hara* [(1946), 88 C.C.C. 74 (B.C.C.A.)].

In *R* v. *Cameron* [(1901), 4 C.C.C. 385 (Ont. H.C.J.)] Mr. Justice MacMahon held that an acquittal by the magistrate on a charge of carnal knowledge because of insufficient evidence is a bar to a further charge of indecent assault in respect of the same occurrence.

5 Prior to the revision in 1954–55, this offence was known as "carnal knowledge," and the older cases use that terminology.

Attempt Sexual Intercourse (Carnal Knowledge) with a Girl under 14
In *R* v. *De Wolfe* [(1904), 9 C.C.C. 38 (N.S. Co. Ct.)] the accused
was charged with both attempted carnal knowledge and indecent assault,
but convicted only of common assault in the absence of any corroboration implicating the accused.

The New Brunswick Supreme Court, Appellate Division, in *R* v.
Langley [(1927), 48 C.C.C. 293 (N.B. App. D.)] upheld a conviction
for indecent assault, and confirmed that a crown attorney may prefer an
indictment for that offence where evidence advanced at the preliminary
hearing was sufficient to support the charge, even though the accused
was committed for trial on a charge of attempted carnal knowledge.

In *R* v. *McLean* [(1931), 57 C.C.C. 239 (N.S.)] the accused was
charged with both attempted carnal knowledge and indecent assault,
and the same evidence was given on both counts; Chief Justice Chisholm
was of the opinion that the jury was wrong to acquit of the former and
convict on the latter. If they believed the girl's story (she was 11) then
they should have convicted the accused of carnal knowledge and if they
did not there should have been no conviction for either offence.

In *R* v. *Stewart* [(1938), 71 C.C.C. 206 (Alta. App. D.)] the
offence occurred when the girl was 10 but she was 13 at the time of the
trial. The court of appeal found prejudicial error and ground for a new
trial in the failure of the trial judge to instruct the jury that in the
absence of proof of the major offence they might convict on the lesser
offence of indecent assault. They quashed the conviction but did not
order a new trial because there was no corroboration of either offence.

In *R* v. *Brown* [(1951), 99 C.C.C. 305 (N.S. App. D.)] an issue
before the court was whether a finding of not guilty of attempted carnal
knowledge precluded a finding of guilty of indecent assault. The testimony of the 11-year-old victim was to the effect that the accused had
pulled off her pants and had sexual intercourse with her. Hughes J. said,

It is possible for a man so to act with a child that she might think he had
intercourse with her when he did not and he might never have intended to
have sexual intercourse.
In such a case, he would not be guilty of an attempt to have sexual intercourse but might be guilty of an indecent assault. In such a case, no corroboration is necessary to convict. [Citing *R* v. *McLean, supra.*]

Sexual Intercourse with a Girl between 14 and 16
The court of appeal in *R* v. *O'Hara* [(1946), 88 C.C.C. 74 (B.C.C.A.)]
substituted a verdict of indecent assault, which does not require corroboration, where the corroborative evidence was insufficient and in part

improperly admitted to support the major offence. (The girl in this case was just under 16.)

Sexual Intercourse with the Feeble-Minded

Where the major charge was sexual intercourse with a feeble-minded person, the court of appeal in *Dupont* v. *R* [(1958) 28 C.R. 146 (Que. App. D.)] held it was *not* open to a trial court to amend the charge to indecent assault because the two offences were totally of a different character. They quashed the conviction on the ground that the indictment as amended was null and void and therefore non-existent. The court pointed out that its action did not constitute an acquittal of a further charge of indecent assault.

In addition to those cases noted above, in all of which there was some evidence of sexual intercourse or an attempt at intercourse, there is another group of cases in which indecent assault has been charged, and which effectively widens the range which the offence covers.

Violent Acts Involving Children

In *R* v. *Tilley* [(1953), 106 C.C.C. 42 (Ont. C.A.)] the accused, 57, "inflicted painful and serious injuries" on the sexual organs of a little girl (aged 7), either by use of hands or otherwise. His conduct towards the little girl was sadistic. Having completed his sexual attack upon her, he told her to get out of the car and threatened that if she did not he would "kill her." (The accused was also tried as a criminal sexual psychopath.) Another case showing aggression is *R* v. *Backshall* [(1956), 115 C.C.C. 221 (Ont. C.A.)], where the accused induced two girls (aged 7 and 8) into his car and drove off (as in the Tilley case). When he stopped, one girl escaped, but the accused "ripped the pants off the second girl" before she too escaped.

Violent and Sadistic Acts Involving Adult Females

In *Cullen* v. *R* [(1949), 94 C.C.C. 337 (S.C.C.)] a 17-year-old female was severely beaten and had been choked into a state of unconsciousness, and in *R* v. *Marion*, cited above, a woman who resisted the accused's advances was dragged from the car and her clothing was badly torn: the crime was committed "after use of much violence." In both of these cases the acts were intentionally directed to sexual intercourse. In *R* v. *Robertson* [(1946), 86 C.C.C. 353 (Ont. C.A.)] the accused had tied up his nude victim and subjected her to "sadistic treatment" the details of which are not given. In this case a conviction on a charge of intent to maim and disfigure was quashed on appeal.

Incestuous Acts

In both *R* v. *Ollech*, cited above, and *Fargnoli* v. *R* [(1957), 117 C.C.C. 359 (S.C.C.)] the indecent assault was directed by the accused against his own daughter.

Fraudulent Acts

In *Thorn* v. *R* [(1952) 15 C.R. 129 (N.B.C.A.)] the accused entered the lower berth of a train while a woman was asleep and attempted to have sexual intercourse with her, pretending he was her husband. The court of appeal indicated that the facts may well have indicated rape or attempted rape but upheld the conviction of indecent assault on this "dastardly and vicious" crime.

Lesbian Acts

In *R* v. *A.B.* [(1955), 113 C.C.C. 325 (Alta. App. D.)] the court of appeal acquitted a woman who had been convicted of this offence in magistrates' court. The accused, who had written a letter to the complainant suggesting lesbian practices, later visited her and attempted to kiss her. The conviction was quashed on the grounds that there was no "hostile act" with circumstances of indecency. The possibility remains of assaults of a lesbian character which may be charged under this offence.

These are, of course, not all of the cases appearing in the reports, but a varied sample which shows that the spread of cases falling under the offence of indecent assault female admits of no easy categorization. This should make us aware that we are not here dealing with any homogeneous entity but with one which presents many facets, each of which would bear separate scrutiny.

Corroboration

The offence of indecent assault is not included under section 131(1) of the Criminal Code as one of the offences which require corroboration. There are many cases which repeat the rule that corroboration is not necessary.[6] But the statement that corroboration is not required in cases falling under this offence is misleading and must be qualified. Section 134 of the Code provides that where the only evidence that implicates the accused is the evidence, given under oath, of the female complainant,

6 *R* v. *Brown* (1951), 99 C.C.C. 305 (N.S. App. D.); *R* v. *O'Hara* (1946), 88 C.C.C. 74 (B.C.C.A.); *Cullen* v. *R* (1949), 94 C.C.C. 337 (S.C.C.); *Fargnoli* v. *R* (1957), 117 C.C.C. 359 (S.C.C.); *R* v. *Terrell* (1947), 88 C.C.C. 369 (B.C.C.A.); *R* v. *Fiset* (1953), 107 C.C.C. 248 (Que. Mag. Ct.); *R* v. *Druz* (1928), 34 O.W.N. 119 (Ont. C.A.).

and where that evidence is not corroborated in a material particular by evidence which implicates the accused, the judge shall instruct the jury that it is not safe to find the accused guilty in the absence of such corroboration, but that they are entitled to do so if they are satisfied beyond a reasonable doubt that her evidence is true. This rule was set out in *R* v. *Jones* [(1925), 19 Cr. App. R. 40],[7] an English decision, and adopted into the Canadian Code in the latest revision.[8] Where the evidence which is forthcoming is not under oath, for example where a child of tender years is involved and is not sworn, then, by the operation of section 566 of the Code, evidence of the child must be corroborated in a material particular by evidence which implicates the accused. The unsworn evidence of a child is admissible under the operation of section 16(1) of the Canada Evidence Act.[9]

Where a judge sits without a jury, he must warn himself of the danger of convicting without corroborating testimony,[10] but it will not be assumed because of the judge's silence on the matter that he did not exercise all of the caution necessary.[11] Although the matter was not raised in a case of indecent assault, in *R* v. *Reeves* [(1941), 77 C.C.C. 89 (B.C.C.A.)], involving a case of rape, it was said by Sloan J.A. at p. 92 that the warning must be given whether or not there was corroborative evidence, and also that the judge must inform the jury what constitutes corroborative testimony. In another rape case, *R* v. *Fennell* [(1957), 29 C.R. 337 (B.C.C.A.)], Bird J.A. was of the opinion (at p. 341) that the instruction to the jury should be specific:

In my view it is settled law that [it is] the duty of a judge in charging a jury in cases of rape where he considers there is evidence independent of that of the complainant capable of corroborating her testimony, to declare in clear terms *what that evidence is* and on the other hand if he considers there is

---

7 For other authorities in support of the rule see Edwards (1954), Crim. L.R. 330. For criticism of the rule, see Glanville Williams, "Corroboration – Accomplices" (1962), Crim. L.R. 588 at 591.
8 This amendment was proposed by J. Diefenbaker, as noted earlier. There was considerable discussion in Hansard about this rule (see Debates, H.C., Canada, 1954, II, 2038 and IV, 3559).
9 Prior to the revision of the Code, unsworn testimony was admissible under the operation of section 1003(1) of the Code as well as section 16(1) of the Canada Evidence Act, but the section in the Code has not been continued. There was a dispute whether the wording of these two sections was co-extensive, but *R* v. *Silverstone* [(1934), 61 C.C.C. 258 (Ont. C.A.)] and *R* v. *Gemmill* [(1924), 43 C.C.C. 360 (Ont. C.A.)] decided that they were. That problem is no longer in issue.
10 *Fargnoli* v. *R* (1957), 117 C.C.C. 359 (S.C.C.).
11 *R* v. *Tolhurst* (1939), 73 C.C.C. 32 (Sask. C.A.).

no such corroborative evidence it is likewise his duty to so declare. [Italics are mine.][12]

It is not enough for the judge to refer the jury to the evidence at large and leave them to decide what evidence, if any, they consider corroborative.[13]

Reading L.C.J., who delivered the judgment of the court of criminal appeal in the leading case of *R* v. *Baskerville* [(1916), 25 Cox C.C. 524 (Ct. Crim. App.)], set out the elements governing corroborative evidence (on p. 91) as follows:

We hold that evidence in corroboration must be independent testimony which affects the accused by connecting or tending to connect him with the crime. In other words, it must be evidence which implicates him, that is, which confirms in some material particular not only the evidence that the crime has been committed, but also that the prisoner committed it.

The evidence must be "independent," that is, it must be found in evidence other than that of the complainant herself, so the fact that she made a complaint or the substance of what was said in the course of her complaint is not and cannot be corroboration.[14] Not infrequently the independent corroboration is found in the testimony or the behaviour of the accused. In *R* v. *Fournier* [(1956) 23 C.R. 363 (Alta. App. D.)] the admission of the accused himself that he seized the woman when she stepped out of the auto was sufficient corroboration of her testimony on which to sustain conviction for indecent assault. In *R* v. *Fontaine*, cited earlier, it was held that where the court was of the opinion that the explanation offered by the accused was an unreasonable one, circumstances admitted by the accused to which he offered an explanation of an exculpatory character might be looked to for corroborative evidence implicating him. In *R* v. *Richmond* [(1945), 84 C.C.C. 289 (B.C.-C.A.)] O'Halloran J.A. was of the opinion that the voluntary statement

---

12 Bird J.A. cites *R* v. *Feigenbaum* (1919), 14 Cr. App. R. 1; *R* v. *Kelso* (1953), 105 C.C.C. 305 (Ont. C.A.); and *R* v. *Smith and Gibson* (1956), 115 C.C.C. 38 (Ont. C.A.). *R* v. *Mitchell* (1958) 28 C.R. 198 (Ont. C.A.) and *R* v. *Clarke and Clarke* (1959), 28 W.W.R. 283 (B.C.C.A.) are to the same effect.
13 The duty of a judge to point out specifically what can be considered as corroborative is more clearly settled in Canada than in England, where it has not been held as a requirement of law that the judge's instructions be specific. See Glanville Williams, "Corroboration – Sexual Cases" (1962), Crim. L.R. 622 at pp. 667, 668. He regards the position as taken in the *Fennel* case as a desirable practice.
14 *R* v. *Plantus* [1957] O.W.N. 388 (Ont. C.A.). For other cases stressing the need for "independent" testimony, see *R* v. *Richmond* (1945), 84 C.C.C. 289 (B.C.C.A.); *R* v. *Hubin* (1927), 48 C.C.C. 172 (S.C.C.); *R* v. *Dyck* (1956), 19 W.W.R. 164 (Sask. C.A.) at p. 172; and *R* v. *Thomas* [1952] 2 S.C.R. 344.

made by the appellant, to the effect that the facts set out in the warrant on a charge of indecent assault were true, constituted corroboration, and not only "tended to connect" him with the crime but actually did "connect" him with it. In *R* v. *Collerman* [[1964] 3 C.C.C. 195 (B.C.C.A.)] Sheppard J.A. sustained the magistrate who held that the giving of false evidence by the accused was corroborative of the complainant's evidence. He also cited with approval the following passage from *MacDonald* v. *R* [(1946), 87 C.C.C. 257 (S.C.C.) at p. 266]. "The behaviour of a witness as well as his contradictory or untrue statement are questions of fact from which a jury may properly infer corroboration." Chief Justice Anglin, in the Supreme Court of Canada decision in *R* v. *Hubin* [(1927), 48 C.C.C. 172 (S.C.C.)], said that if the trial judge had found corroboration in the conduct of the accused at the time he was arrested and when he was identified by the complainant, or in his making two contradictory statements, the court would not have set aside the conviction.[15] In *R* v. *Hober* [(1943), 80 C.C.C. 332 (B.C.C.A.)] the majority of the court of appeal of British Columbia was of the opinion that the accused's admission that he took the child on his lap, though he denied that he had touched her indecently, was not sufficient corroboration of the girl's story.[16]

This leads us back once again to consider the ruling in the *Baskerville* case, that the corroborative evidence must "implicate the accused" in two aspects; it must indicate (*a*) that a crime has been committed and (*b*) that the accused committed it. In *R* v. *Creamer* (Krämer) [(1924), 41 C.C.C. 403 (Alta. App. D.)] Stuart J. pointed out that the phrase must be given a slightly different significance in each of two possible cases. Where the crime has been proved by evidence from a source other than the child, then the question arises as to who did it. In these cases the corroborative evidence must "not so much tend to show that a crime has been committed but rather that the accused was the person who did it." In other cases where the identity of the accused is not in dispute, the question becomes, "Did the accused do something forbidden?"

Examples of the former kind of case can be seen in *Shorten* v. *R* [(1918), 42 D.L.R. 591 (S.C.C.)] and *Steel* v. *R* [(1924), 42 C.C.C. 375 (S.C.C.)], where the fact that the accused was in the girl's company was treated as corroboratory. But in those cases, the fact of the offence

15 The trial judge had found corroboration in the girl's identification of the accused's car, which he admitted was his, but the Supreme Court did not agree that this was corroborative evidence sufficient to implicate him.
16 Chief Justice McDonald was of the opinion that the case "was very close to the line," but preferred to give the accused the benefit of the doubt. See the strong dissenting opinion of O'Halloran J.A.

having been committed by someone was otherwise established. There are a series of cases of the latter kind, which are particularly important because of the obstacle they present to providing the required proof where pedophilic acts have occurred.

In *R* v. *Gee Poy* [(1922), 38 C.C.C. 280 (Alta. App. D.)], a 22-year-old proprietor of a store was accused by a girl aged 9 of inviting her to the back of the store and there running his hand down the front of her dress to her abdomen. The accused admitted taking the girl to the back of the store but denied touching her in this way. Stuart J.A. could find no corroborative evidence for what he regarded as "merely a slightly indecent assault." His brother Hyndman J.A. had this to say (at p. 283):

In most cases of a sexual nature there is undisputed or at least satisfactory evidence of the physical act, such as a patent injury, blood, etc., which doctors will say were caused by physical force administered from without, and which prove an offence by some one. But *until this fact is established* I cannot understand how it can properly be said that any admissions of the accused had any other effect than this, that if an indecent assault had in fact been committed, he had the opportunity of committing it which would be a material particular sufficient to implicate him. There is no evidence corroborative of the girl's story that the man did anything more than place his hand on her shoulder. [Italics are mine.]

The conviction was quashed. In *R* v. *Gemmill* [(1924), 43 C.C.C. 360 (Ont. C.A.)] the girl was 7 and the accused lived on the same street; there was no question of identity or opportunity to commit the act. Magee J.A. said (at p. 362), "In cases of this sort it is not only necessary to corroborate the identity of the accused as the offender but to corroborate the facts of the offence. . . . Here there is no *outside evidence* of any assault at all." (Italics are mine.)

In *R* v. *Hober* (cited above) a 6-year-old girl testified that the janitor at her school had taken her upon his knee and had indecently touched her. The janitor admitted taking the child on his knee and putting his arm around her but denied any indecent contact with her. The conviction was quashed on the ground that there was no corroborative evidence that an indecent assault had occurred. In *R* v. *Rolfe* [(1952), 36 Cr. App. R. 4], an indecent assault case which involved an adult woman, Lord Chief Justice Goddard, on the facts of that particular case, held that no corroboration was necessary, but he passed the opinion (at p. 6) that "where corroboration is necessary on a charge of Indecent Assault it is necessary to corroborate the indecency."

The problem which these cases present is that in many cases involving pedophilic acts where the acts involve looking, touching, fondling, and kissing, there is little likelihood of any physical evidence that the act has occurred, so that the fact that the crime was committed can seldom be proven by outside evidence. Contrary to what Mr. Justice Hyndman said in the *Gee Poy* case, there is in the vast majority of cases little likelihood of "patent injury" or "blood." It is difficult to see how one can get around these cases for they seem to hold firmly that outside evidence of the indecency itself is necessary. Because of the nature of the acts they are most frequently committed in secret, and if outside evidence is insisted upon there may be serious difficulty finding corroborative proof in some cases. Perhaps sufficient attention was not given in these cases to the factor of opportunity. Although mere opportunity alone cannot amount to corroboration, in a bastardy case it has been said that the circumstances and the locality of the opportunity may be such as in themselves amount to corroboration.[17]

In *R* v. *Millar* [[1966] 1 C.C.C. 60 (N.B. App. D.)], a recent decision of the New Brunswick Supreme Court, Appellate Division, involving a case of indecent assault on a 13-year-old girl, Bridges C.J.N.B. said, "I think opportunity under suspicious circumstances affords the required corroboration."[18] In this case, in addition to opportunity, the suspicious circumstances were that the accused was a married man aged 34 and the girl was 13, he had been drinking, and they had driven to an out-of-the-way place in a wooded area.

The decision in the *Baskerville* case warned of the danger of laying down any formula as to the kind of evidence which amounts to corroboration, and perhaps as the courts become more aware of the nature of pedophilic acts there will be less insistence on physical evidence of the act or actual harm done to the child, and more willingness to consider the surrounding circumstances to satisfy the not unreasonable requirement of corroboration.

The question as to whether the unsworn evidence of a child of tender years can be corroborative of the unsworn evidence of another child appears now to be well settled. Estey J., in reviewing the authorities in *Paige* v. *R* [(1948), 92 C.C.C. 32 (S.C.C.)], a case of carnal knowledge of a girl between 14 and 16, said (at p. 37), "It has been repeatedly held that the unsworn evidence of a child of tender years will not constitute corroboration of the evidence of another child of tender

17 *Jones* v. *Thomas* [1934] 1 K.B., 323. The requirement of corroboration in affiliation proceedings rests on a different statutory basis from the Criminal Code. See *Luther* v. *Ryan* (1956), 115 C.C.C. 303 (Nfld. S.C.).
18 Cases cited: *Dawson* v. *McKenzie* (1908), S.C. 648; *R* v. *Newes* (1934), 61 C.C.C. 316 (Alta. App. D.); *R* v. *Richard* (1957), 99 C.C.C. 262 (N.S. App. D.). See also *R* v. *Childs* (1958), 122 C.C.C. 126 (N.B. App. D.).

years whose evidence is also given without oath."[19] The law does not define a child of "tender years." In *R* v. *Duquay* [[1966] 3 C.C.C. 226 (Sask. C.A.)] a girl of 13 was sworn, and then examined as to the nature of the oath before giving testimony, and a second girl, aged 11, was examined and her testimony accepted without the oath being taken, but the record did not reveal the nature and scope of the judge's inquiry.[20] The Court of Appeal held that the testimony of the former was inadmissible and that of the latter improperly received. Culliton C.J.S. said (at p. 267),

The law has long been settled that when a child of tender years is called as a witness, the presiding Judge or Magistrate must first inquire whether or not the child understands the nature of an oath. If it has that understanding it must be sworn in. The inquiry must be made and the oath must not be administered to such child without such inquiry.[21]

The duty of the presiding judge with respect to receiving unsworn testimony is set out in *Sankey* v. *R* [(1927), 48 C.C.C. 97 (S.C.C.)]. In *R* v. *Jones* [[1964] 2 C.C.C. 123 (N.S. App. D.)] it was held that not only is it his duty to make the inquiry, but the transcript should reveal both that the inquiry was made and the nature of the inquiry.[22] Following the *Paige* decision, the court in the *Duquay* case also held that the unsworn testimony of the one child could not be corroborative of the sworn testimony of the other.[23]

Complaints

One of the exceptions to the general rule that "hearsay" evidence is not admissible is "complaints" made by victims in sexual cases. In *R* v. *Lillyman* [(1896), 18 Cox C.C. 346 (Cr. Cas. Res.)] there was an attempt made by the Court for Crown Cases Reserved to clarify some

19 See *R* v. *Whistnant* (1912), 20 C.C.C. 322 (Alta. App. D.); *R* v. *McInulty* (1914), 22 C.C.C. 347 (B.C.C.A.); *R* v. *Lamond* (1925), 45 C.C.C. 200 (Ont. C.A.); *Brule* v. *R* (1929), 48 Que. K.B., 64 (Que. App. D.); *R* v. *Drew* (No. 2) (1933), 60 C.C.C. 229 (Sask. C.A.); *R* v. *Manser* (1934), 25 Cr. App. R. 18.
20 In *R* v. *McKevitt* [(1936), 66 C.C.C. 70 (N.S. App. D.)] a 12-year-old girl, fully developed, was held competent to testify under oath without first being examined as to the nature of the oath, especially where her age was not called to the attention of the court before testimony was given.
21 See also *R* v. *Lebrun* (1951), 100 C.C.C. 16 (Ont. C.A.); *R* v. *Dumont* (1950), 98 C.C.C. 336; *R* v. *Larochelle* (1951), 102 C.C.C. 194 (N.S. App. D.) at p. 201.
22 Evans J.A. in *R* v. *Horsburgh* [[1966] 3 C.C.C. 240 (Ont. C.A.)] at p. 248 disagrees with this view.
23 For a contrary opinion see Lord Goddard's decision in *R* v. *Campbell* (1956), 40 Cr. App. R. 95.

of the earlier confusion, and certain propositions were set down: evidence is admissible of the fact that a complaint is made, provided it was made as speedily after the act complained of as could reasonably be expected; where the fact of a complaint was admissible, particulars of the complaint may be given; and, evidence of the complaint is not admissible as evidence of the fact complained of, which must be established by other evidence (and strictly speaking should be given before evidence of the complaint is admitted). Evidence of the complaint is admissible to establish (*a*) the consistency of the prosecutrix with her story told in the witness box, and (*b*) to show her want of consent to the acts complained of.

The question of whether a complaint was admissible where want of consent was not in issue (for example, where a girl was under 13) was settled by *R* v. *Osborne* [[1905] 1 K.B. 551 (Cr. Cas. Res.)].[24] It was a case of indecent assault which involved a complaint made by a 12-year-old girl. The court decided that as a complaint was admissible to show consistency with a girl's story as well as to negative consent, it was admissible on the first ground even though the second ground did not arise.

It was set down in *R* v. *Osborne* (at p. 561) that a complaint was admissible only when it was made at the first opportunity after the offence which reasonably presented itself. This has proven to be a rather elastic rule, for the courts have given it a wide interpretation. For example, in *R* v. *McGivney* [(1914), 22 C.C.C. 222 (B.C.C.A.)] a complaint made by a 6-year-old girl to her grandmother about two weeks after the event was held admissible.[25] Galligher J.A. (at pp. 230, 231) pointed out that consideration must be given to the youth of the child, the fact that she would not appreciate the nature of the offence and would perhaps fear punishment, that while the lapse of time might be very serious in the case of a person of mature years where the question of consent was involved, in the case of a child it must be regarded in a very different light. In *R* v. *Smith* [(1905), 9 C.C.C. 21 (N.S. Co. Ct.)] a complaint made by a mature woman after a lapse of five days was held admissible, while a lapse of twenty-four hours was held to be too long a time, making the complaint inadmissible in *R* v. *Marsh* [(1940), 74 C.C.C. 312 (B.C.C.A.)], where the girl was 15 years old and had spent the night in her home with her mother and had seen her the following morning. In *R* v. *Barron* [(1905), 9 C.C.C. 196

24 Lawrence J. in *R* v. *Kingham* [(1902), 66 J.P. 393] had held it was not admissible, while Ridley J. in *R* v. *Kiddle* [(1898) 19 Cox C.C. 77 (Gloucestershire Assizes)] had held that it was.
25 There is some uncertainty about the length of time, one reference being "ten days," the other "about two weeks."

(N.S. Co. Ct.)], a complaint was not made by a child of 7 until ten days after the event and the evidence of it was admitted. Wallace C.C.J. expressed the opinion that although some English courts had decided that a complaint must be made immediately, the Canadian courts had not followed them. He argued (at pp. 198, 199) that in cases of rape the prompt complaint is offered and received because it negatived the consent of the girl and confirmed her story, but when consent was not in issue, such evidence was offered for the purpose of confirming her testimony and showing consistency of her conduct. In his view, there was no fixed time in which a complaint must be made, in some cases two days was unreasonable while in others the period might be two weeks. A delay might be due to want of opportunity to disclose, bashfulness, fear, or some physical or mental condition, and if so a lapse of time could be excused. He pointed out that a child was not affected by that indignation and sense of wrong which would naturally lead to a prompt complaint. Although the delay in making the complaint did not affect its admissibility, it did affect the weight which should be given to it. In *Hopkinson* v. *Perdue* [(1904), 8 C.C.C. 286 (Ont. A.C.J.)] (a civil case), a complaint made by a wife to her husband on first seeing him after his return from work but several hours after the assault was held to be admissible. In *R* v. *Nightingale* [(1957), 124 C.C.C. 214 (N.B. App. D.)], a case of rape, the principle was said to be the first reasonable opportunity, "before the girl has had time to devise an untrue accusation."

Lord Goddard C.J., in *R* v. *Cummings* [[1948] 1 All E.R. 551 (Ct. Crim. App.)], a rape case, said, "Who is to decide whether the complaint is made as speedily as could reasonably be expected? Surely it must be the judge who tries the case. There is no-one else who can decide it." He was of the view that a trial judge has all the facts, and if he applies the right principle and directs his mind to the right question, which is whether or not the prosecutrix did what was reasonable, the court of appeal should not interfere.

In *R* v. *Osborne*, cited above, it was said that "only where . . . a complaint [is] not elicited by questions of a leading and inducing or intimidatory character" is it admissible.[26] But it was pointed out in the same case by Ridley J. (at p. 556), that the mere fact that the complaint is made in answer to questions is not in itself sufficient to render a complaint inadmissible. Certain questions of inquiry by a mother or other person in charge which express natural concern would not render a complaint inadmissible, so long as they were not suggestive or leading,

26 This principle was adopted in *R* v. *Spuzzum* [(1906), 12 C.C.C. 287 (B.C.)], a case of rape.

or pointed to a particular person. In each case, the decision rests on the character of the questions, the circumstances, the relationship between the questioner and the complainant, all of which must be left to the discretion of the deciding judge.[27]

It was stressed in the *Lillyman* and *Osborne* cases that the complaint is evidence not of the facts complained of but only of the consistency of the conduct of the prosecutrix with the story told by her in the witness box and of the absence of consent if consent is material.[28] Lord Hewart C.J., in *R* v. *Evans* [(1924), 18 Cr. App. R. 123], said, "It has been pointed out again and again in these cases that evidence of a complaint by the prosecutrix is not corroboration of the evidence against the prisoner. It entirely lacks the essential quality of coming from an independent quarter."[29] This view has been followed in two rape cases decided in Canada, *R* v. *Reeves* [(1941), 77 C.C.C. 89 (B.C.C.A.)] and *R* v. *Bondy* [(1958), 121 C.C.C. 337 (Ont. C.A.)], and would undoubtedly also apply to cases of indecent assault.

Glanville Williams attacks the reasoning in these cases on the grounds that a jury should be entitled to consider any evidence which is persuasive to show that the charge is not a fabrication. He holds, with reason, that it would be extremely unlikely that a girl who ran to her mother in overpowering distress complaining of a sexual attack and named the defendent as the culprit, would have deliberately falsified the charge by substituting the name of the defendent for the real attacker.

It is reported in the Cambridge Study that one-third of the female children between the ages of 8 and 13 who were involved in cases of indecent assault were in fact consenting, and while it could not be said in some of the remaining 150 cases that there was active consent, it likewise could not be said that there was any active opposition.[30] These findings are disturbing and suggest that we have too little information on how in fact such cases come to the attention of the parents. Who tells? Is it the children involved? Is it other children? Do parents become suspicious and cross-examine the child? How frequently do children go directly to their parents to complain? The answers to these questions may prove valuable to us as we reconsider our rules with respect to complaints as well as corroboration.

27 See *R* v. *Norcotte* (1916), 12 Cr. App. R. 166; *R* v. *Wilbourne* (1917), 12 Cr. App. R. 280; *R* v. *Hunt* [1964] 1 C.C.C. 210 (Ont.).
28 See *R* v. *Christie* (1914), 10 Cr. App. R. 141.
29 The same has been expressed with respect to a complaint in the case of indecent assault on a boy: *R* v. *Coulthread* (1933), 24 Cr. App. R. 44.
30 L. Radzinowicz, ed., *English Studies in Criminal Science*, vol. IX, *Sexual Offences* (London, 1957), p. 413. See also p. 86.

Consent

By definition, the crime of indecent assault involves the absence of the victim's consent and the burden of proving this absence rests on the prosecution.[31] In the exceptional case where, for example, the accused severely beats and chokes a girl into unconsciousness (as in *Cullen* v. *R* [(1949), 94 C.C.C. 337 (S.C.C.)], because of the nature of the attack, the element of consent would not be a defence to the charge and consequently need not be negatived by the prosecution.[32] In *R* v. *Giguire* [(1922), 39 C.C.C. 322 (Alta. App. D.)], where the only evidence of want of consent was that of the girl herself, absolutely denied by the accused, the Alberta Court of Appeal considered the character of the girl, her conduct on the occasion complained of, and her subsequent relations with the accused, before deciding that the circumstances were not such as to justify a finding that she did not consent to what took place.[33] The working upon a girl's passions so as to break down her resistance and induce her to consent does not constitute the offence of indecent assault.[34]

By the operation of section 132 in the Criminal Code, the fact that a person under the age of 14 consented to a sexual encounter is not a defence against the charge of indecent assault. This section has been cited and put into effect in both *Descoteau* v. *R* [(1952), 104 C.C.C. 299 (Que. App. D.)] and *R* v. *Jones* [[1964] 2 C.C.C. 123 (N.S. App. D.)]. In the latter case, Coffin J. said (at p. 128), "No consideration should be given to the question whether the girl consented or did not consent to the actions of the appellant, as s. 132 of the Criminal Code expressly excludes consent as a defence to the charge where the offence is 'in respect of a person under the age of fourteen.'" In *Fairclough* v. *Whipp* [(1951), 35 Cr. App. R. 138] Lord Chief Justice Goddard expressed the opinion (at pp. 139–40) that, "The question of consent or non-consent arises only if there is something which, without consent, would be an assault on the latter." Although there is no doubt

31 *Christopherson* v. *Bare* (1848), 11 Q.B. 473, per Lord Denman C.J.: "It is a manifest contradiction in terms to say that the defendant assaulted the plaintiff with his permission." See also *R* v. *Donovan* [1934] 2 K.B., 498 (Ct. Crim. App.). Laidlaw J.A. in *R* v. *Marion* [(1956), 118 C.C.C. 388 (Ont. C.A.)] at p. 389 confirms that the onus is on the Crown to prove there was "no such [consenting] act by the complainant."
32 See also the decision of Hogg J. in the first appeal: *R* v. *Cullen* (1948), 93 C.C.C. 1 (Ont. C.A.).
33 For what is required in rebuttal, see *R* v. *Hart* (1914), 10 Cr. App. R. 176.
34 *R* v. *Landry* (1935), 64 C.C.C. 104 (N.B. App. D.), per Banter C.J., at p. 105: "If consent was obtained otherwise than by threat or fear of bodily harm then the accused could not be convicted."

that the statutory provision nullifying consent in these cases was a deliberate public policy to afford a kind of absolute protection to young girls, the decisions in the "invitation" cases discussed previously have thrown the issue back to a consideration of the concept of assault. As far back as 1925, the *Report of the Departmental Committee on Sexual Offences against Young Children*, prepared under the chairmanship of J. C. Priestly, pointed to the "serious difficulty" of prosecuting in "invitation" cases, and recommended a change in the law.[35] Lord Goddard, the Lord Chief Justice in the *Fairclough* case (at p. 140), suggested a change which in effect would make "indecent conduct in the presence of a child or in relation to a child" an offence, and again in *R* v. *Burrows* [(1951), 35 Cr. App. R. 180] he said that "It might be a very good thing if Parliament altered the law and made it an offence to invite a child to do an indecent act with a grown person." The Cambridge study made similar recommendations.[36] It seems obvious that the mere nullification of "consent" in these cases has not achieved all that was intended. It should be acknowledged that it has gone a long way to providing the kind of protection which seems desirable, but it can be agreed that only a reformulation of the offence, perhaps along the lines suggested by Lord Goddard, is long overdue.

Sentencing

The presentation of facts in the reported cases is not consistent, and it is difficult because of this to make any worthwhile comments about the attitudes expressed by the courts in sentencing, but it is possible none the less to review the cases in order to show, if there be need to show it yet again, the absence of any uniform principles operating in this area.

In *R* v. *Allen* [(1954), 108 C.C.C. 239 (B.C.C.A.)] and in *R* v. *Underhill* [(1955), 114 C.C.C. 320 (N.B. App. D.)] the accused in each case was sentenced to two years for indecent assault on a young girl, and each appealed sentence. In the former case, the term was reduced to time served (a period of a little over three months) while in the latter case the sentence was confirmed, but it is not possible to compare the cases because of the absence of uniform factual data. In the two following cases the Ontario Court of Appeal raised the sentence to a uniform six months definite and twelve months indeterminate. In *R* v. *Backshall* [(1956), 115 C.C.C. 221 (Ont. C.A.)] the sentence at

35 Departmental Committee on Sexual Offences against Young Children, *Report*, Cmnd. 2561 (London, H.M. Stationery Office, 1925), para. 34.
36 L. Radzinowicz, ed., *Sexual Offences*, p. 415.

trial was twenty-four months' probation, while in *R* v. *Jones* [(1956), 115 C.C.C. 273 (Ont. C.A.)] the original sentence was $150 and costs. In the former case, there were elements of aggression (ripping a child's pants off) and they would have merited, the appeal court said, a penitentiary sentence but for a probation officer's report which gave strong support to the magistrate. In the latter case, three children were involved (approximately the same age as in the *Backshall* case), but no details of the offence are reported. It would appear that the court was struggling for some internal consistency in the sentences handed down, but it seems impossible to judge from the cases as reported whether the facts of the two cases merited a uniform sentence.

Although a single court may operate with some consistency, we are a long way from agreement when one compares sentences in different provinces. In *R* v. *Langley* [(1927), 48 C.C.C. 293 (N.B. App. D.)] the original charge was for attempted carnal knowledge of a girl under 14, reduced to indecent assault, and in *R* v. *McLean* [(1931), 57 C.C.C. 239 (N.S.)] the accused was charged with both of these offences but convicted only of the latter. In the *McLean* case, the accused was given a suspended sentence for two years, while in the *Langley* case he was sentenced to two years and it was also ordered that he be given ten lashes at the end of the first year.

In *R* v. *Robertson* [(1946), 86 C.C.C. 353 (Ont. C.A.)] a sentence of fifteen months definite and six months indeterminate was raised to two years, where the case disclosed that there had been sadistic treatment of the female person involved. In *R* v. *Marr* [(1955), 114 C.C.C. 318 (N.B. App. D.)] a 19-year-old had admitted wanting sexual intercourse with a woman of 30, but the charge of rape was not proven and a conviction for indecent assault was registered. He was sentenced to eighteen months. The appeal court which confirmed the sentence noted that the maximum sentence for this offence had recently been raised from two years to five years and took from this that "indecent assault" should be regarded more seriously than previously. But it might well be asked whether in raising the maximum sentence the legislators had in mind this kind of indecent assault or rather cases involving children or adolescent girls; or did they consider all the different kinds of indecent assault and decide no distinction should be made? Or is it possible that they did not consider the various kinds of indecent assault at all, and raised the maximum penalty in the abstract, as it were, leaving it up to the courts to make out of the change what they would? As can be seen from the review of the legislation, no discussion of this increased penalty appears anywhere on the public record. One is left to wonder what information, if any, was available to the legislators when the increased penalty was decided on.

The case of *R* v. *Allen*, cited above, gives a rather full account of the steps taken and the consideration given to sentencing by the British Columbia Court of Appeal in a case of pedophilia. The accused was sentenced to two years in penitentiary rather than the provincial reformatory (Oakalla Prison Farm) because, as the trial judge explained, he was informed that there was a full-time psychiatrist on the staff of the penitentiary.[37] When the appeal from sentence came before the court, counsel asked the court to grant an adjournment so that Dr. Richmond, Medical Officer at the Oakalla Prison Farm, could examine the prisoner. The doctor reported, in brief, that the possibility of repetition "could be disregarded," that the accused was unlikely to profit from imprisonment, that the public was not in his opinion in further danger from this individual, and that the sentence should be reduced on condition that the accused agree to place himself under the advice of a psychiatrist or to be admitted to the Crease Clinic for a course of psychotherapy. The doctor went on to say that the prisoner's health was satisfactory, that he had a history of duodenal ulcer, and that "he wet his bed until he was 10 years old." Regrettably, the doctor did not say how the court should make use of this last piece of information.

The court then sent the prisoner to the Crease Clinic for a two-month period, resolving to determine what course to follow after that time. The clinic reported in due course, saying, "We do not consider that he is a true sexual deviate in that he had not exhibited a pattern of sexually disturbed behaviour," and adding that institutional care either in prison or in mental hospital would be of no particular benefit, that supportive help could be given by a psychiatrist or social service worker on an outpatient basis, and that a recurrence of past behaviour was extremely unlikely.

37 This reasoning shows signs of developing into one of our national correctional myths. Although at the moment there are no statistics available to show how frequently offenders are sent to prison with a recommendation that they receive psychiatric treatment, nor are there figures available to show how often such treatment is in fact given, there seems to be a general expectation that because there are psychiatrists on the staff in some institutions, an offender sent to one of these institutions will receive psychiatric help. In actual fact it is doubtful whether the amount of psychiatric services available at present makes it possible to cope with anything more than the emergency cases as they arise within the prison. In the absence of follow-up studies it is impossible to make any claims for or against the efficacy of psychiatric intervention in correctional institutions, and we are still far from establishing research as a built-in component in service operations.

The court of appeal accepted these reports, for they were uncontradicted by anything offered by the crown. O'Halloran J.A., in giving the judgment of the court, said (at p. 243),

The Court therefore cannot be blind to the clear implication that (a) there is every rational ground to believe that if the appellant does not remain in prison any tendential sexual aberrations towards young girls will most likely be disciplined and cured; but (b) if he goes to prison to serve the maximum sentence intended for acts of a more serious nature than he committed, then the likelihood is he will emerge from prison uncured, embittered, and more likely to be a greater (and certainly no less) danger to young girls and to the community at large than he was when convicted.

The court made special note of the fact that the accused was "not a true sexual deviate" and said that had the report been to the contrary, or neutral or silent or doubtful in this respect, or had it been effectively challenged in any substantial element, the court would have been confronted with an entirely different situation from the one in which it found itself. Bearing in mind the rehabilitation of the accused, the deterrence of this type of crime, and the protection of the public, the court unanimously agreed to reduce sentence to the time spent in jail "as the interest of justice demanded." The decision also noted that the counsel for the accused had informed the court that the appellant recognized the urgency of continuing regular psychiatric treatment and also that the opportunity for so doing was readily available to him.

I have no quarrel with the decision. On the few facts available it appears to be a sensible one. On the surface the case appears to be a sincere effort to arrive at a rational solution to a perplexing problem for the court. My objection is that the court was led along the right path on the basis of expert opinion that, although apparently not challenged, was certainly open to challenge.

On what grounds can a doctor base an opinion that the possibility of repetition "could be disregarded"? The possibility might be low or high, and heterosexual pedophiles as a group are now known to have a low recidivist rate,[38] but in no event can it be disregarded. The accused, said Dr. Richmond, was unlikely to profit from imprisonment, but he could have cited no studies showing that pedophiles did or did not profit from imprisonment or that the results of punishment were better or worse than with other kinds of offenders. In the doctor's opinion the public was not in further danger from this individual, but surely the doctor must have known that no individual is predictable and the most he could have said was that offenders *of this kind* rarely cause further

38 Mohr, *et al.*, *Pedophilia*, 99; compare L. Radzinowicz, *Sexual Offences*, pp. 267 *et seq.*

danger to the community. The information about bed-wetting may be of some esoteric interest but what could a court of appeal be expected *to do* with it and what does it have to do with the problem at hand, standing as bald and uninterpreted as that? Of the Crease Clinic, which reported as a group, it might have been asked, When is a deviate a "true deviate," for in this case three other young girls were involved, and how many acts are required to make a "deviate," and is it the number of acts or the length of time over which they occur which determines a "true deviate"?

The court of appeal took great care in processing this particular case, but there can be no doubt that if this pattern of proceeding were undertaken in every case involving indecent assaults on young girls, all of our mental health facilities could not possibly bear the strain. It is one of the tragic facts of our country that there are not enough mental hospitals, clinics, and psychiatrists available to treat the mentally ill, and it is folly to imagine that we could undertake to provide diagnostic or treatment facilities for all of the sex offenders alone. If the court of appeal felt that the interests of justice demanded a reduction of sentence in this case, does not the same interest of justice demand the same attention and the same treatment in every case of the same kind? Yet such attention is demonstrably impossible. It may not be necessary. It can be granted without question that each case involves a unique individual and that there are unique characteristics, but at the same time there are common characteristics, common features, common circumstances which can be kept track of. Since we will never be in a position to undertake the procedure followed by the court of appeal in every case of this kind before the courts, we are in fact able, if we wish to be of practical assistance to the courts, only to inform them on the common characteristic features found in groups of identifiably similar cases. I doubt that we can feasibly do more than report to the courts what would be the probable result if one form of disposition rather than another is used in relation to persons who can be classed in specified groups. What is to be deplored is that in contrast to medicine, which keeps track of individual cases to learn more about specific disease entities and the probable response to particular forms of treatment, we have not yet learned to do anything remotely similar in the criminal field. We will dissect a point touching on corroboration, for example, with great care, and we have quite properly invested much effort in these and similar problems over the years, becoming more or less skilled and sophisticated at matters of adjudication. Yet, once having made the decision on the question of guilt; we seem to be strangely fumbling and crude and uncertain in the area of sentencing.

Indecent Assault Male

148. Every male person who assaults another person with intent to commit buggery or who indecently assaults another male person is guilty of an indictable offence and is liable to imprisonment for ten years and to be whipped.

The offence of indecent assault male is dealt with under this part rather than with the other homosexual offences because the term "indecent assault" has the same meaning as in the offence of indecent assault female, and many of the problems which arise, such as corroboration and complaint, are exactly the same whether female or male children are involved. It will not be necessary therefore to repeat the entire arguments, but cases which deal with the same problem except that they involve males will be given to demonstrate the application of the same principles.

In *R* v. *Horn* [(1923), 40 C.C.C. 117 (Alta. App. D.)], previously discussed under gross indecency, the accused was convicted of indecent assault on a 4-year-old boy. Although the evidence of the boy was not admissible because of his tender years, in his statement to the police the accused said, "I stopped the car and was feeling bad and took out my penis. I tried to kiss the kid but he jerked his head away." In reaching his decision, Stuart J. (at p. 122) quotes Archbold on *Pleading* (p. 930): " 'An assault includes an attempt to commit a battery,' and a battery 'includes every touching or laying hold (however trifling) of another's person or clothes in an angry, revengeful, rude, insolent or hostile manner (cites 1 Hawk. P.C. ch. 15, s. 2).' " He went on to say,

There is no doubt that this is the law. And when a man confesses to having first taken out his own private organ and then attempted to kiss the child I think there can be no doubt of the rude and insolent manner of the attempt to touch the child's person. It was certainly an attempt to commit a battery which constitutes in law an assault. And it was accompanied by the act of indecency.

In *Beal* v. *Kelley* [(1951), 35 Cr. App. R. 128 (Div. Ct. Cas.)] the accused exposed his penis to a 14-year-old boy and asked the boy to handle it. The boy refused and the accused grabbed hold of the boy's arm and pulled him towards himself and then released him. Lord Goddard C.J. found in the latter act the assault, the hostile act, because the act was against the boy's will and it did not matter that he could not give consent.

In *R* v. *Burrows* [(1951) 35 Cr. App. R. 180] it was alleged that the accused exposed his genitals to a 14-year-old boy and asked him to masturbate him, and the boy testified that the accused had tried to touch his (the boy's) private parts. The trial judge had directed the jury that if either allegation were proved, they could find the accused guilty, which they did. The Court of Criminal Appeal, however, allowed the appeal on the ground that the direction to the jury was wrong. If it were proven that the man had tried to touch the boy, this would have been indecent assault, but the invitation to the boy to touch the accused did not constitute an assault. In the absence of an hostile act against the boy, the accused should not have been convicted of indecent assault. The latter case presents the same problem of the "invitation" cases discussed earlier, and the comments made there regarding the difficulty these cases raise have equal validity here.

Corroboration

The offence of indecent assault male is not included under section 131(1) of the Criminal Code as one of the offences which requires corroboration. Nor is it included under section 134, which requires a warning to be given to a jury regarding the danger of convicting on the uncorroborated testimony of the complainant. It is nevertheless the practice to give warnings in cases involving accomplices, and reference is made to the earlier discussion under the section on buggery.[39] When the evidence against the accused is given by a child of tender years who is not sworn, then by the operation of section 566 of the Code the evidence of the child must be corroborated in a material particular by evidence which implicates the accused.

In *R* v. *Silverstone* [(1934), 61 C.C.C. 258 (Ont. C.A.)] evidence was received under section 16 of the Canada Evidence Act from two children of tender years in corroboration of the testimony given by a 9-year-old boy. Evidence was also received from a medical man, which established that an assault of the kind described by the boy had been committed, but nothing more. The conviction was quashed on the grounds that the unsworn testimony of the two boys could not serve to corroborate the complainant's story, nor was their testimony corroborated in any material respect. The evidence of the doctor as to the fact that the offence had been committed by someone did not "implicate the accused" and so could not be treated as providing the corroboration required.

In *R* v. *Iman Din* [(1910), 18 C.C.C. 82 (B.C.C.A.)] the evidence

---

39 For a critical examination of the rule see Glanville Williams, "Corroboration – Accomplices," 1962 Crim. L.R. 588.

of an 11-year-old boy was taken but the boy was not sworn. The question arose as to whether there was or was not corroboration of the boy's story as required by section 16(2) of the Canada Evidence Act. Two judges, accepting the discrepancies, found corroboration in the unsworn testimony given by a 6-year-old brother, while two others did not, and a new trial was ordered. The position taken by the judges in this case, which was to treat the unsworn evidence of one child as corroborative of the unsworn testimony of another, was contrary to the authorities already discussed, and subsequently in *R* v. *McInulty* [(1914), 22 C.C.C. 347 (B.C.C.A.)][40] the court withdrew from this position.

Complaints

In *R* v. *Camelleri* [(1922), 16 Cr. App. R. 163], discussed earlier under the section on buggery, it was held that the admissibility of complaints which applies in cases involving females also applies in cases involving males. In *R* v. *Lebrun* [(1951), 100 C.C.C. 16 (Ont. C.A.)] Bowlby J.A. stated (at p. 24), "The rule laid down by Lord Hewart C.J. in the *Camelleri* case should be accepted as the law of Canada, with a query as to the age limit of the complainant." The case provides a thorough review of many of the issues raised with respect to the evidence of complaint. In regard to complaints having been elicited by questions of a leading, inducing, or intimidating character, Bowlby J. said (at p. 24):

. . . the Court should not, in my opinion, invoke the well-known principles which are considered when deciding as to the admission or rejection of a confession made by a prisoner. Questions which tend only to elicit the truth from a person who has been sexually assaulted are not objectionable. Questions, however, which are suggestive of the illegal acts or which tend to induce such person to accuse a man, or intimidate such a person into accusing a man, are objectionable and a complaint made as a result of such questions should not be admitted.

The question of admissibility is one of law; Mr. Justice Bowlby warned judges, magistrates, and crown attorneys to be alert in cases of this kind to see that there was no ground for suspecting the good faith of mothers or others putting forward a charge. "The possibility of inciting a child or other person to make such a charge must be ever jealously guarded against." The court should not admit evidence of the complaint until satisfied that it was made at the first opportunity which reasonably presented itself and not one subsequent to and separate and distinct from the first complaint made. It was stressed again that such evidence

40 See also *Paige* v. *R* (1948), 92 C.C.C. 32 (S.C.C.).

did not in the slightest degree corroborate the complainant as to the facts charged, but was to be used merely to assist in determining whether or not the complainant was a creditable witness. Because such testimony only applied to credibility, it was improper to adduce such evidence before the complainant had given his testimony.[41]

Statements Made in the Presence and Hearing of the Accused

Evidence of a statement made in the presence and hearing of an accused may be given for the purpose of showing the conduct or the demeanour of the accused on hearing it. It was said in *R* v. *Christie* [(1914), 10 Cr. App. R. 141 (H.L.)][42] that a statement made under such circumstances, even where one would expect a strong denial, is not proof of the facts stated, except in so far as he accepts the statements so as to make them in effect his own. If he accepts only part of the statement, then only to that extent does it become his statement. Acceptance may be shown by word, conduct, action, or demeanour at the time the statement was made, and it is to these that a jury must look to determine whether or not there was acceptance of the whole or a part. A mere denial does not render a statement inadmissible, because the accused may deny it in such a way and under such circumstances as may lead a jury to disbelieve him, and a denial of this sort may constitute evidence from which acknowledgment may be inferred. Where the accused denies the truth of a statement the trial judge should indicate his opinion to counsel that, although admissible, such a statement would have little weight or value and might unfairly prejudice the jury against the accused. A jury should also be warned that unless they find that there was acknowledgment they ought to disregard the statement.

Similar Acts

In *Makin* v. *Att.-Gen. for New South Wales* [[1894] A.C. 57][43] Lord Herschell L.C. stated (at p. 65), "It is undoubtedly not competent for the prosecution to adduce evidence tending to show that the accused has been guilty of criminal acts other than those covered by the indictment, for the purpose of leading to the conclusion that the accused is a person likely from his criminal conduct or character to have committed the offence for which he was tried." But this evidence is admissible when it is relevant to a question before the jury, for example, when it bears on the question of whether the acts charged in the indictment were designed

41 Cases cited are *R* v. *Guttridges* (1840), 173 Eng. Rep. 916 (Worcester Assizes, 1840), and *R* v. *Lillyman* (1896), 18 Cox C.C. 346 (Cr. Cas. Res.).
42 See L. Radzinowicz, ed., *Sexual Offences*, p. 383.
43 See also *R* v. *Harris* (1952), 36 Cr. App. R. 39 at p. 52.

or accidental. The mere fact that the evidence tends to show another offence does not in itself make it inadmissible. In *R* v. *Iman Din*, cited above, the trial judge admitted evidence of a similar act on another boy, "as it tended to show the nature of the accused." This evidence was held by all of the judges of the court of appeal to be clearly inadmissible, and a new trial was ordered.[44]

In *R* v. *Boynton* [(1934), 63 C.C.C. 95 (Ont. C.A.)], a case of gross indecency, evidence had been adduced at trial that the accused had committed two precisely similar offences with other men, one two days before and the other earlier. Middleton J.A., delivering the judgment of the court, said (at p. 96):

We are of the opinion that the evidence was not properly admitted. It was in no way relevant to any issue before the Court. It is not the case of an ambiguous act which might be innocent or guilty according to the intent. Nor is it a case of identity. The only matter in dispute is the commission of the very act charged. The witness, "the other male person," asserted the act, the prisoner denied it. To admit this evidence would be admitting evidence to show that the accused was a man of evil disposition and likely to commit the crime charged against him and therefore [the evidence] was not properly admitted.[45]

There are many cases where evidence of specific acts or circumstances which connect the accused with particular features of the crime has been held admissible even though it also tends to show him to be of a bad disposition. The issue in these cases as reviewed in *R* v. *Sims* [(1946), 31 Cr. App. R. 158)], involves: the identity of the accused,[46] the nature of the act done by the accused with or to another person,[47] or whether the acts charged in the indictment were designed or accidental; but in the latter instance, as *R* v. *Cole* [(1941), 28 Cr. App. R. 43] shows, it should not be introduced where counsel has made it abundantly clear that the defence does not intend to raise the defence of accident or mistake.[48]

In *R* v. *Cline* [(1956), 115 C.C.C. 18 (Ont. C.A.)] the facts showed that the accused, disguised in dark glasses, had stopped a small boy and asked him to carry his suitcase. When the boy ran away, the man pursued him, caught him, and then let him go after telling him to tell no one what had happened. The court held that the evidence of similar

44 See in particular the judgment of Macdonald C.J.A. at p. 89.
45 Middleton J. cites *R* v. *Shellaker* [1914] 1 K.B., 414 (Ct. Crim. App.).
46 *Thompson* v. *R* (1917), 13 Cr. App. R. 61 (H.L.).
47 *D.P.P.* v. *Ball* (1911), 6 Cr. App. R. 31 (H.L.).
48 See L. Radzinowicz, ed., *Sexual Offences*, pp. 386 *et seq.* for a discussion of the applications of this rule in a variety of different offences.

acts done by the accused, either prior to the offence charged or after-
wards if such acts were not too remote in time, was admissible to show
a pattern of conduct and establish the criminal intent where the acts
complained of were either innocent or equivocal as in the instant case.
The court was also of the opinion that in such cases the prosecution may
advance such evidence in the first instance without waiting for the
accused to set up a specific defence calling for rebuttal.[49] The court set
aside the conviction of indecent assault and substituted a conviction for
attempt indecent assault.[50]

Some idea of the importance of these offences can be had if one considers that the Cambridge study reports that "Eighty per cent of the
victims of indictable offences were involved in indecent assaults, the
vast majority of all indictable sexual offences being indecent assaults of
one sort or another."[51] Of the 1,178 victims of indictable offences
studied, seven out of ten were children under 14 years of age.[52] In the
Metropolitan Toronto study[53] referred to earlier, 41.5 per cent of all
sexual offences, indictable and non-indictable, were cases of indecent
assault female, and a further 7.7 per cent were indecent assault male. It
bears repeating that over 90 per cent of the latter involved boys under
the age of 15, and 50 per cent of the females in the former category
were under the age of 12. It is impossible to escape the conclusion that
children under the age of 14 are predominantly involved in these
offences. It is these cases which are of special concern to us here.

One striking difference which can be seen between cases of indecent
assault female and those of indecent assault male is that the former is
used to cover a wide variety of situations, in terms of both the kinds of
acts involved and the ages of the victims. This variety does not appear
in the cases of indecent assault male. One cannot but become aware that
in the offence of indecent assault female we are confronted not with a
single phenomenon but with a cluster of various kinds of acts which I
submit are prescribed by the statute for a variety of reasons. They can
be grouped as follows: assaults which occur in the pursuit of sexual
intercourse with adult females, prescribed because of the use of force;

49 This same view is expressed by Viscount Simon in *R* v. *Harris*, cited above,
at pp. 53, 54.
50 The court sets out a series of propositions relating to the law of attempts and
to the evidence necessary and admissible to establish the offence.
51 L. Radzinowicz, ed., *Sexual Offences*, p. 110.
52 *Ibid.*, p. 365.
53 J. W. Mohr and A. K. Gigeroff, "A Study of Male Sexual Offenders Charged
in Court over a Twelve Month Period: Report on the Development of the Study
with an Inventory of the Data Collected and Basic Analysis" (Forensic Clinic,
Toronto Psychiatric Hospital, May 1964, mimeographed).

assaults in the pursuit of sexual intercourse with a person in one of the protected age groups, prescribed partly because of the use of force and partly in defence of chastity; assaults, often in pursuit of sexual intercourse, which result in physical harm to children, prescribed because of the personal harm to the child and to protect the child against physically damaging sexual attacks; assaults against female children by their own fathers, prescribed because of the incest taboo; and lastly, assaults against children where there is no attempt at sexual intercourse, no physical harm done, but where immature acts of fondling and touching are usually involved: this is prescribed because of a social taboo against the premature sexual activity of children especially with persons who are outside of the child's peer group, and particularly because it is feared to be a preliminary step to intercourse with the child.

Most of the offences which occur fall within this latter category. The Cambridge study reports that in a large majority – 91 per cent – of offences against 1,994 victims (1,370 of whom were females), no physical consequences resulted from the sexual misbehaviour involved. The report says that this was "largely due to the fact that most of the indecencies were of a minor nature and in many there was *de facto* consent by the victims involved."[54]

It is against this background that we can begin to understand the importance of some of the decisions made in the case law. The decisions in *Fairclough* v. *Whipp*, *D.P.P.* v. *Rogers*, and *R* v. *Burrows* suggest that it is now necessary to show some hostile act or threat in the "invitation" cases, and where the evidence shows no more than an invitation by the accused to the victim to manipulate him, no charge of indecent assault can be supported. The statutory provision withdrawing the defence of consent where the victim is under 14 cannot operate until an "assault" is first proven. The fact that the child accedes to the request of the accused does not, in my view, make the behaviour of the accused less reprehensible, but the construction of the offence, based as it is on "assault," is inadequate to meet these cases. Although the number of cases which can be classed as "invitation" cases is small, nevertheless, as the Departmental Committee on Sexual Offences against Young Persons suggested, "These cases are of a serious nature, and it is not right that there should be any ambiguity about the possibility of prosecuting these offences against girls as well as against boys."[55]

54 L. Radzinowicz, ed., *Sexual Offences*, p. 104. Four in ten of the victims of indictable offences were not actively resisting, resenting, or objecting to the indecencies which occurred.

55 Departmental Committee on Sexual Offences against Young Children, *Report*, para. 34. These statements were made 25 years before the line of cases cited above.

In the *Gee Poy, Gemmil*, and *Hober* cases, the court was looking for corroborative evidence that the indecent assault had occurred, but as the Cambridge study demonstrates, in the vast majority of cases there were no physical consequences. Unless future cases follow the *Millar* and *Childs* cases in stating that corroborative evidence can be found in the suspicious circumstances, the approach taken in the *Gee Poy* case could have equally unsatisfactory results in any other cases in which no physical consequences can be shown.

The difficulty of providing corroboration of the unsworn testimony of a child as required by the Code at present is one of the most important problems in this area. There have been a number of recommendations put forward to allow the unsworn evidence of a child to be corroborated in some circumstances by the unsworn evidence of another child or children.[56] Similarly, as pointed out earlier, Glanville Williams also questions the reasoning behind the rule which holds that complaint to a parent can not be used as corroboration in certain cases. The whole issue of the meaningfulness of the oath, and whether too much reliance is placed on it alone to decide the question of the reliability of children's testimony, needs re-examination, but I am not prepared to enter into this argument here.

A consideration of the case law together with the empirical information available leads one to the firm conclusion that there is good and sufficient ground for separating the offences against children from those against adolescents and adults, and that the long-standing formulation based on the concept of indecent assault is no longer adequate or appropriate in the light of our growing information about these offences.

One of the strongest impressions which remain after a review such as this is that the case law is initially limited in its usefulness to the reformer by the very function it serves, which is in part to clarify the legislation as it already exists. However much it may attempt to raise principles for use in future cases, these of necessity are developed in relation to the existing law. Seldom does a court directly suggest changes, for this is not the court's function. In referring back to previous decisions to support a decision taken or to answer an argument raised by counsel, one cannot but be impressed by the enormous effort that has been expended to consolidate and purify the law as it stands.

One of the difficulties which the case law presents as subject matter for research, especially perhaps in this area, is that there is no systematic reporting of facts, and very often they are only meagerly reported if at

56 Glanville Williams, "The Proof of Guilt," 1955 Crim. L.R. 1236.

all. With all deference to the bench, however much it may be "disagreeable to discuss" or seem that "no useful purpose can be served in reviewing the sordid details," the absence of facts on the records drastically reduces the usefulness of cases for research. (One can hardly imagine a medical journal having much meaning if doctors, for whatever reason, did not describe what they were treating, but gave only the reasons for their decisions.) Consequently, much vital basic information, such as what act was involved, is missing.

Since one cannot use the case law to establish a range of cases, partly because of the drastic prior selection which has been made, partly because the factual situations are frequently not reported, it is impossible to gain any clear impression of the law in operation. Even where the facts are fully reported, there is no way of knowing whether the case described is a typical one or not. It is impossible to determine how frequently the type of situation described in the case occurs, that is, whether it represents a large social problem or a very special isolated one. Where the facts are fully reported, one can see only one example of how the law has been used to cover a particular situation. The case law does not admit of any quantitive breakdown.

Much of the case law in this area is devoted to a discussion of evidentiary and procedural problems involved in the cases, and it would appear to be most valuable in this regard. Many of the evidentiary problems which arise go beyond the subject matter of these cases, of course, and should be considered in the light of their wider application.

It might well be raised in objection to the statements made here that it is ridiculous to expect the case law to serve a function it was never designed to fulfil, and that it is pointless to attempt to extract from it the kind of information which it cannot possibly give. There can be no disagreement to either proposition, but the objection merely emphasizes the main argument made here. It seems obvious that to get some of the information which would be useful for reform, it is necessary to reach deeper towards the everyday decisions of the courts and not be satisfied only with the reported decisions.

Each case is essentially involved in reaching a decision with regard to the particular facts before the court. Criminal law reform must, on the other hand, be concerned with a dimension of the problem which is more than the individual case. It cannot look at each reported case as an isolated and unrelated event, and any attempt to reconstruct the criminal law on this basis alone would be an unrewarding one. We must view reported cases as an indication of possible patterns of crimes in the community, without relying on them alone for our conclusions, for they cannot tell us in detail what the patterns are. To establish these patterns, it is vital to "marshal the facts." Lawyers are familiar with this process in individual cases, but what the reformer needs to learn and undertake is the "marshalling of facts" across a range of similar cases. The cases which daily flow through the trial courts can be made to serve as a reservoir to provide a body of abundant, readily available resource material.

4

Analysing and Structuring Factual Data:
Gross Indecency as an Example

The Dominion Bureau of Statistics reported that in 1961, 384 persons were convicted under the category of "buggery or bestiality, gross indecency."[1] Setting aside all questions of whether or not these statistics are complete, one is immediately confronted with the problem of how many of these 384 convictions can be assigned to each category. Regardless of what other breakdown is given, whether with respect to age, occupation, educational level, marital status, place of crime, or sentence, the statistic is of little use because one does not know in the first place such basic information as whether these offences were committed against males, females, adults, adolescents, children, animals, or other living creatures.

It becomes obvious that to organize information in a more meaningful way it is necessary to begin with much smaller groupings. It is the aim of this part to examine the single offence of gross indecency as an illustration of a method for structuring factual data. The object in doing so is to come to a better understanding of what is involved in the offence and how this section is being used by the courts.

The raw data used herein was gathered at the Forensic Clinic, Toronto Psychiatric Hospital, in a research project, "A Study of Male Sexual Offenders Charged in Court over a Twelve Month Period."[2]

1 Dominion Bureau of Statistics, "Statistics of Criminal and Other Offences," *Annual Report*, 1961, p. 52.
2 J. W. Mohr and A. K. Gigeroff, "A Study of Male Sexual Offenders Charged in Court over a Twelve Month Period: Report on the Development of the Study with an Inventory of the Data Collected and Basic Analysis" (Forensic Clinic, Toronto Psychiatric Hospital, May 1964, mimeographed).

Gathering Information

The study referred to above was designed to gather information on every person charged with any one of fourteen sexual offences in the Metropolitan Toronto courts. Court calendars were received daily from each of the magistrates' courts of Metropolitan Toronto, and all of the appropriate cases under the charges enumerated were selected. On all cases, the Metropolitan Toronto Police provided photostat copies of the offence report, together with a copy of the criminal record; the courts provided information on the nature of the proceedings, the presiding magistrate, and the dispositions. (Other information was gathered through a series of interviews with some of the accused persons, but it is not relevant to the present discussion.) The collection of cases was started on November 1, 1961, and completed on October 31, 1962.

There were 597 persons in the study population, 75 of whom had multiple charges so that the total number of offences covered was 715. Of the total population, 72 persons, or 12 per cent, were charged with a total of 82 offences of gross indecency. A number of charges were withdrawn, and others dismissed so that the net total of persons convicted was 60, or roughly speaking four out of every five persons who were originally charged. These 60 were convicted of a total of 68 charges. It is with respect to the convicted group that the following breakdown is made.

Analysis of Cases

A list of the 68 cases was made, on which was noted a selection of elementary data such as the age of the offender, the act which took place, the place where the act occurred, and what other person was involved, avoiding for the moment the designation of "victim." All of the facts taken for consideration were objective and did not involve any of the information which had been obtained from interviews with the accused persons after their conviction. The approach taken was to divide the cases in ways which readily suggested themselves; for example, those which involved acts between adult males were separated from those involving heterosexual partners, and those which involved adults only were separated from those which involved adolescents or children.[1]

1 For a full example of the methodology used in a phenomenological analysis see J. W. Mohr, R. E. Turner, and M. B. Jerry, *Pedophilia and Exhibitionism* (Toronto, 1964). For a consideration of the theoretical problems in this area, see J. W. Mohr, "Terminology and Nosology: A Central Problem in Research of Criminal Phenomena," *Canadian Journal of Corrections*, vol. 5, no. 4, 1963; "Notes on the Development of an Empirical Basis for Criminal Legislation," *Criminal Law Quarterly*, vol. 8, no. 4, 1966; "Towards Phenomenological Models of Criminal Transactions: Actus Reus Reconsidered," Fifth International Criminological Congress, Montreal, August 1965.

Cases Involving Adult Male Partners

Of the 68 cases, 30 resulted from 15 transactions in which both parties were consenting adult males, both of whom were charged and convicted. In ten instances, the acts had taken place in public washrooms situated in a public building or a restaurant; in three cases, the events occurred in a park; one took place in a jail cell, and the remaining one in a parked car near a parkway. A breakdown of the 15 events showed six acts of fellatio, three of mutual masturbation, one of mutual masturbation and fellatio, and one of masturbation.[2] In the remaining case, which occurred at 6:00 A.M. in a parked car, one man was lying on top of the other, both had the front of their pants open, and, as the police report stated, they were "trying to have sexual intercourse" with each other.

These cases represent 50 per cent of the persons charged with this offence, and about 44 per cent of the total number of convictions registered. The cases were alike in that (a) with one exception, the jail cell, the acts occurred in a public place, (b) the same kind of act was involved in each, and (c) the parties were consenting adult males.

There was one case in which, though two parties were charged, both adults, only one was convicted. The place was a public park and the nature of the act was the same as in the other cases. In three cases, only one of the parties was apprehended and convicted (the other party escaped and consequently no information on him is available). The nature of the act in each case was the same, fellatio; in two cases the acts occurred in parks, and in one, in a public washroom.

Cases Involving Male Persons between 14 and 21

Nine adults were charged with a total of 16 offences; of these, seven were for single offences, one was for two offences, and the remaining accused had seven convictions. In five of the cases, the younger person was also charged and convicted, and in one unusual case, discussed at the end of this section, only the youth was charged and convicted.

2 The term "masturbation" in this context refers to the manual handling and touching of one person's genitals by another person.

These cases can be divided into two groups, those in which the youth was between 19 and 21, and those which involved adolescents between 14 and 18. In the former group, there were three cases in which both parties were charged and convicted. The events appeared to be the same as those between consenting adults discussed above. The ages of the parties were 23 and 20, 24 and 20, and 35 and 19; the acts were mutual fellatio, mutual masturbation and fellatio; the places where the act was committed were a truck parked in a field, a park, and the rear of a theatre. These cases might well be seen as forming part of the same group as those involving consenting adult partners, discussed above.

In the cases involving youths between 14 and 18, six adults were convicted of a total number of 13 offences, and two of the younger persons were also convicted. One person, aged 29, was convicted of seven charges, and two youths involved with him, aged 17 and 16, were also convicted. In the remaining five cases, the age of the younger person was as follows: two at 17, and one each at 14, 15, and 16. In all of these cases, the older man had given something to the youths, usually money but in one case cigarettes. The act had been repeated numerous times in three of the cases. One man, aged 39, was convicted of two charges for acts committed with two 17-year-olds. In the remaining four cases, the ages of the boys were 14, 15, 16, and 17, and in the latter case there had been numerous occurrences. The acts in all cases involving youths between 14 and 18 were reported as fellatio committed by the older on the younger person.

What is significantly different in these cases is the place where the offence occurred; in ten cases, it was the residence of the older man, in one in a motel room, in one at a drive-in theatre, and in the remaining case, involving the 14-year-old boy, in a public washroom.

In the one case where the adolescent was charged but not the adult, the facts are most unusual. The boy of 18 and the man of 25 walked voluntarily into a police station where the boy told the police he had allowed the older man to commit fellatio on him on the promise of being paid $5.00. He claimed the man would not pay him after this, unless he performed the same act on the older man. The adult denied the story. The youth claimed that the act had occurred in a parked car in a parking lot. The youth was convicted, while the adult was not charged.

Up to this point, we have discussed a total of 56 convictions registered against 49 persons. The remaining 11 persons were convicted of 12 offences. These cases do not admit of any large grouping.

Cases Involving Heterosexual Adult Partners

There were four persons convicted who fall under this grouping, three males and one female.

In two cases, only the male person was convicted of the offence. One case involving a 52-year-old man and the second a 25-year-old. In both cases, the male persons, while in their cars downtown at night, were approached by females who were being watched by the police for soliciting as prostitutes (one female was a known prostitute). In each case, the woman got into the car and the party drove to a parking lot. The acts in both cases involved fellatio.

In the remaining case, both male and female were convicted. The male, aged 24, and a female companion, aged 26, had been observed on a public beach in the middle of the afternoon, where the female performed fellatio.

Cases Involving Children

Three cases can be grouped under this category. In one, a 16-year-old boy was convicted of two charges, both involving a 5-year-old girl, his cousin, in her own home. The boy, on two separate occasions, placed his penis between the girl's legs and at one point forced her head down to his genitals, almost choking her in the process. Although from the age of the parties this appears to be a heterosexual pedophilic act, the attempt at intercourse and the elements of violence suggest a more serious deviation.

In the second case, a 27-year-old male involved an 8-year-old boy by committing fellatio on him and paying him ten cents. The act took place in some bushes at Riverdale Park, Toronto. This is classifiable as a homosexual pedophilic act.

In the remaining case, a 39-year-old male walked into the kitchen of a home, exposed himself and masturbated in front of a 10-year-old girl. On the facts available, it would appear to be more in the nature of an exhibitionistic act than one of pedophilia. There is no indication that the child played any other part than that of spectator.

Other Cases

Three men, aged 23, 21, and 18, were convicted of gross indecency. They had offered a 16-year-old girl $150.00 to pose for nude pictures. They drove to the home of one of the males, and while one of them took pictures the girl posed with the others in various positions including "putting their face to her privates" (cunnilingus). The girl was not convicted.

In the final case, a 32-year-old male was convicted of gross indecency after police searched his room and found a large quantity of obscene pictures. Two photographs revealed the accused committing fellatio on an unidentified male.

Summary

In 60 cases involving persons convicted of gross indecency, the breakdown into the various divisions is as follows:

	n	%
Cases involving adult males*	40	66.7
Cases involving persons between 14 and 18		
adults	6	10
adolescents	3	5
Cases involving children	3	5
Cases involving heterosexual adults		
males	3	5
females	1	1.6
Others	4	6.6
	60	100.0

*Included in this category are those cases where three participants were aged 20, 20 and 19. "Adult," as used here, means over 18.

Using this basic structure, it is possible to build up other useful information systematically. For example, the ages of the parties under the first group distribute themselves as follows:

	n	%
18–20*	3	7.5
21–24	6	15
25–29	8	20
30–34	6	15
35–39	9	22.5
40–44	4	10
45–49	1	2.5
50–54	1	2.5
55–59	—	—
60 plus†	2	5
	40	100.0

*This category covers only 3 years.
†Specific ages are 75 and 71.

If a criminal category shared the same degree of homogeneity as the cases herein, it would be possible to extract this kind of information periodically to determine whether the ages of persons becoming involved in this offence remained the same, decreased, or increased.

Similar constructions can be made with respect to the adults who become involved with adolescents, or to the adolescent "victims" themselves. It is possible also to structure information as to the dispositions handed down by the various courts.

Without repeating the details here, we may recall with what difficulty this section was discussed by members of parliament and by the Senate Banking and Commerce Committee in 1952, when the Criminal Code was being revised (Senator Roebuck, the chairman, asking, "What is Gross Indecency? I don't know, it has never been defined"); by Judge Egbert of the Supreme Court of Alberta, who attempted to give some guidelines in *R* v. *K. and H.*; in the comments of J. Sedgwick and R. E. Megarry; and, finally, by the foreman juror in *R* v. *A.B.* (see Appendix I), who, after listening to a tortured address by a Crown Attorney, asked, "Is there a definition in law as to what constitutes gross indecency?"

That the term "gross indecency" is vague is obvious; the breakdown of cases convicted shows the results. What merit can there be in maintaining an offence phrased and structured in such a way that it covers at the same time a 75-year-old man committing fellatio in a public washroom and a 16-year-old boy who forcibly assaults his 5-year-old cousin in her own home?

It may be argued that the sample given here is a biased one, referring only to the Metropolitan Toronto area and reflecting the policy of the police force there. To some extent this is true, but a consideration of 32 cases covering a four-year period, taken from the files of the Ontario Provincial Police, shows that the tendency throughout the province is, if anything, to include even more pedophilic acts under this offence. Convictions were registered against nine persons for acts committed with thirteen male children (under 14), eight of whom were under 10 years old, and with five female children under 8 years old. If one were to add these cases into the sample already analysed, there undoubtedly would be a shift in the relative sizes of the various categories. But this would not alter the meaning of the categories already established. It would strengthen the pedophilic and also the adolescent (14 to 18) categories, but only slightly, since it must be remembered that the 32 cases covered a four-year period.

In 1961 the Dominion Bureau of Statistics reported 384 convictions for buggery, bestiality, and gross indecency without reporting specifically the number of convictions for each offence. Estimating the number of gross indecency cases in that figure at 300, the sample herein (60 cases) would represent 20 per cent, or one out of every five cases, which is more than sufficient to establish a pattern. The addition of further cases would likely alter the relative groupings slightly in one way or another but the basic distribution would not essentially change. Once the factual data relied upon to determine the groups had been decided, the total national picture could be more readily obtained through the use of punch cards – but this facility is not as yet available.

The information exists in the courtrooms and the police services across the country; there is a methodology for analysing and structuring the data in meaningful ways; the technology necessary is widely used in government and industry. What is missing? There is an unfamiliarity with and skepticism over the possible application of scientific methods to what have been regarded traditionally as legal problems. It follows that there is also a failure to appreciate the relevance of empirical studies and to utilize these in the formulation of criminal legislation. There is perhaps an understandable hesitancy over considering a balance sheet on the operation and effectiveness of previous legislative efforts in criminal law, where there is no precedence for ever having done so in the past.

Conclusions

Offences committed against the laws controlling homosexual, exhibitionistic, and pedophilic acts form but a small proportion of crimes, but these offences represent the major sexual deviant offences and the large majority of all sexual offences in the community. I have approached the problem presented by these offences from several perspectives; I have dealt with their historical formulation, their legislative evolution, and the treatment accorded them by the courts as represented by the case law; in the previous chapter I have presented an example of a phenomenological analysis of one of the offences. To follow this procedure was of course to become aware of other dimensions of the problems, and this inquiry led me to consider the treatment given these sections by parliament (as reported in Hansard and other committee reports), the process followed in the latest revision of the Code, the evidentiary problems which impinge upon a study of the substantive side of the law, as well as incidental comparative studies of similar provisions and some of the wider social factors which have great importance in a reconsideration of normative rules. By confining the study to a few sections of the Code (they number exactly five), and by pursuing this method, it was possible to examine the various stages in the latest revision and not only to show specifically the inadequate treatment given these offences by the members of parliament and the royal commissioners, but to raise the more important question of criminal law reform in general. There may be some who deal with the criminal law, either on the bench or at the bar, or in police stations or law schools, who do not think we are in need of criminal law reform, but I do not share this view. For those who do see the need for reform, the problem is not whether the bell should be tied around the cat's neck but who should do it and how it should be done.

This study has attempted to show that no simple or single approach to these offences could possibly yield the kind of information one would wish or need to have in order to reformulate them. Each phase of the study presents a different facet of the problem, or to put it differently, each shows another part of the refraction which results when a group of offences is subjected to this process. That the areas refracted are all interrelated goes without saying, and I have attempted to show that history, legislative evolution, and case law do not provide a sufficient basis on which to determine the direction of future moves.

It is necessary also to determine what occurs when current cases are subjected to a phenomenological analysis in hopes of bringing us closer to the reality of the acts behind the offences that are daily processed by the courts. Comparative study is of course most helpful when one is aware of the phenomena underlying particular statutes before one compares them with the normative rules in other jurisdictions where similar information may not be available. It is also evident that any reappraisal that is meaningful for one's own time must involve an assessment of the offences against the larger backdrop of social facts. Each of these areas has not been explored in the same detail here, but I am convinced that each of them is essential to any future reform and that this method has validity and is applicable to any other group of related offences under the Code.

Why then do I not offer a solution to the problems presented by the offence of gross indecency? The information available following the phenomenological analysis indicates that, as at present constructed, the offence covers an indefinite ground and takes within its bounds a wide variety of acts. There is not enough information available to show how the other offences related to it are used by the courts. It may be found that certain acts which are included at times under the offence of gross indecency are also included under other sections, so that there is an area of overlap, the extent of which should be known. To raze the one section and construct something in its place without being aware of its relationship to other sections in this area is to create problems which will only have to be faced in the future. For reasons of unity, internal structure, and harmony, all the sex offences should be reconsidered together. Being unable to offer at this time comparable and comprehensive data on all of the sex offences, I do not propose to single out one offence and treat it separately from the others. I believe it would be a mistake to do so. If a study of the history of criminal law reform in this country teaches us anything, it is that we are long past the stage when we can afford to tinker with individual sections.

The phenomenological analysis of offences is of particular importance to this process because it provides us with a means of looking behind the legislation, beyond the case law, and it confronts us with a new dimension of the problem of sexual deviations and the law. It presents us with a picture of the legislation *in operation*, and it taps the untouched resources of the unpublished cases. It adds something more than this. It enables us to conceive of the problem not on the basis of the act alone but on the basis of the "event." Using a tri-polar configuration of offender, victim, and act, one is able to become aware of important differences between various kinds of cases. The meaning of the act changes, not only for the parties, but for society as well, when the victim is a child rather than an adolescent or an adult. The character of the "event" is different again when force is present and when it is not. Our concern should also be different when the offender is a young adolescent with a lifetime ahead of him, from when he is an old man with an exemplary life behind him. I stress the importance of this kind of analysis because of the colossal blunders committed without it in the most thorough modern reform of criminal law, the American Model Penal Code. For example, section 213.2, "Deviate Sexual Intercourse by Force or Imposition," includes under one section anal intercourse, fellatio, any sexual intercourse per os or per anum with an animal forced on one person by another, if force or threats or drugs are used, or if the victim is unconscious, or in any event if the victim is under 10. This is patently a melange of strikingly different events quite unrelated in character; it covers, to give but one example, both homosexual pedophilic acts and acts of forceful heterosexual anal intercourse. Granted both acts merit a proscription, but it makes no sense to lump them together since the participants, extent of harm done, and chance of recidivism all differ. When statistics are compiled on section 213.2, will the adopters of the Code know whether children or adults or heterosexual or homosexual partners were involved, or to what extent bestiality played a part? It is an absurd construction and a proposal which we can well avoid.

This kind of analysis admittedly leads one away from the strictly legal study of the criminal law. But before dismissing this kind of inquiry, it is well to consider some remarks made by Professor Johannes Andenaes in 1954 in proposing an institute of criminology and criminal law in Oslo: "It may safely be said that our legislative efforts in this field [criminal legislation] are insufficiently based on empirical investigations, and have to an unnecessary extent been made in the dark."[1] Consider also the observation of Jerome Hall: "Unless we are to confine our work to analysis of ideas, the factual side of law must engage equal attention."[2]

When our society is confronted by the danger presented by the

1 Johannes Andenaes, *Institute of Criminology and Criminal Law, 1954-1964* (University of Oslo, Norway), p. 2.
2 Jerome Hall, "Three Fundamental Aspects of Criminal Law," in Gerhard O. W. Mueller, ed., *Essays in Criminal Science* (New Jersey, London, 1961), p. 159.

presence of automobiles on the street, we make detailed studies of the danger points as they reveal themselves in traffic accidents, and from the information gathered we improve the motor car, the brakes, the lights, the bumpers; we improve the street signs and street lights, the markings on the street, the curves and the corners, the crosswalks; and we promote driver and pedestrian education, starting with the pre-schoolers. We do not set about meeting the problem by dealing *only* with the people who have accidents, although we do that as well. With the criminal "events" in our midst we continue with our antiquated "literary" Code, as Stephen described it, continue to see each "crime" as an isolated event of human behaviour, and bend our efforts to punish or reform each offender in a variety of ways, without much information about which form works with which kind of offender. We do not keep detailed studies of the "events" as they occur. We overcrowd our jails, overtax the probation officers, fail to establish anything like an adequate parole service, and then conceptualize the problem as one of corrections. The appointment of the Canadian Committee on Corrections by the Department of Justice is a case in point. Yet we have only the haziest idea, or no idea at all, of the very different kinds of cases under each offence category. Without this breakdown we cannot know what kinds of cases the courts are funnelling to what correctional facility and how those decisions work out in practice. We have an extensive arsenal of alternative dispositions but no one is able on the basis of our present formulations to inform a magistrate which weapons to use, when to use them, or why. We must return to the essential ingredients of each offence, to learn who and what are involved in the "events," to consider what other measures can be taken to prevent particular crimes, or whether we should still make criminal proscriptions in these situations, and if so, which alternatives are available, what kind and degree of intervention are called for. We shall have to decide these questions on the basis of the facts we learn about the various acts involved, not on the basis of uninformed imagination.

In my opinion, we cannot make any appreciable progress in this direction until the government undertakes to establish a permanent body, adequately financed and staffed to plan a systematic reform of the substantive criminal law and the related evidentiary and procedural rules. Such a body must either undertake the necessary research itself or allocate aspects for particular study to individuals, schools, or institutes of higher learning on a priority basis. What is called for is a systematic, continuous long-range study conducted under well-known and established machinery for reform, so that experience gained in working in one area can be used in the adjacent areas to ensure unity of approach and continuity with a consistent well-enunciated set of guiding principles and strategy. The Uniformity Commissioners, a fairly homogeneous group of senior administrative personnel from the various provinces, are neither representative enough nor sufficiently conversant with other aspects of the relevant problems to fill this role.

One begins to realize that the work which is necessary now cannot be done by one man or one royal commission working in one place in a limited period of time. Sir James Fitzjames Stephen did prepare a *Digest* alone, which a royal commission turned into a draft code, but one might ask, on the shoulders of how many royal commissions working for how many decades did he stand? Someday, hopefully sooner than later, some public resources will be directed towards the preparation of a new criminal code. We have yet to bear the full cost of criminal law reform in this country.

Appendix I

REGINA v. A.B. and C.D.

Note

The following is a full transcript of a trial on a charge of gross indecency which took place at Toronto in 1965. Although the material herein is part of the public record the names of the parties and the dates have been changed to prevent any embarrassment to the persons involved.

IN THE GENERAL SESSIONS OF THE PEACE IN AND FOR THE COUNTY OF YORK

Regina v. A.B. and C.D.

Before his Honour JUDGE J.

Appearances:

CROWN ATTORNEY
for the Crown

MR. X.
for the Accused C.D.

MR. Y.
for the Accused A.B.

Toronto, Ontario
Thursday, April 18, 1965

Jury panel absent from Court room.

CROWN ATTORNEY

May it please your Honour, my learned friend MR. X. acts for the accused C.D. and my learned friend MR. Y. acts for the accused A.B. MR. X. wishes to place himself upon the mercy of the Court and I believe my other learned friend has instructions to plead not guilty.

I was wondering if we could dispose of my learned friend's plea prior to taking the hearing?

THE COURT

Arraign him.

CLERK OF COURT

C.D. and A.B., you are both charged that: "On or about the fifth day of November, in the year 1964, at the Municipality of Metropolitan Toronto, in the County of York, [you] committed an act of gross indecency one with the other, contrary to the Criminal Code." On this charge, C.D., how do you plead, guilty or not guilty?

ACCUSED C.D.

Guilty.

CLERK OF COURT

A.B., how do you plead?

ACCUSED A.B.

Not guilty.

The Court upon hearing evidence disposed of the case against C.D. Jury panel called in to the courtroom.

MR. Y.

Your Honour, there need be no notation of the previous case on the indictment if the jury is taking it with them.

THE COURT

All right, leave it out.

Jury called and sworn.

CLERK OF COURT

Gentlemen of the jury, look upon the prisoner and harken to his charge. He stands charged in the name of A.B. in that he did: "On or about the 5th day of November, in the year 1964, at the Municipality of Metropolitan Toronto, in the County of York, commit . . . an act of gross indecency one with the other, contrary to the Criminal Code." Upon this indictment he has pleaded not guilty and for his trial has placed himself upon his country which country you are and it is your duty, therefore, to inquire whether he be guilty or not guilty and harken to the evidence.

Will you retire to the jury room and hang up your hats and coats and come right back.

Jury retired.

MR. Y.

May I address you before the jury return, which might save time? There has been some indication before your Honour as to the evidence that will be heard and there is a great deal of evidence that the other man c.d. was standing on a street corner and rubbing his private parts. I do not know what inferences may be drawn about that, but eventually there will be evidence that a.b. came driving by.

It is my submission all the evidence about watching c.d. prior to the accused a.b. is not relevant to the accused a.b. and I do not know what suggestion can be made – perhaps some moral suggestion – and while it does not apply to a.b. it is my submission that evidence ought not to be heard. I do not see any useful purpose. a.b. was not even there.

The other question is, there is evidence of a wig apparently found in a.b.'s car, and, with respect, I do not know that that evidence, if it is going to be submitted by the Crown as an exhibit, could properly be admitted. I do not know that it bears any relevance to the act itself, the act of gross indecency between the parties, and it certainly will prejudice and might prejudice the accused and may be more detrimental than probative.

The evidence, I understand, of the police officer will be he viewed the act between one c.d. and one a.b. and I anticipate that will be his evidence and certainly that is all that is required of the Crown to rely on and the other evidence would have no effect. I would say all the evidence prior with reference to c.d. ought to be omitted and the evidence of the wig in connection with a.b. ought to be omitted as well.

THE COURT

The wig, I suppose, was found in a.b.'s car?

CROWN ATTORNEY

Yes.

MR. Y.

I do not know that it has any probative value.

THE COURT

I do not know. What does the Crown say?

CROWN ATTORNEY

In my respectful submission, your Honour will probably know what the evidence will be because you heard the evidence with reference to c.d. When the accused pleads not guilty I assume one of the possible defences is the officer had eye trouble at the time he saw what was taking place.

The Crown's evidence will be and it is my submission the two accused are homosexuals and in my submission from the observation with reference to the accused C.D. it would appear he was standing in the rain and every time a lone male driver would come up Yonge Street he would rub himself in the area of his privates. The officers felt, "Here we have something," and finally parked further along Yonge Street and he lured the accused A.B. into his clutches and they went in the car and committed an act of gross indecency.

Also I might advise your Honour when the accused's apartment was searched they found pictures of males dressed in women's clothing, some scantily and some not quite so scantily and the wig and it would all tend to show the accused is a homosexual and there was no mistake in the officer's observation and I think the authorities will back me up, especially *Regina and Thompson*, the powder puff case, the accused was charged with indecently assaulting young males and the powder puffs and pictures found in the apartment, it all goes to show how the accused's mind operates.

If my learned friend said, "The defence is going to be this is not gross indecency, the evidence is admitted but not gross indecency," he might have some merit because it is all relevant and if the Jury thinks not they can disregard it.

MR. Y.

The pictures were not found on A.B., they were found on C.D.

CROWN ATTORNEY

I apologize, that is right. I would not introduce them.

MR. Y.

In the powder puff case there was evidence of a similar kind of procedure of similar acts, certainly, but here the act of having a wig and the act of gross indecency are separate and that ought not to be affected as far as the probative value.

I am aware of the case my friend quoted and I think they can be distinguished in that in the case quoted there were a series of transactions of a similar nature so it was admitted to show the series of transactions of a similar nature.

THE COURT

I cannot say this evidence to be tendered by the Crown is inadmissible. I do not think it has much probative value but it is not inadmissible. I do not think it is inadmissible. I will let it in.

Call the jury in.

MR. Y.

Could we have the witnesses excluded?

THE COURT

How many are there?

CROWN ATTORNEY

Two.

THE COURT

The first witness is to assist the Crown and the other one will give evidence. You can have the Defence witnesses excluded if you like.

Jury returned.

CROWN ATTORNEY

Your Honour and members of the jury, it is my privilege to address you briefly at the outset of this trial. I am acting for the Crown and my learned friend is acting for the accused or representing the accused, and in case some of you have never sat on a trial of this nature before, perhaps before I outline the facts I should describe the mechanics of a trial.

First, I have the right to call witnesses and in this case I will be calling two. I put them in the box and question them and my learned friend has the right to cross-examine and by cross-examining my witnesses he can see whether they remember or are telling lies or part of the truth. That is one of the weapons available to the Defence. Then, at the end of the case he has the opportunity to either call a defence or no defence. In the latter case if he calls no defence I have to sum up my case and he addresses you last. This is sometimes a psychological advantage in that he might think of something that the Crown might not have anticipated during the case. Or he may call a defence and if he calls a defence he addresses you briefly and calls witnesses and then calls his evidence. Then I have the right to speak to you on the whole case.

During the course of my remarks if I give you any view of the evidence, what I say is not evidence, just what you hear from the witness box.

This is a simple case and we should not be here too long on it. It is alleged on Thursday, November 5 of this year, about one o'clock in the morning, two detectives were in an unmarked car on Yonge Street when they observed this man near Birch Avenue and due to the fact he was alone at that hour of the morning and appeared nervous, they were rather suspicious; they thought he was watching out for something. So they took up observation. It was raining and he did not have a raincoat on. One of the officers will advise you when a car with a lone male driver came up Yonge Street he would rub himself in the area of his privates.

Finally, the accused before you today drove up Yonge Street and apparently the other man went through this gesture and before you know it he and the accused are in the same car and quite by accident they went to the parking lot where one of the officers, in order to get out of the rain, had hidden himself when he noticed something happening in the car. He went over to the car and investigated and found the accused before the Court with the other gentleman's penis in his mouth, doing something. That is really all it is about. That is gross indecency. I will call the first witness, Witness One.

WITNESS ONE, *sworn, examined by* CROWN ATTORNEY.

Q. Sir, you are a detective with the Metropolitan Toronto Police Force?

A. Yes, sir.

Q. How long have you been on the Force?

A. Twenty-one years past.

Q. I believe on Thursday, November 5, one o'clock in the morning, you were on duty in plain clothes with Detective Witness Two.

A. I was.

Q. Driving north on Yonge Street in an unmarked car.

A. Yes, sir.

Q. You made observations on a lone male.

A. I did.

Q. Near Birch Street.

A. Yes.

Q. Whereabouts is that, actually?

A. Birch Avenue is the first street north of the C.P.R. tracks running west off Yonge Street.

Q. That is near the Ports of Call.

A. Just south of the Ports of Call Tavern.

Q. Would you describe to the jury what you saw?

A. Your Honour, Gentlemen of the Jury, at the time in question my attention was drawn to the man standing on the northwest corner of Birch Avenue and Yonge Street owing to the fact that it was raining slightly at the time and this man was standing on the sidewalk right at the edge of the curb and my partner and I decided to watch him.

So, we parked the unmarked police car in the Liquor Control Board lot on the east side of Yonge Street just right opposite Birch Avenue. In watching this man, I observed each time a car passed him with a lone male occupant this man put his hand in the area of his privates and rubbed himself. Also, on each occasion when a car turned west along Birch Avenue this man would walk directly to the corner of Birch Avenue and appeared to watch the westbound auto.

At approximately 1:10, ten minutes later, there was a 1959 Pontiac with a lone male driver who drove south on Yonge Street and then turned west on Birch Avenue and stopped the car about 150 to 175 feet west of Yonge Street. This man left the corner, walked up to the car in question, got into the passenger's side. The lights in the car were turned out. This man stayed in the car for approximately five to eight minutes and got out of the car and returned to the corner of Yonge and Birch Avenue.

We continued observation on this man and again observed each time a lone male occupant drove by that he rubbed the front of his body in the area of his privates.

At 1:45 A.M. I got out of the police car and I climbed over a fence into a parking lot of the Ports of Call, walked north through the lot to Shaftesbury Avenue, then walked west across Yonge Street, south on Yonge Street passing the man in question and I concealed myself behind a sign board on the southwest corner of Yonge and Birch. I kept this man under observation and he continued in this same process each time a male occupant alone in a car passed.

It started to rain harder, so when this man was facing north on Yonge Street I crossed Birch Avenue and concealed myself in the parking lot of number 10 Birch Avenue. At 2:00 A.M. a 1963 Volkswagen, licence number 123456, proceeded west on Birch Avenue from Yonge Street very slow. The driver of this car was the accused man before the Court this date, MR. A.B.

The accused man backed the Volkswagen car into the driveway of the Marathon Equipment Company on the south side of Birch Avenue and this man we had kept under observation for some time proceeded west on Birch Avenue from the corner, walked over directly to the passenger's side of the accused man's auto. He got into the passenger's side, appeared to be [in] a very short conversation, and then the accused man drove the car across Birch Avenue and right into the parking lot where I was standing. I had concealed myself in beside a garage – there is a slight indentation in the garage doorway where I concealed myself and the accused man drove within three to four feet of me. He parked the car on the west side of the lot and turned the lights out.

Q. How far would he be away from you at this stage?

A. The lot is a very small lot approximately 40 feet wide. I would be no more than 24 feet from the back of the car.

Q. Incidentally, what was the other man wearing?

A. The other man was wearing a sweater coat type, dark sweater coat. I observed that the passenger of the car put his arm around the accused man, the driver of the car, and then the accused man's head bent forward towards the passenger and therefore out of my sight.

Then I approached the car in question on the passenger's side and upon looking in the window I saw the accused man bent over and he had the passenger's penis in his mouth. The passenger had an erection and the accused man was moving his head up and down sucking the passenger's penis.

I then opened the door, turned my flashlight on the accused man and the passenger, told them I was a police officer and immediately the accused man remarked, "Please leave us alone. It will cause trouble. Just leave us alone. We will go away." I informed the accused man he and the other party were both under arrest and would have to accompany me to the police station.

By that time, within moments, my partner Detective Witness Two arrived on the scene and placed the accused man and the passenger in the police car. I then obtained the keys for the Volkswagen car in question from the accused man A.B. He also produced on my request the ownership for the car in question.

On a search of the glove compartment of the car in question I found a black lady's wig. I took this in my possession and the accused man and the second man were then removed to 57 Police Station where they were charged with this offence.

Q. Thank you. Your witness.

Cross-examination by MR. Y.

Q. How old would you say that the other man was that was with the accused?

A. About 26 or 27 years of age.

Q. You ascertained that the accused was about 30, is that correct?

A. I believe so, yes.

Q. I take it you also ascertained the accused man had had no previous convictions, is that correct? For any offence whatsoever?

A. That is right, yes.

Q. When you examined him did he tell you he was gainfully employed?

A. He did.

Q. You had no reason to suspect otherwise, did you?

A. No, sir.

Q. You have been employed with the Police Force for a period of 21 years and I take it over that period you have made a number of arrests. Have you ever charged anyone with gross indecency who has committed adultery?

A. Would you repeat that?

Q. Have you ever charged any person with gross indecency who has committed adultery?

A. I am afraid I am not in a position to answer that. I do not understand it.

Q. You have charged a number of people with gross indecency.

A. Yes, I have.

Q. Have you ever charged anyone with gross indecency because you found they committed adultery?

A. That all depends on your definition of adultery. I don't connect the two at all.

Q. Have you ever charged anyone with gross indecency because of an act of fornication?

A. You mean fornication in the true sense of the word?

Q. Yes.

A. No, I have not.

Q. Have you ever charged anyone with gross indecency because of an act of masturbation?

A. No, I have not.

Q. I have no further questions.

THE COURT

Gentlemen of the jury, I am going to excuse you for the night now. I want you to be very careful not to discuss this case with anybody in your absence from the Court room because you must decide on the guilt or innocence of this man from the evidence you hear in this witness box, that and that alone. If you were to hear anything else outside the court room it might be difficult to disassociate that from your mind, so you must not discuss it with anyone. You are now excused until tomorrow morning.

Jury retired.

Friday, April 19, 1965

On resuming.
Same appearances as heretofore noted.

Jury returned.

CROWN ATTORNEY

I have one very short witness, Detective Witness Two.

DETECTIVE WITNESS TWO, *sworn, examined by* CROWN ATTORNEY.

Q. You are a detective on the Metropolitan Toronto Police Force?

A. That is correct.

Q. I believe on Thursday, November 5, last year, at one o'clock in the morning, you were the partner with the previous witness Detective Sergeant Witness One.

A. That is correct.

Q. Could you briefly state to the jury just what you saw without going into great detail?

A. About 1:00 A.M. that date we made observations on a gentleman who was standing on the corner of Birch and Yonge Street. He was drawn to our attention by his actions. He was watching cars which were going up and down Yonge and turned on to Birch. He kept rubbing his privates with his left hand during all this time he was under observation from one o'clock to approximately two o'clock. During that time he got into one car which came south on Yonge Street and turned right on to Birch and stopped a short distance from the corner. He was in that car for five or eight minutes. He got out again, came back to the corner of Birch and Yonge where he walked up and down as before.

About 1:45 the Detective Sergeant left the car on foot to make observations on this man. The other man disappeared from view.

About two o'clock a Volkswagen bearing licence number 123456 for 1964 made a turn on to Birch Avenue. It stopped about 50 to 60 feet along Birch Avenue up into a driveway on the south side of Birch. At that time the lights went out and this man we had been making observations on he left the corner of Yonge and Birch and went up to this car and around on the passenger's side, then the car started up and crossed from a parking lot from the south side across Birch to a parking lot on the north side.

At this time I was in the Scout car on my own parked on the east side of Yonge Street in the Liquor Control Board. After this car had moved from the south side of the street to the north side of the street, about five minutes after that I decided to go look for the Detective Sergeant. At that time I went on to this lot where the car was parked and the Detective Sergeant was having a conversation with the accused man A.B. and another man by the name of C.D. At that time they were both under arrest, placed in the Scout car and taken to Number 57 Station and further investigated.

Q. Originally, why did you stop to observe this person?

A. This was one o'clock in the morning, practically no pedestrians on Yonge Street, a very fine drizzle of rain falling which a short time later turned into quite a heavy rain. This man was walking up and down, appeared to be waiting for someone or something and his actions were rather suspicious.

Q. You were not looking for this sort of thing.

A. No.

Q. Thank you.

Cross-examination by MR. Y.

Q. Officer, just to be clear, the man you first observed walking up and down Yonge Street was not the accused, is that correct?

A. That is correct.

Q. I take it because there were very few pedestrians, if any, and because it was raining that night there were very few pedestrians, if any, on Yonge Street?

A. That is correct.

Q. And this parking lot, is it behind some stores on Yonge Street?

A. Yes, it would be immediately behind the first two or three stores on the northwest corner of Yonge and Birch.

Q. There were no pedestrians in the parking lot?

A. No.

Q. Were you there when the questioning took place? Did you question the accused at all?

A. No, I didn't question him. I had some conversation with him at the police station.

Q. Did you have a conversation with him about his occupation?

A. I did.

Q. Did he tell you he was – he worked with a church?

A. If I remember correctly he told me he was a musician and did mention a church.

Q. Did he tell you he was a choir director with a church.

A. Yes.

Q. Did he tell you he had been associated with the church in that occupation for a great many years?

A. I can't tell you definitely the number of years but he did leave me to believe he had been there for some time.

Q. You checked and found this man has never had any criminal convictions?

A. To the best of my knowledge that is correct.

Q. That is all.

CROWN ATTORNEY

That is the case for the Crown, your Honour.

THE COURT

Defence?

MR. Y.

May I address the Court perhaps in the absence of the jury?

THE COURT

You have a motion?

MR. Y.

Yes, I have a motion.

THE COURT

All right, take the jury out.

Jury retired 10:20 A.M.

MR. Y.

Your Honour, my motion is to the effect that the Crown has not proven its case. The obligation of the Crown is to bring in some evidence as to indecency and gross indecency. It would seem that indecency of gross or gross indecency is a matter of degree according to the very norm of our society. I would think, your Honour, that when the Crown was to prove its case it would have to show what decency means in our society by perhaps calling some scientific evidence or modern scientific evidence that would say according to the customs and morals of our time this is indecent or this is what the customs and morals of our time is and this is the behaviour and beyond that this is gross behaviour or behaviour beyond that.

The only fact before your Honour is a physical act. There is nothing more. There is nothing to say it is indecent. There is nothing to give that physical act any colour whatsoever; in order to find that, your Honour must take some kind of judicial notice, in my submission, as to what the norms of our society are or what the customs of our society are, and I submit the Crown should have brought that evidence.

In view of the recent findings in the Wolfenden Report and the Kinsey Report I do not think evidence of this kind is indecent, that the Court can take judicial notice that it is indecent behaviour or homosexual behaviour is indecent. The Wolfenden Report indicates 37 per cent of all males have some form of homosexual behaviour and that Report says this kind of conduct the criminal law should not associate itself with.

THE COURT

Does it differentiate between an act of this kind taking place in public than in private?

MR. Y.

The Wolfenden Report does, but in so doing it says this kind of behaviour is not necessarily criminal, so I think the obligation of the Crown is to establish this is criminal. The customs of our society are not so clear.

THE COURT

You mean it should not be criminal.

MR. Y.

My view is it should not be criminal. The Criminal Code says it is gross indecency. Indecency is a matter of custom and the Crown should have to show the normal range of behaviour before it can term this conduct "gross."

THE COURT

I would have to have a public inquiry to hear from about fifty different people.

MR. Y.

If that is so, your Honour, in order to properly determine that, then your Honour has to take the same kind of judicial notice as if a public inquiry has held that this is gross indecency.

I take it then that would be the position of the Crown that you can take some judicial notice of what is notorious in our community as to behaviour that is normal or behaviour that is gross.

THE COURT

I will have to leave that for the jury. You will have to argue that before them.

Call back the jury.

MR. Y.

I will not be calling any evidence, your Honour.

Jury recalled.

CROWN ATTORNEY

Members of the jury, that will be all the evidence you will be hearing. I think that is only common sense. I do not think there is anything else to this case.

You are going to have to decide whether the accused is guilty beyond a reasonable doubt. I cannot comment on the law; his

Honour will direct you on that. He is the sole judge of the law. However, you are the sole judges of the facts of the evidence you have heard in that witness box and no other evidence. What I say is not evidence and what my learned friend says is not evidence. So I would direct your attention to that.

I think it is common sense what gross indecency is. First, I suppose it is indecent and the gross part is question of degree and there may or may not be, I do not know, a side issue here in that some people feel that this should not be law. In other words, if two consenting males perform such an act in private it should not be condemned by law. I am not prepared to comment upon that law, first, whether it is in private or not in private, that is the law and even if the accused – if somebody came out and said – came up to the police station and said, "I am a homosexual and I have done these acts of perversion," and wrote out a statement and nobody saw him, he came and purged his conscience – that is an extreme example, I suppose – but he could be convicted on that statement alone. That seems a little extreme but that is the way it is and perhaps it is a good thing that the law is this way because in my respectful submission anything unnatural should not be fostered in our community.

I think anything that happens between a male and female providing they have consent, I suppose that is perfectly all right providing it is done in private, in my submission that is natural. But in my submission the unnatural part – and I do not think I need dwell upon this – is when it happens between two males. It is my respectful submission that is abnormal and unnatural and something that should not be condoned because it may be – I should not dwell on it too much, but it is done and I do not think [it] should be more or less sanctioned.

In literature there has been a trend to discuss this sort of thing and in so far as the public press is concerned. However, as a public issue the press has got a point, but I think you know in many societies they are slowly but surely petering out. This thing has happened towards the latter stages and I do not think whatever my learned friend says should be taken into consideration in that account.

I do not have the last word with you and I have to anticipate that he is going to argue that this is not indecent and, secondly, if it is indecent it is not gross indecency because the Kinsey Report and the Wolfenden Report have been received and that Report has been in the press and I do not want to comment upon that save and except all they did was to refer to the statistics, they did not really recommend, in my submission, anything except this should be kept – the law should be confined to acts that take place in public, and it is my respectful submission if it takes place in private it is bound to take place in public, and aside from that you are all gentlemen and I am sure you would know the type of effect of this type of behaviour if it is fostered.

I will leave it with you and let his Honour direct you as to your verdict.

MR. Y. addresses the jury.

MR. Y.

May it please Your Honour and gentlemen of the jury, it is my turn in the course of these proceedings to now address you. It is my duty to address you upon the facts and it is His Honour's duty to address you upon the law and if what I might say to you in any way contradicts the law to what His Honour gives you, you must take the law from His Honour and not what I say.

I have listened, gentlemen of the jury, to my learned friend; we stopped burning witches a long time ago. The onus is upon the Crown to prove beyond a reasonable doubt that this man committed an act of gross indecency. You gentlemen of the jury have been chosen to pronounce upon that act. You are here to judge A.B., but in a very much larger sense you are here to judge this society and to judge every man who may be brought before the Court in a like or similar offence. You must at all times remember that this is a criminal act which you are judging, it is an offence under the Criminal Code, and before you judge A.B., a man whom you have heard has no previous convictions, is not a convicted criminal and a man who has been associated with a church for a great number of years, you must consider that he is a criminal, that he has committed a criminal indecent act and an act that is criminally gross because if you convict him he will stand condemned as any murderer, arsonist, rapist, thief, or armed robber, and that is the kind of conduct you must associate A.B. with.

So that I must caution you before you so charge him and before you link him with that part of our society regard completely and through your minds to what I may have to say to you and what my friend has said to you.

It is our submission that the Crown has not proven that this act is gross and they must so prove beyond a reasonable doubt that that act is indecent. There is no evidence before you as to what our society considers decent. Therefore, it is our submission it is very difficult for you to find out to say what is indecent. I would have thought the Crown would have presented evidence before you to show the norms and morals and customs of our society and there is psychiatric evidence they might present in that regard but they chose not to call anyone. I wonder why. I wonder why there is no sociologist or psychiatrists on behalf of the Crown to say this is what is decent in our society and the behaviour that you have heard about today is indecent. Perhaps they have not found it because they stopped burning witches, as I say, a long time ago.

Our society in the past number of years has exhibited a great deal of tolerance. It has become a touchstone of our society we no longer judge a man because of his race, we no longer judge a man because of his colour, and that has become more and more evident every day, and we no longer judge a man because of his creed. A man may be a Catholic, Protestant, Jew, Unitarian, and he may be an atheist, and he is tolerated in our society and, in fact, accepted, and there are laws to that effect, and that is a mark of our society, that is a mark of a democratic society and that is a mark of the society which can differentiate decency from indecency.

While our society is doing all those things our society also has made great strides in the advancement of medicine. Not only are we finding cures for polio, not only are great attacks being made on cancer, but psychiatrically and sociologically evidence is also finding and bringing out many things about the sexual behaviour in our society, things which were not known before.

My friend mentioned Doctor Kinsey, he has mentioned the Wolfenden Report, and the Wolfenden Report has said that it is not the function of the criminal law to enter into the private lives of some citizens under certain conditions, and Doctor Kinsey has suggested that there is a large segment of our society that exhibits homosexual tendencies between the ages of 16 and 65 and in fact there is a segment of our society that is homosexual. But homosexuality is not criminal conduct *per se* as my friend would have you believe. My friend has not brought before this Court a grain of law to say because you are a homosexual you are a criminal. We are much more advanced in this society.

Our court requires an act of gross indecency and the inference may very well be that because our act does not convict and does not specifically set out homosexuals as criminals in the same way as anyone who commits murder and rape, the inference may be drawn that our act and our Criminal Code and our society tolerates a homosexual and homosexual behaviour is not a crime. Our act says what is indecent is a crime and what is gross indecency is a crime. No matter what you may feel morally, no matter what your own particular feelings are, no matter how against your taste the particular act might be – and let us not become so zealous as to say, "Because I do not believe in that act, it is against my taste, therefore, it is criminal." You cannot do that. You might consider it immoral but [it] need not be criminal. In your own private taste what you may see in public and private and what you might consider as a reflection on good behaviour ought not to enter into this case.

This man may be held for examination by society and perhaps that is all the more reason why you should find his conduct criminal. Do not let your private zeal run over and spill into the criminal law so as to bring a man within the framework of the Criminal Code and have him wear the brand of a criminal for the rest of his life. There is a very great distinction between what is criminal and what may be immoral and what may lack face in your own private mind.

It is our submission as well with the growth of sex education in the schools, with the ability to discuss sex freely among men and women, with literature, public medical literature, with the freedom to read books that we now have, with all this great freedom there ought to be a responsibility on the Crown to prove beyond a reasonable doubt what is indecent and to show you what is indecent, for them to have someone come in to show what is indecent because there are different segments of our society that think differently, as you are well aware. There are some segments of our society that might find an act such as this indecent and there are some segments perhaps – while I am not putting in a consensus – but there are people who can say, and people who have studied, and psychologists right at the University of Toronto, doctors and psychiatrists who could come into the courtroom to tell you what is indecent behaviour. If you do not know what is decent, how can you say beyond reasonable doubt, gentlemen – because that is your function – what is indecent? And I submit the Crown has not proved beyond a reasonable doubt that this act is indecent, they have not brought these people before you to determine what is decency and what is indecency.

Fornication in some quarters may be considered indecent; masturbation may be considered indecent, and one of the most indecent acts of our society is adultery. It is one of the few acts for which you can get a divorce in this country. These gentlemen could not get a divorce for gross indecency but no one is ever arrested for adultery. What sort of value has that in our community? Are you prepared to prosecute people as criminals for adultery and, if not, surely gross indecency which the law and the legislature considers less offensive should not be considered as criminal. How can you rationalize that value in your own minds. Let us assume you disagree with their use, you are going to find an act indecent, you then come to the next hurdle, that is, is it gross indecency. Is it gross? One dictionary gives a synonym for gross as monstrous. His Honour may give you other definitions of gross such as flagrant, but is it monstrous?

Let us assume you find this act is indecent. What does gross mean? What does gross mean so as to define this act? Remember, gross is a word we all learn in public school. It is a comparative word. There is decency and indecency but we must find this gross and assuming the conduct you have heard about is true and assuming you find it indecent within the meaning of the Code, what is gross? There are no children involved, there are no children before the Court. The evidence is clear they were two males, one 27 and one 30. No one under the age of 21 – two adult males. There were no pedestrians, no other people. This was not on the street. This was not on the City Hall steps. What is gross? Who was affected by it? Who did they insult? If they had gone up a lane and urinated in private would it have been gross? It may very well be a teen-aged couple who are copulating in a car in a parking lot are not committing an act of gross indecency but it very well may be if they stand on the City Hall steps and do the same thing then it will become gross. What is that quality gross? How can we give to this act the quality of grossness? Surely grossness or monstrous must be something that extends beyond a private act between two consenting male adults.

It is my submission the Crown has not proved beyond a reasonable doubt that this act is gross. You must be satisfied it is gross. His Honour will tell you time and circumstances may make certain acts gross. My friend mentioned the Wolfenden Report. The Wolfenden Report has said in England that this act in private is not even gross indecency. They have suggested it be removed from the Criminal Code after months of listening to psychiatrists, sociologists, sexologists, and everyone including lawyers and everyone who had

a great deal of experience – that committee was made up of a number of clergymen, a number of lawyers – and they have said in
private, they have recommended that act not be considered gross
indecency and be removed from the Criminal Code because the
Code should not bring the private lives of citizens within its sphere.

Our law does not differentiate. It leaves it up to you gentlemen to
make up your minds about it and I suggest that the evidence you
have before you and from what you know in society that this is not
a monstrous act that this is not a monstrously indecent act, that it
did not affect children, it did not affect the public. There were two
consenting males at two o'clock in the morning in a parking lot on
Yonge Street in a car out of the way of everyone. It is just a question
of degree.

Had this occurred on Yonge Street in broad daylight you might
very well have considered it monstrous. Had it occurred in your
children's classroom you might have considered it gross, but who
did it affect so as to consider it gross?

Gentlemen of the jury, this is a most difficult case, but as I have
said, the act was not unnatural and abnormal. I do not know what
books he reads. I do not read some books; perhaps we do not read
the same things, I do not know. I have the Wolfenden Report in
my briefcase and after months of testimony those acts were not
considered by that committee to be abnormal or unnatural.

Gentlemen of the Jury, A.B. has come before you; he is a man
who is not a criminal, he is a man whom you may meet in your
everyday life, he is a man who has had a good record, he is a man
who is being charged with a criminal offence. Gentlemen, I think
A.B. is entitled to say to you that on all the facts and all the evidence
the Crown has not proved beyond a reasonable doubt that A.B. is a
criminal. Thank you.

Charge to the Jury.

THE COURT

Gentlemen of the jury, we have now come to the end of this case
where we must determine whether or not the accused man is guilty
or innocent of this offence. While that is our joint duty, it is my
special duty to explain the law to you as pertains to the case and
you must accept the law from me as I give it to you and from no
one else because I am supreme in that field.

On the other hand, you are supreme so far as the facts are

concerned. In the course of my remarks to you I may have occasion to pass my opinion upon the evidence and I do that to assist you and for no other reason and you are entirely at liberty to reject any opinion I pass upon the evidence.

I hope you obeyed my instructions not to discuss this case in your absence from this court room because you must decide on the guilt or innocence of this man entirely on the evidence you have heard from that witness box, that and that alone. You must approach this matter with entire impartiality, without fear, favour, or prejudice of any kind. If you have any prejudices in a matter of this kind you must banish them from your mind so that this man gets a fair and impartial trial in the best traditions of British justice.

You have had an opportunity of hearing and seeing the witnesses and I do not think there is much doubt about what they say and what they related in the witness box and I think you will have no trouble in accepting what they said as being the truth; at least, it is not contradicted in any way. In every criminal case there are two kinds of evidence; one is direct evidence and the other is circumstantial evidence. It is from that circumstantial evidence you can draw deductions or inferences as to the guilt or innocence of the accused man, but there is an important rule in regard to circumstantial evidence. Before you can convict an accused person on circumstantial evidence you must be satisfied not only that the circumstances are such as to be consistent with his having committed the act but you must also be satisfied the circumstances are such as to be inconsistent with any other rational conclusion than that he is guilty of the act charged.

Another important rule is the onus of proof. The onus of proving the accused man guilty rests from beginning to end upon the Crown. That onus never shifts and the Crown must prove every ingredient of the offence beyond a reasonable doubt and if there is a reasonable doubt created by the evidence then you must give the benefit of that doubt to the accused man.

Now, what is the charge with which the accused man stands indicted? He stands indicted that, "On or about the fifth day of November, in the year 1964, at the Municipality of Metropolitan Toronto, in the County of York, he committed an act of gross indecency, contrary to the Criminal Code." You have heard the evidence in this matter, gentlemen of the Jury, and I do not think there is any dispute on the facts. It is only a question whether this particular act which was committed in this case was not an act of gross indecency. That is the defence in this matter.

Well, of course, no witness has been called to give evidence as to what constitutes gross indecency. It is not defined in the Criminal Code. It is for you as a cross section of the citizens of this country to decide whether or not you think this particular act is grossly indecent. Grossly indecent means very indecent or a great amount of indecency, and that is what you must determine. You heard what the CROWN ATTORNEY has said and MR. Y. has said on this subject and it is up to you to decide whether or not you consider the act which was committed by the accused man one of gross indecency. Of course, gross indecency, probably if such an act was committed in private, committed in the privacy of their own homes you might not consider the act grossly indecent, whereas you might consider the act grossly indecent if committed in public or where it was committed in this case, but I say that is a question for you as jury-men representing the citizens of this country to decide whether or not you think the act committed in this case is an act of gross indecency. That is all I can say about it, gentlemen, I will leave it to you.

I must warn you, in order to convict this man or acquit, all twelve of you must agree. You cannot be divided in your opinion and either convict or acquit. You do not have to be unanimous but in that case there would be a disagreement and it would probably require a new trial, so I want to strongly urge you to come to a unanimous decision either one way or the other. When you retire to your jury room select from among you a foreman and return your verdict to me.

Jury retired 10:55.

THE COURT

Any objections, MR. Y.?

MR. Y.

I wonder if your Honour might consider recalling the jury and telling them it is dangerous to convict on a sexual offence on uncorroborated testimony of only one person. There is no corroboration.

THE COURT

Where do you get that law?

MR. Y.

There is some law to that effect. I was reading a set of lectures on jury trials and I believe there is a case referred to by Mr. Martin or Mr. Long dealing with sexual offences and the case is reported in the Criminal Appeal Records and I could make that available.

THE COURT

There are certain sections of the Code in which that is referred to and it says without corroboration it is dangerous to convict, but gross indecency is not one of them.

MR. Y.

I wish to make that point at this particular time and would ask the jury to be called back for the purpose of the record.

The second consideration that I have is that your Honour mentioned to the members of the jury that they might not consider this gross indecency if it occurred in private but they may if committed in public. There is a case I believe, *R* v. *Jay*, 170 Criminal Cases, where there was an act of fellatio between a woman and a girl in a car in a park and the Court felt the circumstances were different and psychiatric evidence was called and in that particular case there was a finding upheld on appeal it was not an act of gross indecency. I do not know in that case whether the act occurred in public in the sense that in the same light it might very well be taken to reflect to the jury that if this act did in fact not occur in private it was an act of gross indecency, where using that case as an analogy they could find it was not gross indecency even if it occurred in public, and I think your Honour might point that out to the jury.

THE COURT

It is like a negligence case, MR. Y. You can't define when a person is negligent or not negligent, it is only a matter of opinion.

MR. Y.

I am concerned your Honour, the jury might draw from your remarks the inference if this had not occurred in private it would be gross indecency.

THE COURT

I said you might consider this act not grossly indecent if done in private and you might consider it grossly indecent if done in public. I do not see anything wrong saying that to the jury.

MR. Y

I just wished to make that objection.

THE COURT

Have you any objection?

CROWN ATTORNEY

No, your Honour.

THE COURT

We will adjourn and wait for the jury.

Court recessed.

On resuming 12:05 P.M., jury returned.

CLERK OF COURT

I understand you have a question to ask his Honour.

FOREMAN JUROR

Your Honour, there are three points on which we are having a little trouble and we thought we could get some guidance from the Court. One of them is, is there a definition in law as to what gross indecency is?

THE COURT

No.

FOREMAN JUROR

The law does not specifically define gross indecency. Secondly, are there any precedents to this case and what role would a decision in this case play as a precedent in other similar cases?

THE COURT

A certain act which is committed may under certain circumstances be grossly indecent and in other circumstances it may not be grossly indecent. That is for you to decide and adjudicate upon. You can understand a certain act being performed under certain circumstances where it might not be grossly indecent but the same act under other circumstances might be grossly indecent.

FOREMAN JUROR

In your opinion are there precedents that would help us?

THE COURT

No.

FOREMAN JUROR

Is it possible for the jury to make a decision with a recommendation especially if that decision is not guilty.

THE COURT

To make a decision what?

FOREMAN JUROR

Is it possible to make a recommendation even if the decision is not guilty?

THE COURT

You can make a recommendation.

FOREMAN JUROR

Does the Court usually take this into account?

THE COURT

    Yes, they certainly do.

FOREMAN JUROR

    I think that covers the questions.

THE COURT

    Do you think you will be very long?

FOREMAN JUROR

    It is very difficult to say.

THE COURT

    All right.

Jury retired 12:08 P.M.

Court adjourned.

On resuming, 2:30 P.M., jury returned.

CLERK OF THE COURT

    Gentlemen of the jury, have you agreed upon your verdict? How say you, do you find the prisoner at the bar guilty or not guilty?

FOREMAN JUROR

    We find the defendant guilty as charged. We would like to strongly recommend leniency and treatment.

CLERK OF THE COURT

    Gentlemen of the jury, harken to your verdict as the Court hath recorded it. You say you find the prisoner at the bar guilty as charged and strongly recommend leniency and treatment. So say you all.

CROWN ATTORNEY

    May it please your Honour, perhaps for the edification of the jury I should mention at this stage the other accused pleaded guilty and was fined $200.00 and had a previous conviction for the same act. It may be of some edification for my learned friend, I had the privilege about three years ago to be in the Old Country where I saw two accused being sentenced for much the same thing as this. They were doing it jointly. The one accused was an admitted homosexual with a long list of convictions and he received six months. The other accused had never been in trouble and the Court saw fit to give him eighteen months. That is how the courts in England sometimes view this.

THE COURT

    What do you want to say, MR. Y.?

MR. Y.

    In view of the previous sentence when there was a plea of guilty

and a second conviction your Honour saw fit to impose a fine of
$200. This gentleman has never been in trouble before and has a
good record in the community, working for a church and other
organizations, a responsible and respectable citizen. In view of the
previous sentence and in view of the jury's recommendations I have
spoken to Doctor Stokes of the Forensic Clinic and spoken to the
accused and he is prepared to attend for treatment. I would recommend to Your Honour the accused be given suspended sentence
and attend the Forensic Clinic for treatment for whatever term they
see fit.

THE COURT

Anything further to say?

CROWN ATTORNEY

No.

THE COURT

Well, A.B., the jury has found you guilty of this offence. It is your
first offence and I suppose there is strong hope you won't repeat it
so I am going to put you on suspended sentence for two years and
put you on probation, a condition of which is you attend for treatment at the clinic whenever you are required to do so. This does not
mean the end of this offence. It means if you commit another
offence of any kind within the next two years you can be brought
back here and sentenced to jail for this offence. Do you understand
this?

THE ACCUSED

Yes.

THE COURT

Are you content?

THE ACCUSED

Yes, your Honour.

THE COURT

All right, two years' probation.

MR. Y.

There is bail.

THE COURT

They will attend to that in the Clerk's office.

Court adjourned.

Appendix II

On December 21, 1967, the Minister of Justice Pierre Elliott Trudeau introduced in Parliament a variety of amendments to the Criminal Code and other statutes in what became widely known as the "omnibus bill."[1] Clause 7 of this bill relates to the offences of buggery and bestiality (s. 147) and gross indecency (s. 149) and reads as follows:

"149. 1 Sections 147 and 149 do not apply to any act committed in private between

(a) a husband and his wife, or

(b) any two persons, each of whom is twenty-one, both of whom consent to the commission of the act.

2 For the purposes of subsection (1),

(a) an act shall be deemed not to have been committed in private if it is committed in a public place, or if more than two persons take part or are present; and

(b) a person shall be deemed not to consent to the commission of an act

  (i) if the consent is extorted by threats or fear of bodily harm or is obtained by false and fraudulent misrepresentations as to the nature and quality of the act, or

  (ii) if that person is, and the other party to the commission of the act knows or has good reason to believe that that person is feebleminded, insane, or an idiot or imbecile."

The explanatory note accompanying the clause simply states:

"This amendment would make the provisions of sections 147 and 149 inapplicable to acts done in private between husband and wife or any two adults if the parties thereto consent."

Sections 147 and 149 at present read as follows:

"147. Every one who commits buggery or bestiality is guilty of an indictable offence and is liable to imprisonment for fourteen years.

1 Bill C-195 bore the title "An Act to Amend the Criminal Code, the Parole Act, the Penitentiary Act, the Prisons and Reformatories Act, and to Make Certain Consequential Amendments to the Combines Investigation Act and the Customs Tariff." Parliament was dissolved in the spring of 1968 before this bill was debated, and its reintroduction into a new session of parliament was required before a formal debate could take place.

149. Every one who commits an act of gross indecency with another person is guilty of an indictable offence and is liable to imprisonment for five years."

If adopted, what would be the effect of the change? The analysis of the 60 cases of persons convicted of gross indecency in the study described in Part IV herein shows that if these cases were to arise under the new proposals, 59 of them could still be convicted for the offence of gross indecency. In the one remaining case where police found photographs of the accused committing fellatio on an unidentified male there is not enough information to decide if it would still fall under the section. If the unidentified male was under 21 years of age, or another person was present (such as a photographer) and even if the place was private, there could still be a conviction for gross indecency. Assuming that a conviction was not registered in the one case, the result would be the same in 98.3 per cent of the cases. The net effect in terms of actual convictions would be that the law would operate virtually as it does now. It can be said that the change merely ratifies the already existing use of this section by the police and by the courts. There are of course cases where the section has been used to convict persons involved in homosexual acts in private, but these are extremely rare. The proposed amendment is nevertheless significant and important. It does eliminate what are (to slightly shift the meaning of Bentham's phrase) "imaginary offences." That is, there is a great deal of sexual behaviour in private between heterosexual parties as well as homosexuals which under the law as it stands at present could be prosecuted, was thought to be a crime, and theoretically was a crime, but in reality was not charged by the police or convicted by the courts. Since 1954 when the section was last amended there have been undoubtedly untold numbers of these "illegal" acts, but only a small handful of cases have been prosecuted as a result. What the legislation proposes to do is to remove the remote possibility of prosecution for this behaviour when it occurs in private.

Would the change as it is proposed significantly alter either heterosexual or homosexual practices? It would seem unlikely. Sexual behaviour has powerful biological, psychological, and social determinants, and is an enormously complex process along each of these dimensions. As a research question, it would be well nigh impossible to isolate and measure what part the strictly legal provisions, standing as an unenforced threat, play in that process. Certainly the removal of the legal proscription will not in itself remove the social controls in terms of existing mores of sexual behaviour; in all probability these will continue to have their social as well as psychological impact. There is no evidence to show that the presence of the law has either increased or decreased the amount of homosexual behaviour or in itself affected the kind of sexual acts engaged in by heterosexual parties. What is taken as an increase in homosexuality, as evidenced by the increased numbers of stereotype homosexuals seen in public, may well be a matter of increased visibility. The large majority of homosexual people do not exhibit these traits and are not identifiable by their physical appearance, speech, dress, or social behaviour. Along with this it should be considered that there has been over the last 20 years a shift in the social attitudes towards sexual matters, at least in terms of more open discussion about sex and a more open display of its existence.

The proposals made are a welcome addition to the development of the law, but only as a preliminary first step in the clarification of these sections. Much more important is the fact that the proposals open up this area of the law for public discussion and education. With an increased public awareness of the provisions of the law, hopefully a growing understanding of the social problems we have will follow. We need to develop a wider consensus about what we want to control in ourselves as a society in order to assist and give greater direction to the legislators, the police, and the courts.

Although the proposals, if accepted, would bring the written law into greater conformity with present practice, and this may be all that was intended and can be expected at this stage, a question that remains is whether the proposals go far enough in reforming or clarifying the existing law. I do not think that they do. Without ever spelling out clearly what gross indecency means, without ever specifying what behaviour it was intended to control, without ever defining the terms, it is now proposed that this unknown shall not be applicable to certain classes of people in certain situations. "Gross indecency" is still as vague a formulation as it ever was.

If the proposition is accepted that sexual behaviour in private between certain parties is a moral question for them and not for the law to decide, that we ought not to legislate in relation to morals, that "the law has no place in the bedrooms of the nation," then we must be quite clear about the reason for retaining the law which would apply to the remaining cases, virtually all the cases which are tried now. If the reason for retaining the law is not founded in morality, then what is the justification for it? What is it we are trying to prevent or protect? What is it we object to and why? It is here that information about how the existing law is being used, and empirical data about the acts concerned, can provide us with a concrete starting point for discussion. For example: most court cases, as the study referred to shows, arise out of homosexual acts between consenting adults in public places. From certain perspectives the acts may be regarded as immoral, but if it is accepted that the law ought not to legislate in relation to morals, then are there other grounds which justify a proscription in these cases? It can be considered that almost all sexual behaviour, heterosexual as well homosexual, occurs in private. Our society would be a very different one if there was not such a high degree of consensus to abide by this standard of privacy in sexual behaviour. There is, I think, a general regard for public order along this dimension, widely subscribed to, from which everyone gains some measure of freedom to pursue other activities of life. In this regard I think that in general there are certain similarities between heterosexual and homosexual acts in public.

If this is an acceptable ground on which to base the legislation, how should the law be enforced? This question turns on the meaning we would give to the words "in public." An absolute proscription would result if "in public" were defined in terms of "public place," so that the determining factor would be the place where the act occurred. If the place was public, the act could be said to be "in public." On the opposite end of the scale, "in public" might be defined to mean "in a public place in the presence of one or more persons," and prosecution might be allowed only on the basis of actual complaints received from members of the public. On this basis the onus is placed on members of the public to complain publicly in court. An alternative method might define the act to be an offence if it occurs "in a public place where members of the public are likely to see or would probably see the act," so that "in public" is made an open question to be determined by the evidence presented to a presiding judge, magistrate, or jury. The study referred to above shows that at present almost all of these cases arise out of charges laid by the police. Members of the public have not made specific complaints in most of the cases, although one of the cases involving a heterosexual couple on a beach did arise from a specific complaint. The question comes down to whether we wish to place the responsibility with ourselves as members of the public, or with the police to "do it for us," or whether we prefer to leave the decision open as an issue to be decided by the courts in each instance. This of course is not a question which can be settled by looking to research findings; it turns on how we conceive the public's role in the administration of justice in relation to that of the police and the courts. I believe that in the process of determining justice in the courtrooms of the nation it is better for the members of the public to be more directly involved. In this way the community's problems can be continually presented as living issues for the magistrate and all who may be present in the court. The person charged is not confronted only by the police and the law on a statute book, but by a fellow citizen who voices his complaint. The person who complains should be required to stand up and do so, and not anonymously step back behind the police and force them to carry the burden of presenting evidence alone.

There also arises the question of the maximum sentence in the Code, which the present proposal does not alter. As the majority of cases are of the "public indecency" type, is it still desirable to continue the maximum penalty of five years? In the 40 cases of homosexual acts in public examined in the study, 30 were fined, five were placed on probation, two were given suspended sentence only, and three received jail terms of 10, 30, and 60 days each. The span between the five-year maximum in the law and the actual practice of the courts appears to be unsupportable in such cases, and yet the proposal does not touch on this question. It may be that a five-year maximum is necessary where the offence involves a child or an adolescent, but this is a very good reason why we ought to distinguish between the different kinds of cases involved.

A great deal more can, and undoubtedly will, be said about these proposals. I have attempted here once again to illustrate the relevance and importance of empirical data as an informational base from which we can construct our legal categories, or as a factual picture in relation to which we can examine our ideas. We have come a long way in identifying most of the important elements in the offences under consideration – marriage, age, force, fraud, mental capacity to consent, publicity – which quite rightly I think should play a part in our considerations. Each of these elements is an abstraction. We can approach the problem by imagining how these elements come together, or we can look to see how they have in fact come together in the cases we have been prosecuting.

I have said nothing specifically about the changes to the offences of buggery and bestiality, but from what has been said it can be inferred that the process of unravelling these offences and relating the empirical findings to the legal concepts is exactly the same. To continue including these two very different behavioural acts in one section, however elaborate we may allow the exclusion clauses to become, is to carry on into the future, once again, the formulations of the middle ages as discussed by Coke and set out in the opening pages of this book.

Hopefully, both those who would now praise the proposed amendments as a great reform and those who would reject them out of a concern that they will lead to society's degeneration will become more aware that the proposals as they stand will not in actuality change what we have been doing. Regrettably, neither do they reach far enough to dissipate the essential vagueness of the term "gross indecency." The task as I see it is initially to demystify this terminology. Our aim is to construct legal provisions that are less dependent on the subjective value judgments of particular individuals, that are less abstract, more conscious, deliberate, and specific. We recognize, I think, that part of our difficulty in dealing with these areas of sexual deviation is the fact that they are emotionally charged and that popular myths are made to serve as the currency of informational exchange. For these very reasons it is all the more important to have access to factual studies which can serve as a guideline in discussions, and to build into our legal provisions (which endure over such long periods of time) as much rationality as we can muster. Public discussion and criticism of the existing law has played a part in prompting these proposals; their emergence now requires a more widespread consideration of the problems at their base. The issues involved are of a kind which ought not to be handed over to a committee of legal or any other single kind of experts to resolve. The experts have a responsibility to present data and information, to express opinions, but the essential positions to be taken should be thrashed out in our public forums. Informed public opinion is our safest guide, and can be made a more integral part of the making of criminal law. The effort of achieving it can at the same time play an even more vital role in the social process of general public education and social cohesion.

Table of Cases

GLASSBORO STATE COLLEGE